Ask Ms. Class

Ask Ms. Class

Susan Ohanian

Stenhouse Publishers
York, Maine

Stenhouse Publishers, 226 York Street, York, Maine 03909

Library of Congress Cataloging-in-Publication Data

Ohanian, Susan.
    Ask Ms. Class / Susan Ohanian.
      p.   cm.
    Includes bibliographical references.
    ISBN 1-57110-025-3 (alk. paper)
     1. Teachers—United States—Miscellanea.   2. Teaching—United States—Miscellanea.   I. Title.
LB1775.2.O43   1995
371.1′02—dc20   95-20511
                                       CIP

Published simultaneously in Canada by
Pembrooke Publishers Limited
538 Hood Road
Markham, Ontario L3R 3K9
ISBN 1-55138-064-1

Cover and interior design by Catherine Hawkes
Typeset by T'NT

Manufactured in the United States of America on acid-free paper
99 98 97 96 8 7 6 5 4 3 2 1

In memory of

Bill Knapp, my sixth-grade teacher
James Grimes, my high school English teacher
Bill Broderick, my principal at three different schools

in gratitude for their celebration of different drummers.

Contents

Dd

Ee

Ff

Gg

Hh

Ii

Jj

Kk

Ll

Mm

Nn

Oo

Pp

Qq

Rr

Ss

Tt

Uu

Vv

Introduction

Who wouldn't want to be Ms. Class? Flip and fervent at the same time, she's the alter ego of every committed teacher who has sat meekly and silently in the teacher's lounge while a colleague espouses yet another goofy idea about students and learning.

When I have sat quietly fuming in meetings with other educators, needing some comfort, I've often returned to the ideas of Susan Ohanian. The author of more than ten books and three hundred articles on teaching, learning, and curriculum, Susan has always relished a good, fair fight over ideas. Her writing has appeared in everything from scholarly journals to the op-ed page in newspapers like *USA Today*.

When I first read the manuscript of *Ask Ms. Class*, I was charmed, repulsed, and ultimately, hooked. But I ended my reading wanting to know more about the genesis of this book. There's no one quite like Ms. Class in education, and I wondered where she came from and how she connects with the rest of Susan Ohanian's work. I anticipated many readers would have similar questions, so I decided to ask the author. We agreed to do an interview by fax one morning about Ms. Class. Whenever I talk with Susan, I'm always prepared to be delightedly provoked. I wasn't disappointed.

Brenda: Where does Ms. Class come from? Can you think back to the moment when she leapt out of your imagination?

Susan: One of my early reading memories is the "Can This Marriage Be Saved?" column in one of those ladies magazines. My eight-year-old self loved that column, loved the delicious details of people's misbehavior and the way the advice giver always brought warring spouses back to compatibility. Then one day I caught my husband reading "Dear Abby," and I realized this delight in reading about other people's perversities must be universal. God knows, teachers have lots of problems and few places to unload them. One thing you have to realize: if Ms. Class in all her hauteur springs from some corner of my own psyche, so do all the people asking for advice. The editor surprised me by writing a marginal note on the manuscript suggesting that perhaps Ms. Class had not sufficiently squashed some "obnoxious" teacher. Hey, I was that teacher, revealing some frustration. Okay, it was one of my really bad days, but I'd never really thought of that persona as obnoxious. Troubled, yes; obnoxious, no. Dare I admit that there's probably not one question or opinion expressed in this book that has not passed through my mind for at least sixteen seconds? I guess what makes me somewhat unique in education circles is that I'm willing to admit it.

Brenda: Tell me more about the persona of Ms. Class. Does she have hobbies?

Susan: I know some readers will suspect she spends a lot of time standing in front of a mirror, asking "Who is the wisest in the land?" Actually, she spends an inordinate amount of time writing letters to editors, pointing out the error of their ways.

Brenda: I do think there's a kind of perverse false modesty or self-abasement among many teachers. It doesn't seem to be acceptable in many teachers lounges to present wisdom in response to others or an opposing view or even to acknowledge you have strengths that your colleagues might lack. "Who the hell does she think she is?" in response to Ms. Class also translates into "No teacher can express opinions this boldly, because I sure can't."

Susan: Yes, but I don't think it's perversity as much as self-preservation. I mean, you have to work in the same building, with some pretense of cordiality. As a teacher I find it more worthwhile to fight for specific needs of individual children—for the right of a deaf student to remain in my classroom or the right of an obnoxious kid to go on a field trip—than to point out a colleague's weaknesses. Figuring out your own pedagogy is so difficult. When would you have time to argue with your colleagues about theirs? On the one occasion that I let myself be drawn into an argument about pedagogy, the result was humiliating. Somehow, a second-grade teacher and I started talking about the importance, or lack thereof, of teaching the use of comma in apposition. Honest to god, that was the focus of our attention. She was so insistent, and I was so unable to convince her of the error of her ways, that I burst into tears. People who read my work probably don't take me for the sort of person who would cry over a comma. I can tell that people are always surprised to meet me and discover I'm quiet, even shy. Perhaps it's the coward's way out, but I have learned to save my vitriol for print, not the faculty room.

Brenda: I think this may be why this is *Ask Ms. Class,* not *Ask Susan Ohanian.*

Susan: You bet. Ms. Class likes burning bridges. I am a bit more cautious.

Brenda: As I read the book, I found myself alternating between belly laughs, epiphanies from connecting my experience with Ms. Class's, and shaking my head in disagreement. What is your response to someone who disagrees more than she laughs, finding Ms. Class truly offensive?

Susan: Ms. Class truly offensive? Surely you jest. Actually, I can think of seven people in the United States, Canada, Central America, and Guam who will probably be offended. I will refrain from naming names but would point out that people who are "truly offended" are people who cannot hold two opposed ideas in their minds at the same time and still function. F. Scott Fitzgerald, by the way, called this ability "the test of a first-rate mind." That is, of course, Ms. Class talking. I had to restrain her from naming those seven names. I think most teachers will thank Ms. Class for refusing to talk the talk so common in professional development courses, for choosing instead to speak the unspeakable.

Brenda: I'm tempted to use the book as a litmus test. My hunch is that colleagues who take offense are the ones who are always preaching at me.

Susan: Yes, it is a temptation. And I'll confess to having a few private litmus tests that I spring on people occasionally. But the frustration of a litmus test is that you spring it and then you have to keep your mouth shut. It must remain your private little secret. You just can't go around proclaiming with glee, "Aha! You failed!" Interesting, isn't it, that we can label kids as failures but not colleagues?

Brenda: How is Ms. Class able to seem so sure of herself?

Susan: Ms. Class knows her place. She is paid to keep a stiff upper lip and a glib tongue, not to let her hair down and cry in her beer.

Brenda: Do you have any final advice for readers of *Ask Ms. Class?*

Susan: Ms. Class and I hope readers will take from this book a renewed recognition that teaching is a craft surrounded by ambiguity, not certainty. Too many people comment on education as if they knew how we should proceed. Ms. Class and I believe we must take teaching one day at a time. And pray for a little luck.

Brenda Power

ADAPTOR PLUG AFFIRMATIVE ACTION

Dear Ms. Class:

I teach in an old school. We have modern audiovisual equipment but there never seems to be an adaptor plug when I need one. Do you have some sort of solution to this?

— Duluth, MN

Dear Duluth:

There are only seventeen adaptor plugs in the world. This means that one will be assigned to your school for four and a half minutes every ninety-three years. Maintain good relations with the custodian. He will know where it is.

ADMINISTRATIVE ANGST

Dear Ms. Class:

I like my principal, but he has a motor mouth. I don't know how to tell him that I don't want to stand in my doorway and hear about his son's testicular disorder or his opinion of doctors, auto mechanics, members of Congress, or professional baseball players—especially when I should be inside teaching! Please help me! But don't identify my location: It's a small town and everybody will know who it is.

— Anonymous

Dear Anonymous:

There is no cure for administrators who regard silence as the hand-maiden of guilt. Don't try to stop your principal. Keep him talking. Invite him into the classroom to talk to your students. A few invitations along the line of "Boys and girls, wouldn't you like to know Mr. X's opinion of the Mesopotamian trade route?" will divert him—and gain you a guest lecturer.

Dear Ms. Class:
  Why are administrators so ignorant?

— Akron, OH

Dear Akron:
  If they were any smarter, a lot of people would be out of a job.

Dear Ms. Class:
  My principal never makes a decision until he tests the waters. It's more important for him to be popular than to be right. The result is that things never get done.
When the principal should be in the cafeteria keeping the lid on, he's out taking
straw polls of the faculty.

— Asheville, NC

Dear Asheville:
  There are two kinds of administrators: those who listen to everybody
and those who listen to nobody. Which type a teacher prefers depends on
whether she is an extrovert or an introvert, a conservative or a liberal, a
Platonist or an Aristotelian, a fan of John Denver or Ice-T.
  Ms. Class cautions the troubled teacher to tread carefully. Although it
is understandable that in desperate moments a beleaguered teacher may
occasionally wish for a Mussolini who can get the bells ringing on time and
the students marching silently in the cafeteria line, be careful what you
wish for. You may get it.

Dear Ms. Class:
  In fifteen years of teaching I've never encountered an administrator who offered
one bit of advice on pedagogy. I wonder how they spend their days.

— Hillsboro, OR

Dear Hillsboro:
  The supply of administrators does seem to exceed the demand. Remember: some administrators are wise. The rest are otherwise. Ninety percent
of administrators give the other ten percent a bad name. The amount of
time administrators spend on a problem is inversely proportional to its
educational value. That's why principals spend half the day in the cafeteria
and the other half counting petty cash. But keep in mind: the administrator
who doesn't do anything can't be criticized for doing the wrong thing.

Dear Ms. Class:
  You are unduly hard on administrators. If you could walk in my shoes for a day,
than you wouldn't be so eager to cast aspersions. I deal with teachers who are

dominated by a union that doesn't care about education, students whose parents don't nurture them, and a public who think they could do it better.

— Paterson, NJ

Dear Paterson:

Ms. Class acknowledges that she casts aspersions and that she enjoys doing so. Ms. Class further acknowledges that administrators suffer so much in this world that there is probably no hell for them in the next. The truth is that school administrators are no more inept than any other class of professionals. The novelist John Gardner once pointed out that it's a "law of the universe that ninety-seven percent of all people in all professions are incompetent." Ms. Class acknowledges that these statistics apply to brain surgeons and advice columnists as well as school administrators.

Dear Ms. Class:

I am a first-year principal, and I am excited about setting up innovative and creative reading and science programs. Do you have any advice for how I might bring the faculty along on this creative change process journey?

— San Jose, CA

Dear San Jose:

No. People who decide to become administrators have no business trying to be clever and creative.

ANSWERS DOWNLOADING

Dear Ms. Class:

I've noticed that you frequently use humor to avoid answering questions. I wonder why you don't give up the advice business and take a job as a stand-up comedienne.

— Juneau, AK

Dear Juneau:

Ms. Class notices that you didn't ask a question. Nonetheless, she will provide an answer. She thinks it's more important to know some of the important questions than to know all of the trivial answers. The eminent news commentator Edward R. Murrow once observed that "our major obligation is not to mistake slogans for solutions." Ms. Class feels that too many answers in education are really slogans in drag.

One of the most important things a teacher can say is "I don't know." Ms. Class has observed that when most teachers ask "What do you think?" they don't really want you to think. They want you to agree or disagree. As

Robert Frost pointed out, "Thinking isn't agreeing or disagreeing. That's voting."

APOSTROPHIC RISK TAKING

Dear Ms. Class:

My third graders are enthusiastic writers. They do a good job of editing. The one thing that causes grief is the apostrophe. Even the best students make bad apostrophic errors. What can I do about this?

— Eugene, OR

Dear Eugene:

Apostrophe Advice, Part 1

Every morning on arising, repeat to yourself: "Lord, help me accept those things I cannot change." If a teacher takes apostrophes seriously, she will surely go mad.

Since Piaget did not address the developmental aspects of apostrophe control, Ms. Class will. She has a modest proposal: forbid apostrophe use by children until they reach the age of sixteen. When teens get their driver's licenses the distinction between possession and plurality sometimes becomes more apparent. There are exceptions, of course. The distinction eludes some people forever.

If you would like information on a grass-roots movement to eliminate apostrophes from administrative memos, please send a stamped, self-addressed envelope.

Apostrophe Advice, Part 2

Teachers would do well to learn from the lessons of history: Emily Dickinson did not use apostrophes. George Bernard Shaw referred to them as "uncouth bacilli" and advocated using one only when omitting it would cause confusion—such as making a distinction between he'll and hell.

APTITUDE FOR TEACHING FAST-FORWARD

Dear Ms. Class:

I hear a lot of talk about "temperament of the trade" and "necessary skills" for teachers. What do you think? What does the ideal teacher look like?

— Orlando, FL

Dear Orlando:

First of all, after chasing hamsters, interrogating boys about the toilet paper wads on the lavatory ceiling, and listening to "I'm telling" all day, she probably looks tired.

Looks aside, the ideal teacher can make a mistake. She does not find it necessary to convince her students that she knows everything, that she could win on both *Jeopardy* and *Wheel of Fortune.*

Some teachers cry when their students walk out the door on the last day of school without looking back. Other teachers put an eight-year-old's desk in the dumpster when he lollygags in the lavatory. Ms. Class has not met the teacher who is all good or all bad, all skill or all heart. Ambiguity, thy name is teacher.

AQUARIUM MAINTENANCE BENCHMARKS

Dear Ms. Class:

Help! I am a primary teacher with no talent for small animals. I tried hatching eggs and it was a disaster. Two chicks were born deformed and Mama Hen killed another. Can you imagine explaining to second graders why Mama Hen ate her babies? Can you recommend a classroom pet that's easier and less traumatic?

— Waukegan, IL

Dear Waukegan:

Ms. Class recommends turtles. It's hard to tell if they are alive or dead.

Dear Ms. Class:

Turtles are a singularly inappropriate classroom pet. Why not recommend fish?

— Chico, CA

Dear Chico:

Ms. Class concedes you may be right about turtles. Certainly the rules of aquarium maintenance are easy:

- If you fail to feed and fertilize the fish, they will die.
- If you feed and fertilize the fish, they will die.

Although some immutable law of the universe is undoubtedly at work, the sight of one of the big fishies eating seven of the baby fishies is traumatic to Ms. Class, never mind eight-year-olds.

ARACHIBUTYROPHOBIA POSTTRAUMATIC STRESS DISORDER

Dear Ms. Class:

What do you think: is teaching a profession or not? If it isn't, what will it take to make it one?

— Walla Walla, WA

Dear Walla Walla:

Teaching cannot become a profession until teachers overcome their fear of arachibutyrophobia—the fear of peanut butter sticking to the roof of one's mouth. For this to occur, teachers must be allotted more than twenty-seven minutes (minus five minutes of leading children to the cafeteria) for lunch.

Some will take Ms. Class's words as jest. Please know that Ms. Class is a very solemn person, one who rarely jests. Ninety-nine point nine percent of the people who write about teaching as a profession never mention the twenty-seven-minute lunch or the absence of Perrier with a twist of lime in the faculty room. The truth is that we have a plethora of books about the conceptualization of teaching and a paucity of those in touch with the daily reality.

ASSESSMENT, AUTHENTIC AND FLIMFLAM

Dear Ms. Class:

I keep hearing about authentic assessment but I can't see that it means much more than keeping students' work in a folder. How am I ever going to sell this to parents, who want to know how their children measure up to children around the country?

— Pueblo, CO

Dear Pueblo:

Ms. Class sympathizes with your cynicism. Those who want to be truly authentic let the students choose what goes in the folders.

Ms. Class does take offense, however, at your willingness to go along with the idea of measuring children against other children. Why is it that we are are so obsessed with measuring children? At the same time we are obsessed with measuring our children from age five to eighteen, we ignore the abilities of parents, policemen, politicians, media pundits. Are the parents of your students willing to take a test to see how they measure up with other parents around the country? Do you want your SAT scores posted on the schoolhouse door?

The irony of assessment, be it authentic or otherwise, is that it doesn't reveal as much about students as people think it does. The worth of any assessment is in the eye of the perpetrator.

ATTACK OF THE GREEN SLIME

Dear Ms. Class:
I'd like to ask you a personal question. I don't understand how you can be so thick-skinned. If people attacked me the way they attack you, I'd just crumble. Don't you care if people don't like you?

— Laredo, TX

Dear Laredo:
Ms. Class appreciates your concern. She is as thin-skinned as anyone else but she has discovered this important fact about herself: Ms. Class would rather be attacked than ignored.

Teachers need to realize that rejection is not altogether a bad thing. Rejections help teachers discover what's worth fighting for. Nobel prize–winner Saul Bellow put it this way: Rejections "teach a writer to rely on his own judgment and to say in his heart of hearts, 'To hell with you.'" Ms. Class considers this the prime justification for encouraging teachers to write—so they will cultivate that to-hell-with-you attitude.

ATTENTION DEFICIT DISORDER TRUTH IN DISCLOSURE

Dear Ms. Class: ·
John yells out comments when I'm trying to talk, rarely finishes one task before starting another, has difficulty following directions, and can't sit still. I wonder if he has attention deficit disorder.

— Lexington, MA

Dear Lexington:
Worried teacher, you didn't mention John's age. Ms. Class wonders if he is your student or your principal. Or perhaps a colleague. The behavior you describe fits what Ms. Class has observed of her colleagues' conduct during faculty meetings. That said, Ms. Class acknowledges that the U.S. Department of Education estimates that from three to five percent of children under age eighteen have a condition known as attention deficit disorder. The DOE has produced two videos that give teachers and parents tips on what can be done about children who are easily distracted. For more information, call 800-328-0272 (ADD is a real concern, and this is a real telephone number).

As for easily distracted administrators and colleagues, Ms. Class advises a good sense of humor.

AUDIOVISUAL READINESS INDICATORS

Dear Ms. Class:

We don't seem to be able to keep a phonograph, tape recorder, or VCR in working order in our school. Do other people have this problem, or is it just us? Are we the only school in the United States that still uses phonographs?

— Scranton, PA

Dear Scranton:

You are not alone. Ms. Class's solution is based on an in-depth, transcontinental study of school equipment requiring a plug. Leave it alone and it will repair itself. If you try to fix mechanical devices yourself, you delay their self-generative power. Anything sent to the audiovisual department for repair will never work again. Kicking equipment does it no good, but it makes you feel better.

Dear Ms. Class:

You seem to have a complex about plugs. What's your problem?

— Des Moines, IA

Dear Des Moines:

Ms. Class is just cautious. She is not willing to let machinery ever get the upper hand in her life.

BASAL DEFENSE FUND

Dear Ms. Class:

Our primary-grade teachers voted to buy trade books instead of basal texts for our classrooms. The assistant superintendent in charge of curriculum vetoed our vote on the grounds that textbooks show the public that we have standards. I just wonder if you can top this as idiotic justification for spending thousands of dollars on books that nobody wants. Please sign me—

— Anonymous

Dear Anonymous:

Sad to say, Ms. Class can indeed top your story, but she's not proud of it. Ms. Class knows a teacher who was given permission to spend her classroom text budget on trade books. Then two days later this permission was withdrawn and the teacher was told, "We have to buy the basals. You don't have to use them, but we have to buy a set for your classroom."

The teacher asked why, and the administrator replied, "In case you drop dead. The substitute will need them."

This is the clean underwear theory of reading instruction, and Ms. Class doesn't think she's ever heard a better justification for buying a class set of basals: just in case the teacher drops dead. But Ms. Class believes most teachers want more on their tombstones than *Clean underwear and every basal in its place.*

BASIC SKILLS WITNESS PROTECTION PROGRAM

Dear Ms. Class:

I have instituted a constructivist mathematics program in my second-grade classroom. Children have the opportunity to explore mathematics and build their own understanding of basic principles. My problem is that parents are outraged that their children aren't memorizing number facts. Do you have any suggestions?

— Phoenix, AZ

Dear Phoenix:

Number facts are to mathematics as spelling is to writing. That is to say, there is less than meets the eye. Nonetheless, Ms. Class advocates Friday spelling quizzes and math facts memorization. A teacher needs to recognize when it is easier—and more productive—to yield than to fight. When you take away the two school rituals that parents understand—math facts and spelling quizzes—you scare them to death. Scared parents suspect and challenge everything you do. So give parents these two small things and they will hold bake sales to buy math manipulatives for your classroom and pay for author visits.

BEHAVIOR CHECKLIST DESTABILIZATION

Dear Ms. Class:

The LD teacher is trying to help me mainstream an emotionally disturbed boy into my third-grade class. She keeps precise checklists on all the students when they are in her classroom, marking their behavior every ten minutes. When Charles comes to my classroom she asks only that I mark his behavior at the end of the period with a smiley face or a frowny face. Even though I am one hundred percent opposed to this type of system, I have a lot of respect for the LD teacher. She has been a lot of help to me and to Charles too. He is a seriously disturbed little boy, and his charts do seem to help him keep on track. Do you think it's wrong of me to use this behavioral system with him when I don't use it with other children? Is it hypocritical to use it with Charles when I oppose it philosophically for other children?

— Schenectady, NY

Dear Schenectady:

Teaching, like life, is a compromise. Ms. Class is willing to bet no student, including Charles, ever questions why you employ this system only with him. Every student in your class knows that Charles is different. Charles is more aware of this than anybody. Children have a great desire to be regular. Nobody in your class wants to be like Charles. Charles doesn't want to be like Charles.

Teacher education courses promulgate two great myths. One myth is that all children expect or need to be treated the same. The second myth is that there are certainties in the schoolhouse. Benjamin Franklin said nothing is certain but death and taxes. In the schoolhouse, nothing is certain and no one is equal.

Ms. Class is as nervous about those smiley faces as you are, but she doesn't think you should lose any sleep over them. Regard them as a temporary measure, one that you and Charles will dispense with quickly.

Dear Ms. Class:

The LD teacher in my school has been working with me on a behavioral checklist for a few students. I guess it helps them. But it doesn't help me. I still am very upset by their obnoxious behavior.

— Stockton, CA

Dear Stockton:

Ms. Class believes there's no point in having a behavior problem in your class if he/she doesn't make you miserable.

BEHAVIORAL OBJECTIVE TERRADIDDLE

Dear Ms. Class:

I have trouble writing my lesson plans in the (required) form of behavioral objectives. Can you offer any advice?

— Nashville, TN

Dear Nashville:

No.

The person who can write "The student will. . . " is either suffering from delusions or is an out-and-out liar. Ms. Class taught seventh graders for ten years; then she taught third graders. She knows that on a good day the best a teacher can claim is "the student might."

Just remember this: a behavioral objective is wishful thinking with delusions of grandeur.

BIAS AND BEGONIAS

Dear Ms. Class:

I am shocked that you could present such a biased point of view on so many issues. Teachers deserve better. We need someone who can give an impartial judgment on the serious matters we face daily. Instead of answering so many questions, you need to ask yourself one: why are you so angry?

— Athens, GA

Dear Athens:

Of course Ms. Class is biased. She would feel ashamed not to be. If you want neutrality, buy a begonia. Ms. Class herself clings to her prejudices. They are both a comfort and a source of strength.

Anger suggests love. The person who is angered by nothing cares about nothing. If she is to survive, endure, and triumph, a teacher must have great capacity for indignation.

BIRD IN THE WINDOW REDUX

Dear Ms. Class:

I am an education major. Next semester we will go into classrooms as student teachers, and I'm scared to death. My professor says we need to find a metaphor for our life's work. Can you help me?

— Omaha, NE

Dear Omaha:

Ms. Class thinks fear is a healthy emotion. Better fearful than smugly confident.

Your professor is wise as well as right. Metaphors are important. Ms. Class confesses to being as pleased as punch that you asked her. At the risk of incurring the wrath of her husband, who says he's very very tired of hearing about the bird in the window, here it is.

Early in her career, Ms. Class was fortunate to encounter a beautiful little essay titled "The Bird in the Window," written by the philosopher/science educator David Hawkins. The metaphor has remained her guiding principle and passion for more than twenty years. Hawkins points out that there is an essential lack of predictability about what's going to happen in a good classroom, not because there's no control but precisely because there is control, of the right kind—the teacher bases her decisions on her observation of actual children in actual situations.

Such a classroom makes room for accidents, the unexpected happening that directs attention in some new way. Suddenly there it is. The bird flies in the window, and that's the miracle you needed. If the teacher is ready for and is able to make educational capital out of the interests and choices of children and out of this accidental appearance of the bird, then great things happen. If the bird coming in the window is just a nuisance, interrupting your planned lesson, then you don't deserve it, and in fact, it never happens. If you deserve it, the bird *will* fly in the window.

Ms. Class treasured this metaphor for years, and then one day there was a bird in her window. Well, close to the window. She noticed that Pete, the second most obnoxious student who had ever graced her classroom, was staring out the window. This wasn't unusual. Since Pete could not read and could barely write, he looked for other things to occupy his attention. Ms. Class asked Pete, "What's up?" and he pointed out that for several days he'd been watching a bird sitting in a nest with three eggs.

Pete was shocked when Ms. Class handed him a Polaroid and told him to go outside and take a picture of that bird's nest and eggs. Pete knew as well as Ms. Class that a sacred rule of the school was *Never let any kid out of your classroom*—particularly a kid like Pete.

Ms. Class told Pete: "I'm writing you a pass that says you are outside the building on essential business. If any adult gives you a hard time, be polite, but tell him to take it up with me. Tell him I said this is an extraordinary circumstance; tell him it's an emergency. That's exactly what I'm writing: EMERGENCY PROJECT."

After all, how many times does a teacher have a robin's nest right outside her window? Ms. Class never doubted that Pete had to go take that picture. Here she was, a teacher who had tried to work under the principle of a bird in the window for twelve years. And now she had one, and she certainly wasn't going to ignore it.

Pete thought Ms. Class was nuts. He did not return to class and write a five-hundred-word essay on birds' nesting habits. He did not read a book about robins. But he seemed pleased by the picture he took. When he thought nobody was looking, he took it out of his pocket and looked at it. And he grinned. And Ms. Class noticed that he didn't curse for six days.

Dear Ms. Class:

Not to throw cold water on a good story—and I have to concede that you do tell a good story—but just what is the point of all this soulful recollection? What good are your sentimentalities to teachers struggling to become professional?

— Springfield, MA

Dear Springfield:

Don't discount stories. By turning pedagogy into narrative, a teacher can address the ambiguities and frustrations of teaching. More than that, narrative can contain these ambiguities and frustrations, at least for the moment, keep them from from running wild. *New York Times* book reviewer Anatole Broyard wrote, "Always in emergencies we invent narratives." What is teaching, if not day-to-day emergencies? Ms. Class knows that every school would be a better place if teachers told their stories and those of the children.

BLACKLINE MASTER TOXIC BUILDUP

Dear Ms. Class:

I've been teaching for fifteen years, and I have run out of storage space in my classroom. I no longer have any place to put my blackline masters and other valuable papers.

— Wilmington, DE

Dear Wilmington:

Pardon me? Other valuable papers? Valuable papers are papers you need. Valuable papers belong in a safe deposit box.

In the classroom, dittos and blackline masters expand to fit all available space. A good rule of thumb is: every time an untenured teacher runs off a blackline master, she should throw away two old ones. Tenured teachers have further to go. They should throw away eight old worksheets for every new reproducible used. This practice clears the mind as well as the shelves.

BOARD OF EDUCATION BROUHAHA

Dear Ms. Class:

Several members of our board of education have set themselves up as preservers of public morality. They are pulling books they find objectionable off library shelves. Their choices are as silly as you might imagine: *Little Red Riding Hood* because there is wine in the basket she carries to her grandmother, *The Great Gilly Hopkins* because there's profanity, and so on. These are the same people who for two years have voted a freeze on all library purchases, insisting we have enough books. I guess we can't do anything about the budget, but do we have any rights against censorship?

— Salem, MA

Dear Salem:

If God had intended for the literacy rate to rise, he would never have created boards of education.

Nonetheless, you are protected by the Bill of Rights. Contact the American Library Association and the National Council of Teachers of English for information on how you can protect yourselves against people who do not believe in free inquiry.

On the other hand, you can also protect yourselves by advising colleagues to forgo presenting Stephen King's *Carrie* as the novel every seventh grader should read.

Dear Ms. Class:

As usual, you exaggerate. No teacher would assign a Stephen King novel for class reading, but to suggest censorship is to let the censors win. You do not help the cause of free expression by pointing to ludicrous examples.

— Richmond, VA

Dear Richmond:

Bite your tongue and bottle your bile. As Ms. Class has pointed out on numerous occasions, she likes writing about education because she never has to make anything up. A teacher who would assign Stephen King to seventh graders is beyond your imagination? Well, Ms. Class could name names. She refrains from doing so because she believes guilty parties may one day be repentant and does not want to make it difficult for them to build a new life.

Be that as it may, Ms. Class once instigated the removal of Judy Blume's *Forever* from a middle school library. Because she herself read *Forever Amber* the summer she was eleven, Ms. Class knows that smut will find its readers. Kids have a right to their dirty little secrets. Schools should not up the ante and upset delicate prepubescent urges for independence and rebellion by bringing those secrets out of the closet. Please don't write attacking Ms. Class's prudery. She prefers not to march for the right of ten- and eleven-year-olds to read library books that treat sexual organs as so much plumbing.

Dear Ms. Class:

Our board of education is an embarrassment as well as a menace. They use their meetings to denounce teachers and to come up with zany ideas. Their latest plan is to bring $1,000,000 (that's one million dollars) in cash to a board meeting so that teachers who are asking for a four percent raise (we have been working without a contract for fourteen months) can "see the value of a dollar."

— Troy, NY

Dear Troy:

A board of education is democracy at its most rampant. If your board wants teachers to see one million of something they would do better to bring in their beer tab collections. At least then they wouldn't have to hire armed guards to protect the exhibit. Ms. Class's best advice to you is to stay away from that meeting. Every hoodlum in upstate New York will be tempted to stage a heist.

As to the real issue you raise, the hearts and minds of school board members: people who get elected to school boards usually do so on the strength of an issue having little to do with the intellectual development of children—busing, prayer, sex education, athletics, and, of course, saving money. Ms. Class has never heard of anyone's getting elected to a school board because he thought there should be more books in the library.

Schools are the only postindustrial institutions run by a vigilante committee, sixty-seven percent of whose members are hoping to get even with a professional class they feel did them wrong—teachers. The other thirty-three percent got elected on the platform of firing the superintendent because the high school hasn't had a winning football team in ten years.

The medical equivalent would be to have Christian Scientists running the hospitals.

Dear Ms. Class:

You are unduly harsh on school boards. You are also unfair. I have devoted twenty-five years of my life to serving on the local school board, and let me tell you, we rarely receive any thank-yous, but we do receive plenty of complaints. People like you, with all your negativity, certainly don't help matters.

— Alexandria, VA

Dear Alexandria:

Of course Ms. Class is unfair. Twenty years as a school teacher has taught her that life is unfair. She would think that twenty-five years as a school board member would have taught you the same lesson.

Ms. Class does recognize the function of school boards. Without them, we would have no way to put off until 2001 what we should have done yesterday. She only wishes to suggest that having been unpopular in high school should not be considered sufficient qualification for serving on a school board.

BOOK BAGS R US

Dear Ms. Class:

I wonder how teachers can leave the building empty-handed. I am permanently stoop-shouldered from carrying home student journals, professional journals, and so on.

— Topeka, KS

Dear Topeka:

Ms. Class suspects it's mostly "and so on." Even though Ms. Class is herself an overpacker and suffers from a book bag-induced frozen shoulder, she has come to know that one of the forty-three important lessons a teacher should learn is that her worth cannot be measured by the weight of the book bag she carries.

Ms. Class suspects that the book bag syndrome is related to the clean underwear syndrome: in case you're hit by a car, you want all your valuables with you. Instead of the motto "When it doubt, pack it," Ms. Class suggests repeating the mantra "When in doubt, leave it out."

Here is a three-step book bag-withdrawal program.

- *Week one:* run a seam across the bag halfway up.

- *Week two:* run another seam down the middle of the bag.

- *Week three:* seal the opening with duct tape.

BOOK CLUB BONANZA

Dear Ms. Class:

Most of the primary teachers in my school belong to school book clubs and encourage their students to order books. I don't see the point of this. Our students are disadvantaged and can't really afford books. I'd rather we put our efforts into getting them to appreciate the library.

— Los Angeles, CA

Dear Los Angeles:

Ms. Class agrees with John Ruskin, who once pointed out that if a book is worth reading, it is worth buying. Ms. Class forgives book clubs for all the posters and other junk they sell because they make the joy of book ownership possible for every student.

Ms. Class suspects you are using the label "disadvantaged" as an excuse to avoid paperwork, but fear not. It is Ms. Class's experience that book clubs have the best-run organizations in the world. Somehow they manage to interpret the teacher's sloppiest bookkeeping and they do make wonderful books available to every child.

BOYS AND GIRLS REFORM INITIATIVE

Dear Ms. Class:

I resent all the cries for recruiting more males into teaching. I wonder if the people pleading for males in education have ever sat in a junior high faculty room.

— Albany, NY

Dear Albany:

You are right that junior highs reinforce the old maxim that "boys will be boys." Isn't it odd that the "good old boys" seem to last forever but "the girls" usually grow up some time in their thirties?

BULLETIN BOARD BARGAIN HUNTER

Dear Ms. Class:

Our school seems to be involved in a bulletin board beauty queen contest. People who never lift a finger to do anything outside of school hours come in on weekends and spend hours creating artistic gems. I don't want to engage in this sort of insanity, but it's hard being regarded as the Orphan Annie of classroom displays.

— Park Ridge, IL

Dear Park Ridge:

Ms. Class feels compelled to present this truth-in-advice disclosure: Ms. Class once raided her husband's closet for a bunch of paisley neckties, which she converted into a quite striking turkey for her Thanksgiving bulletin board. Dougie was the only one of her third graders who seemed to notice Ms. Class's flight of fancy. He said, "Hey, that looks like maybe it could be a peacock!" When Ms. Class prodded, "Remember what month this is?" Dougie reconsidered and said, "Or maybe a turkey?" Ms. Class refrained from falling to her knees and kissing Dougie's feet. Instead, she gave him an all-day pass to the library, with stopovers at the nurse's office.

It's easy to sneer at bulletin boards, but a six-week stint teaching someone else's ninth-grade honors English class taught Ms. Class that ninth-grade intellectuals need the chance both to create some handiwork and to display it. Ms. Class was appalled by the bareness of the room so she asked students to create art work to accompany their interpretation of the literature they were reading. As she posted gravestone rubbings, African masks, and other art, the room acquired the comfortable, cluttered look characteristic of every place she has taught. Students were enthusiastic as they began to read the walls as well as the books. Ms. Class discovered that high school honors students are just as pleased to see their peers admiring their work as are third-grade rotten readers.

BUREAUCRACY BELLWETHER CURVE

Dear Ms. Class:

I wonder if I'm going to make it as a teacher. When I'm not floundering from crisis to crisis, I'm filling out papers—lesson plans, student referrals, and so on. Don't mistake me: I do have moments of satisfaction, but I fear the joy in teaching is passing me by—or getting buried in a paper pile.

— Shreveport, LA

Dear Shreveport:

Your day sounds normal. What they didn't tell you in your college preparatory courses is that a teacher's day is half bureaucracy, half crisis, half monotony, and one-eightieth epiphany. Never mind the arithmetic.

Don't despair. By some miracle, the paperwork gets easier. It doesn't go away, but it does get easier. The strongest memory Ms. Class has of her first year of teaching is the school secretary's shaking her finger and threatening, "You will not leave the building until your student absentee days add up." Tears did no good. Ms. Class had to make the days add up. The best thing the teachers union did, a decade later, was to put clerks in charge of adding up the days each student was absent. (See Figure 1).

FIGURE 1

Attendance Code

⊿	Full attendance.
PA	Absent—postcard sent.
L⊿	Late—pupil presents late pass during AM official period.
L⊿A	Pupil presents late pass during PM official period—L in RED ink.
4⊿	Pupil present but excused after fourth period.
A⊿3	Pupil absent during AM official period but reported in time for more than two periods. Number in RED.
R	Absent for religious observance.
TA	Absence referred to Bureau of Attendance.

Dear Ms. Class:

As a new teacher, I'm amazed that nobody really pays attention to what I do. Our district requires that the district mission statement be posted on every classroom wall, but nobody ever comes around to see if I'm implementing it.

— Jefferson City, MO

Dear Jefferson City:

Seal your lips from such loose talk. Do this immediately. Inefficiency is what prevents a bureaucracy from oppressing the people who work in its thrall.

Ms. Class would point out that one of the great benefits of teaching is that people do not check up on what you're doing. This is how Ms. Class was able to use trade books instead of the basal and replace one-third of the social studies curriculum with E. B. White's *The Trumpet of the Swan*.

CAFETERIA QUANDARY

Dear Ms. Class:

My principal is not available from 10:30 A.M. to 2 P.M. because she's trying to keep order in the cafeteria. Doesn't this seem like a terrible waste of administrative salary?

— Cleveland, OH

Dear Cleveland:

Be grateful. If your principal weren't otherwise occupied, she would have three and a half more hours to check up on what you're doing.

Dear Ms. Class:

I wonder if cafeteria food is uniquely bad at our school or if it's the same all around the country. I think some entrepreneur could make money providing better lunches for teachers.

— Utica, NY

Dear Utica:

You were expecting pâté? chateaubriand? Ms. Class is alarmed, O Hungry One. Didn't your university preparation warn you never to eat school food products? An optimist is someone who eats pizza in the cafeteria. Silly Putty was invented by a federal hot lunch committee when the mashed potatoes sat undisturbed for fifteen minutes. School lunches are designed to punish teachers for not getting up in time to make their own lunches. Teaching is hazardous enough without engaging in the unnecessary risky behavior of eating school mystery meat.

Please, teacher, if you find yourself in the desperate position of needing to eat something from the cafeteria, Ms. Class recommends applying the street-vendor-in-Bogatá food rule: don't eat any food in the cafeteria unless it is bottled or you peel it yourself. If following this rule proves impossible, then heed the advice of Miss Piggy: "Never eat more than you can lift."

Dear Ms. Class:

I wonder why you would waste time discussing what teachers eat for lunch. Children and teachers themselves are much more important than food. Why don't you spend your time on what matters?

— Pasadena, CA

Dear Pasadena:

People more important than food? True, Ms. Class would rate her principal higher than, say, an anchovy, but who could rank higher than chocolate mousse?

This could be a new diversion for the faculty room: rank how your enemies and friends measure up against Hamburger Helper, Spaghetti-O's, raw cauliflower with Cheez-Whiz, mayonnaise and red onion sandwiches (on white bread), tuna patty melt, lima beans, cottage cheese with catsup, liver with mint sauce, tofu burgers, pineapple and guacamole pizza, potato chips from a can, mashed potatoes from a box, french fries from a freezer, refried beans, nonalcoholic beer, grits, turnip greens, sourdough bread, sole à la dieppoise, thirty-garlic chicken, sushi, salmon with cranberry-leek sauce, goobers marinated in Coke, artichoke brownies, coconut fritters, peanut butter puffs, Poptarts, Froot Loops, Twinkies à la mode, Ben & Jerry's Cherry Garcia . . . .

Dear Ms. Class:

I'm thinking of volunteering for cafeteria duty, but I'm bothered by the pay. The school board is offering teachers the same pay as yearbook advisers to do cafeteria duty. Athletic coaches get more. Is there any legal recourse to this inequity?

— Albany, NY

Dear Albany:

Why would you consider such a thing at any price? Cafeteria duty is ruinous to your health. Ms. Class agrees that the teacher taking on such a job should receive hazardous-duty pay, but, that said, you should know there is not enough money available to make cafeteria duty worth the hazards.

Have you noticed you never see any TV commercials with beautiful actors posing as cheerful cafeteria attendants? No one should volunteer for it. The meek (and the untenured) will inherit it.

CAREER LADDER BAD HAIR DAY

Dear Ms. Class:

Whatever happened to career ladders? I don't hear about them any more.

— Niskayuna, NY

Dear Niskayuna:

Count your blessings. Career ladders are alive and well in various parts of the country, though they travel under a variety of names: master teacher, mentor teacher, and so on. Ms. Class talked to one whose claim to the title seemed to indicate she had mastered the evaluation system. She couldn't figure out why she hadn't earned enough points the first time she applied for the title master teacher. So she asked two colleagues to come to her classroom and evaluate her teaching according to the master teacher checklist. She also had herself videotaped so she could measure her performance against the list.

After a second failure to meet the official standards, she finally figured out the problem. "My class was too well behaved. My students didn't provide me with the opportunity to prove I could handle a discipline problem—so I didn't earn any points in that category."

Before she performed for the judges for the third time, this teacher made sure she had a behavior problem in her class. She borrowed a student from another teacher, one who would add the needed bit of spice to her well-practiced lesson, but who could also be easily controlled.

Depending on one's grip on classroom reality, the story has a happy or a ludicrous ending. The candidate is now an officially certified master teacher. In her long, detailed explanation of her eighteen-month pursuit of the mastery certificate, this teacher never once mentioned who or what she taught. For all the preparation for three official examinations, she has never measured herself by anything but someone else's checklist.

Ms. Class doesn't know if this teacher can identify the Treaty of Ghent, the uses of flax, or the location of Madagascar. Nor does she care. What disturbs Ms. Class is that she talked to this teacher for an hour and has no indication of a temperament for the trade, not a hint of the three Cs of our craft: caring, compassion, and commitment to children. Does she laugh with them? cry with them? Will she stand up for them? We must ask of ourselves: mastery of what? and for whom?

CENSORSHIP CREDIT LINE

Dear Ms. Class:

Judy Blume is my students' favorite author. But a local parent group is militant about getting Blume, Zindel, and Cormier removed from the library shelves. I wonder if I dare go on reading Judy Blume novels aloud.

— Birmingham, AL

Dear Birmingham:

Ms. Class believes that censors are textual perverts. But she wonders why you would read aloud authors whose books students already read on their own. Why not expose them to literature they might not otherwise encounter?

Dear Ms. Class:

I am stunned that you would encourage teachers to yield to censors by avoiding reading such authors as Judy Blume aloud. I think the answer to censorship is for every teacher to read Blume aloud.

— Osceola, MI

Dear Osceola:

What a dreary prospect. Ms. Class respects children's desire to read Blume or Zindel or the Babysitters Club or assorted vampire tales. Bad books find their audience. They don't need teachers to distribute them—or read them aloud. Blume's books, to name just one example of bad books, have world wide sales of around thirty million copies. No other author comes close.

Michele Landberg hits the nail on the head in her *Guide to Children's Books* when she points out that what is objectionable about Blume's books is "her bland and unquestioning acceptance of majority values, of conformity, consumerism, materialism, unbounded narcissism and flat, sloppy, ungrammatical, inexpressive speech."

Ms. Class is strong enough in her own convictions that she does not fear occasional agreement with right-wing crazies about a book. Certainly the fact that Ms. Blume is singled out by book-banners is not reason enough to read her works aloud.

CERTIFICATION FACTOR ANALYSIS

Dear Ms. Class:

I'm trying to find out if I have met the requirements for a new certification. My problem is that every time I phone the Bureau of Teacher Certification I get a busy signal.

— Schenectady, NY

Dear Schenectady:

After extensive research, Ms. Class has discovered that in your state when employees of the Department of Motor Vehicles are forced out on mental health disability, they go to work for Bureau of Teacher Certification. The bureau opens its phone lines at 1:00 P.M. They close these phone lines at 1:08 P.M. Employees spend the rest of the day shredding college transcripts that prospective teachers send them. One teacher who took a week's sick leave so he could visit the bureau phoned in that he had located the office. He was never heard from again.

Before you write and chastize Ms. Class for exaggeration, let her point out that she has personal experience with the shredding policies of the New York State Bureau of Certification.

Dear Ms. Class:

Our PE teacher was laid off in a budget squeeze last year, and now we classroom teachers are expected to lead our classes in a physical education program twice a week. I'm not exactly athletic and don't feel I can keep up with, let alone lead, my active class of twenty-eight ten-year-olds. I am worried about someone's getting hurt. Can the board of education continue to require me to do this?

— Lincoln, CA

Dear Lincoln:

Ms. Class actually got through to the Bureau of Certification in your state. They said, as an elementary teacher, you are automatically certified to teach physical education (as well as sex education, swish-and-spit dental hygiene, drug awareness, self-esteem, creative imaging, music, art, and all the other programs whose mandates were once supported by auxiliary personnel). Since you are certified, you can indeed be required to do almost anything.

Be not of faint heart. Ms. Class would wager her unabridged dictionary that you can find a colleague who would rather teach PE than, say, mathematics or social studies. Arrange a swap.

CHANNELING BARGAIN BASEMENT

Dear Ms. Class:

My school has the chance to get fifty thousand dollars worth of sophisticated television equipment and access to a daily news program. It is offered by Channel One. People are pressuring the board of education because they say it's wrong for schools to expose kids to two minutes of commercials that are part of Channel One's twelve-minute news program. I can't believe we'd turn down fifty thousand dollars because of two minutes of ads.

— Topeka, KS

Dear Topeka:

Ms. Class wonders what you would want a school to do, having set its price of whoredom, when, say, the National Rifle Association, Greenpeace, the Palestine Liberation Organization, Planned Parenthood, Daughters of the American Revolution, the Flat Earth Society, the Gay Alliance, vivisectionists, vegetarians, Rotarians, Rosicrucians, Scientologists, or the local skinheads show up at the schoolhouse door with fifty thousand dollars and their individual curriculums to save America?

The issue, dear teacher, is not fifty thousand dollars; it's not even the two minutes of ads. The issue is that a twelve-minute TV show amounts to twenty-four percent of the instructional time of a fifty-minute class period. Ms. Class won't harangue you with the observation that the Channel One show is the progeny of a backstreet liaison between *A Current Affair* and Trivial Pursuit. What she does want you to consider is if you really want to sell your students and your own expertise so cheaply.

Ms. Class trusts that you and your school will have the courage to just say no to Cracker Jack prizes and other bribes.

CHARACTER CLARIFICATION

Dear Ms. Class:

Our primary-grade team has received a special grant to teach character education. I wonder if there is a values clarification program for primary graders.

— Las Vegas, NV

Dear Las Vegas:

Ms. Class feels grateful not to know about a values clarification program for primary graders. But it probably exists. The first rule of education is that if somebody will fund it, somebody will do it. The second rule of education is that once something is funded, workbooks will follow.

For character education, Ms. Class recommends reading *Ramona the Brave* to first graders, *Charlotte's Web* to second graders, and *Where the Sidewalk Ends* to third graders. She does not recommend interrogating students after these readings. Let the strong moral content embedded in wonderful language engulf students as the entertainment it was meant to be.

CHRISTMAS CAPERS DOWNSIZING

Dear Ms. Class:
  I wonder if you have any suggestions for lessening the Christmas hysteria that builds up the last two weeks or so before vacation. I teach third grade and would appreciate any craft ideas you have for Christmas, Hanukkah, or Kwanza.

— Des Moines, IA

Dear Des Moines:
  Ms. Class must confess that she gives more attention to Ground Hog Day than to any of the holidays you mention. In her twenty years of teaching she has never made a milk-carton Santa or spun a dreidel. She feels religious holidays are already commercialized enough and do not need her participation to further debase them.
  Ms. Class does celebrate a variety of holidays with her students: Halloween, Valentine's Day, winter and spring solstices are constants. Other holidays Ms. Class has been known to celebrate intermittently include: Clean Out Your Desk Week in January, Pencil Week in February, First Oreo Cookie Sale in March, Library Week in April, International Pickle Week in May, Whale Appreciation Month and National Dog-Bite Prevention Week in June, Dictionary Day in October, and International Cat Week in November.
  As for December, in addition to the winter solstice, you can honor Alexandre Gustave Eiffel's birth on December 15 with a toothpick or straw tower-building contest. Or honor the births of Isaac Newton on December 25 and Johannes Kepler on December 27 with studies of prisms, pendulums, the solar system, tessellations, and a host of other things that children find fascinating. Any child will prefer making a tessellation or a solar system mobile to making a milk-carton Santa. And tessellations and mobiles can be justified pedagogically. Three-foot-high candy canes and toilet-paper-roll angels have no justification.

CLASSICS CODE

Dear Ms. Class:
  I really don't understand what you have against the classics. We need to help our children gain values, and the classics can help!

— Fairbanks, AK

Dear Fairbanks:

Ms. Class says, "God bless the classics, every one." She reads Kipling and Stevenson and E. B. White aloud to her own third-grade students. But she would support a Constitutional amendment declaring that any teacher caught assigning Dickens to a person under the age of twenty-five would be required to contribute one hundred hours of community service. Libraries can always use volunteer help shelving books. It might be instructive for teachers to see what people read when they get a choice.

Because Ms. Class herself recently got up the nerve to reread *Moby Dick* (a book carefully avoided since her college days), she thinks the punishment for premature assignment should be harsher. Here is a grand book—definitely written for the over-forty set. Besides going on and on about fishy matters, Melville rails at God about the inevitability of death, hardly a notion accessible to twelve-year-olds or eighteen-year-olds or twenty-five-year-olds.

A *New York Times* columnist once suggested that classics could be revitalized by having modern authors rewrite them. Consider the possibilities: *Little Women* by Vladimir Nabokov, *Huckleberry Finn* by James Baldwin, *A Tale of Two Cities* by Joseph Heller, *Wuthering Heights* by Tennessee Williams, *The Iliad* by Norman Mailer.

Dear Ms. Class:

Minority children don't need the classics rewritten; they need to be introduced to the ethnic literature that will show them their roots.

— San Francisco, CA

Dear San Francisco:

Maybe so. But consider this: one of Franklin Delano Roosevelt's favorite books as a child was Rudyard Kipling's *Plain Tales from the Hills*. Need Ms. Class point out that the hills referred to were not those around Hyde Park? Young Harry Truman loved George Eliot and Mark Twain. Mark Twain might have been close to home for a boy from Missouri, but George Eliot certainly was not. And consider this: when Colin Powell, the former Chairman of the Joint Chiefs of Staff, was asked about the book he most remembered from his early years as a black boy growing up in The Bronx, he cited *My Antonia* by Willa Cather. This regional novel, in case you need reminding, gained fame early in the century; it's a coming-of-age story set in Nebraska.

CLASSROOM MANAGEMENT FLAPDOODLE

Dear Ms. Class:

From reading your advice for years, I can guess your attitude about assertive discipline, but surely you believe in some sort of strategies for achieving effective classroom management.

— Billings, MT

Dear Billings:

Yes, indeed. Ms. Class appreciates the way you ask a question. Not wishing to sound alarmist, Ms. Class has devised some cautionary precepts regarding classroom management.

- *The first law of classroom management:* all the theory in the world does not prepare you for classroom vomit.

- *The second law of classroom management:* children never throw up in the lavatory.

- *The third law of classroom management:* there is no convenient time for a child to throw up.

- *The fourth law of classroom management:* whenever a child vomits, the custodian has just left the building.

Finally, you should remember that a teacher invented the phrase *calm before the storm.* She was describing third graders, not weather patterns.

Dear Ms. Class:

As a longtime principal, I can tell you that the difference between a successful teacher and an unsuccessful one is, pure and simple, classroom management.

— Moscow, ID

Dear Moscow:

Nothing about teaching is either pure or simple. Ms. Class resists any notion that classrooms should look alike. Management is, after all, a matter of definition. One teacher's management system is another teacher's definition of prison. One teacher's system of shared decision making would be described by another teacher as pandemonium.

Ms. Class thinks an effective principal is one who is able to recognize and appreciate teachers' diverse working styles and to acknowledge that there are many different ways to get the job done.

CLOSURE CORRELATIONS

Dear Ms. Class:
I wonder if you have any tips on how to bring closure to a lesson. I always seem to run out of time. A lesson is going great, my ninth graders are enthusiastic, and then the bell rings, and they leave without having reached closure.

— Knoxville, TN

Dear Knoxville:
Ms. Class thinks it's great that ninth graders leave your classroom feeling enthusiastic. Ms. Class is reluctant to inquire why anyone would want closure, even in the presence of teenagers.

CLOZE ENCOUNTERS

Dear Ms. Class:
I wanted to get my students ready for the Cloze reading test administered by my district, so we practiced Cloze reading for half an hour each day. I don't understand why my students had the lowest scores of all the sixth grades.

— Tallahassee, FL

Dear Tallahassee:
How would you __(1)__ to the printed page if you were __(2)__ to read __(3)__ __(4)__ every day?

1) a) repel
   b) react
   c) readjust
   d) reactivate

2) a) responded
   b) reminded
   c) required
   d) readjusted

3) a) tedious
   b) meaningless
   c) disjointed
   d) wretched

4) a) love letters
   b) gossip
   c) sex manuals
   d) worksheets

COFFEE CUP EMINENT DOMAIN

Dear Ms. Class:
I know this sounds petty, but it drives me crazy and I hope you can help. Like most teachers, I have conditioned my digestive systems to handle just about anything. I'm used to the coffee in the faculty room tasting like dishwater mixed with drain cleaner, but I can't stand the powdered whitener. So every Monday I bring in a pint of milk. It would last me all week—if people didn't steal it. I have put "private

property" signs on the carton; I have tried hiding the milk in a yogurt container. Nothing works. People continue to steal my milk. Help!

— Philadelphia, PA

Dear Philly:

Ms. Class had exactly the same problem, and she decided a petty problem deserved a petty solution. She bought a one-half pint milk container in the cafeteria and kept it in her classroom. She was able to use milk from the carton for a couple of days. When it spoiled, she moved the old carton to the faculty room refrigerator and bought a new one in the cafeteria.

COLLABORATION SUBGROUP CRIME PREVENTION

Dear Ms. Class:

One of my fourth graders is a terrific writer. Jackie's problem is he hates working in a group. He wants to go off in a corner to write. He refuses to show his draft to anyone. How can I help Jackie learn to collaborate?

— Dover, DE

Dear Dover:

Perhaps, as young as he is, Jackie has already discovered what the prolific and astute writer Paul Theroux noted, "Few books get written or paintings get painted in communes."

Eeyore also had words that serve us well to remember: "We can't all, and some of us don't. That's all there is to it." When Sam Pickering, the model for the teacher in *Dead Poets Society,* went to the middle school for a parent-teacher conference, the teacher told him his son was "getting better at working with others."

Pickering's reaction was not enthusiastic. "What," he exclaimed, "I hope not. Arrogance runs in my family, and until now I thought Francis inherited a saving dose of it. Nothing would upset me more than seeing him at ease amid the undistinguished herd."

COMFORT STATIONS

Dear Ms. Class:

Help! My school district is trying to force me to make an involuntary transfer to a school across town. I have taught sixth grade in my present school for fifteen years. I am comfortable here. Not only do I know the neighborhood, I can't imagine moving fifteen years worth of supplies.

What can I do to fight this?

— Springfield, IL

Dear Springfield:

Ms. Class advises you to switch rather than fight. Ms. Class believes that every teacher should change schools every four years. This will encourage teachers to clean their desks and also enable them to keep telling the same stories in the faculty room.

COMPUTER-ASSISTED LEARNING ULTRALITE

Dear Ms. Class:

Our school has recently established a lab for computer-assisted learning. Teachers are supposed to identify language arts skills in which their students are deficient and cycle them through the lab until they master these skills. My principal says this is "individualized learning," but I have my doubts.

— Madison, WI

Dear Madison:

This is an example of a teacher's need to ask herself, "Is this an advancement or an exaggeration?" A workbook skill is made no better for being able to light up, dance a jig, and whistle "Home on the Range." When all is said and done, a consonant blend that lights up and zaps wicked invaders is still a consonant blend. A student would get more pleasure and just as much information about language from sucking on jujubes.

This, too, will pass when teachers stop clinging to their floppy disks, right or wrong, and realize that one-size-fits-all does not work any better with computer instruction than it does with apparel.

Dear Ms. Class:

Our school board recently declared that books are obsolete. They voted to freeze book funds and to move computers into the library and cycle students through. They want students to "test out" on minimum competency reading skills. I'm heartsick and don't know what to do.

— Troy, NY

Dear Troy:

You are right in resisting the transformation of your library into a technodrill dump, which is a triumph of technology over culture. Do not go gentle into that transistorized maze. Resist much. You need not do this alone. People who want to replace books with disks are themselves not readers. Look for literate support in the community: the PTO, League of Women Voters, Junior League, Chamber of Commerce, and the newspaper are places to start.

CONDOM LITERACY SKILL MAINTENANCE

Dear Ms. Class:

I teach on the fifth-grade team. Like it or not, we are trying to deal with the fact that a number of our students will soon be active sexually, if they aren't already. We are encountering right-wing extremists who oppose our condom literacy program. Do you have any suggestions for combating this kind of parochial resistance?

— Newark, NJ

Dear Newark:

Ms. Class would caution you that when you brand people who disagree with you as "right-wing extremists" you ensure that no discussion can take place. Ms. Class confesses to being disquieted by the information that all ten-year-olds in a school would be subjected to something called condom literacy. Does this mean you ask them to read about condoms? Ask them to read the directions on prophylactic packages? Or are you using "literacy" in one of those neo-chic ways that has nothing to do with print and requires students to practice putting condoms on a banana?

Ms. Class believes schools must stop promising to take on the responsibility for the whole child. She would suggest giving the condoms to the parents of your fifth graders and asking them to assume responsibility for distribution and use.

CONFIDENCE COUNTDOWN

Dear Ms. Class:

I've been teaching for seven years. I love teaching, at least I think I do. What I want to know is: why am I nervous every day? Every day I go into that classroom worrying that I won't know how to deal with the children in my care. When I think about it, when I look back on the past six years, I can think of many wonderful classroom moments. So why am I so apprehensive?

— Buffalo, NY

Dear Buffalo:

From your very own words, Ms. Class knows you have the essential quality of good teacher: humility. Being a teacher means knowing that at any moment you can behave badly.

Teachers rarely experience triumphs in their classrooms, because there is no time to stop and catch their breath, never mind rejoice. The triumphs of teaching are incidents remembered and reflected on during the tranquility of days off, which is why it's a bad idea for teachers to teach summer school.

CONSULTANT CONTEXT INTERSECTION

Dear Ms. Class:

Because of a failed bond election, our board of education put a freeze on teacher travel to conferences. I'm a taxpayer, too, and I appreciate the need to save money. But the district is still hiring high-priced consultants for inservice training. I don't understand why we don't tap the talents of our own personnel. Ironically, some of our teachers are hired as consultants in other districts—but never here.

— Lincoln, CA

Dear Lincoln:

Although the best consultants are simply teachers with business cards and frequent flier miles, the first rule of consulting is that consultants come from somewhere else. People used to say a consultant had to come from thirty miles distance. This distance increases in direct proportion to the number of consultants available and the amount of money the district is willing to spend.

The fact is that whether or not consultants are truly beneficial, they are not what education is about. As Phillip Lopate, New York City teacher and writer, observed in *Against Joie de Vivre,* "What else was being a teacher but trying to respond as humanly as possible to problems that would not wait for an expert."

CONTENT AREA, PERIMETER, AND VOLUME

Dear Ms. Class:

I recently received my M.A. degree in content-area reading. I'm looking for advice on the best region of the country to seek employment. Where are content-area reading specialists most in demand?

— Lexington, KY

Dear Lexington:

Wait just one moment. What, pray tell, is noncontent reading?

CONTINUUM CHASM

Dear Ms. Class:

Our curriculum materials are generated specifically for non-value-laden, individualized instruction to move students along a continuum of carefully structured skills toward a clear goal. We would like your readers to know that we are looking for teachers and administrators with similar goals.

— Charlotte, NC

Dear Charlotte:

Ms. Class appreciates your need for co-conspirators. Ms. Class recommends that you read the ads in such professional journals as *Educational Leadership*, a journal with plenty of continuums and one in which, one may safely assume, Ms. Class will not find her words published.

CONTROL OVERFLOW

Dear Ms. Class:

My colleagues let the children decorate the hallways without any supervision. The result is a messy hodgepodge that makes me shudder every time I walk down the hall. I feel it is irresponsible to allow misspelled papers—and worse—to go on public display. I worry about the bad example this sets for my students and about the terrible impression it gives parents or school board members who might see it.

— Waterbury, CT

Dear Waterbury:

You pose one of those quintessential dilemmas of the schoolhouse. As Henry Adams observed in *The Education of Henry Adams,* "Chaos often breeds life, when order breeds habit." Forty-six percent of a given faculty choose habit over life; twenty-eight percent choose life over habit, and twenty-six percent avoid choosing anything.

So much for the pedagogical underpinnings of bulletin boards. That said, Waterbury, please remember: a misspelling is not the eighth deadly sin. Please take Ms. Class's questionnaire to determine if you are a control freak:

- Do you go in to school on the weekend so you can line up the chairs and alphabetize the administrative memos you've received during the week?

- Do you carefully fold crepe paper borders and pack them away so you can reuse them year after year?

- Can you find these borders when you need them?

- Do you decline parents' offers of refreshments for classroom parties because you think cups and napkins should match and you don't want orange juice and Oreos spoiling your color theme?

If you answered yes to any of the above, Ms. Class hopes, dear teacher, that you get a life.

CRITICAL THINKING PRETEST

Dear Ms. Class:

Whatever happened to critical thinking? A few years ago we heard a lot about it, but it seems to have disappeared.

Developmentally, when can children learn to be critical thinkers?

— Hanover, NH

Dear Hanover:

Ms. Class believes that in schools all thinking is critical as well as rare. The question is not at what age children can do something but at what age teachers are willing to acknowledge it.

Here is an example of what Ms. Class means: second graders in Baton Rouge were asked to figure out how many vans would be needed to carry twenty children and two adults back to school if seven passengers could fit into each van. Students offered the following answers, along with explanations.

Vans

4	Twenty children and two adults need twenty-two places.
3	We can squeeze eight people into one of the vans. It would be wasteful to use four vans and have one van with only one person in it.
2	We all have to fit in two vans because there are only two teachers. We can't go in a van without a teacher.
1	It's only a few blocks. My mom would cram us all into one van.

A teacher who looks only for the algorithmically correct answer will miss knowing that eight-year-olds are thinkers.

CULTURAL LITERACY WINDSHEAR

Dear Ms. Class:

I worry about the lack of cultural literacy in my second graders. They don't even know common nursery rhymes. I wonder how one best goes about catching children up on the vital parts of our culture.

— Pawtucket, RI

Dear Pawtucket:

First, one has to decide what is vital. That's no easy task. Professor E. D. Hirsch got famous identifying the five thousand things one must know in order to be culturally literate. Contending that knowledge is sequential, that small bits of information lead to larger pieces of essential understanding, Hirsch insists, "If there's one nursery rhyme you don't know it might not matter. But multiply 'Humpty Dumpty' by one thousand and eventually you'll be missing what you need to know to understand more demanding material and to make progress."

To which Ms. Class replies, "Hogwash!"

Ms. Class finds it wonderfully loony to posit "Old Mother Hubbard" as a critical first step in the systematic acquisition of a college degree, a two-car garage, and a favorable balance of trade. Children love to parrot nursery rhymes, but they don't understand them. And neither do adults, unless they search out a scholarly annotation that explains obscure historical and political references. Nursery rhymes do not endure for the information they contain; nursery rhymes endure for the pleasure children find in the rollicking rhymes, the irresistible rhythm, and the pure nonsense of it all. It's the sound that matters, not the sense.

More than that, it is wrong to choose a four-year-old's bedtime story or a second grader's read-aloud with an eye on his SAT scores and her acceptance to law school. Treat children's exposure to literature as an information delivery system, treat it as a duty or a means to an end, and you will kill their pleasure in books. We must read to children for the joy of it—our joy and theirs.

CURRICULUM GATES AND HURDLES

Dear Ms. Class:

I am a second-grade teacher, working on a primary-grade curriculum committee. We hope that if our students see school as a job, we will get them ready for life, ready to enter the work force as productive members of our twenty-first century society, and they will be more serious about their assignments. We have set up a market economy linking mathematics and social studies. We wonder if you can suggest some resources for real-life curriculum in language arts.

— Baltimore, MD

Dear Baltimore:

No, no, a thousand times no. Please dismiss any notion of getting second graders ready for life. A second-grade teacher should not even worry about getting her students ready for third grade. The proper concern of every primary-grade teacher must be the current lives of the children in her care.

Ms. Class entreats you to nurture children as children, not as miniature stockbrokers and bankers. Life is today, not tomorrow. Primary teachers should concern themselves not with good results, but with good beginnings.

A good place for your committee to start is to place a moratorium on the use of the term *twenty-first century.*

Dear Ms. Class:

Our math coordinator is an ex-football coach who has never read the NCTM *Standards.* He listens to conservative members of the board of education and insists we follow a curriculum guide based on a strict skills sequence. I teach third grade and believe in a discovery approach to math, but I don't have tenure, so I'm worried about bucking city hall. Any suggestions?

— Buffalo, NY

Dear Buffalo:

Ms. Class has the same respect for her district curriculum guidelines that Jack Nicholson had for restaurant menus. Remember that classic scene in *Five Easy Pieces?* Nicholson orders two pieces of wheat toast. The waitress informs him wheat toast isn't on the menu and there's no way the cook can prepare anything not on the menu. Nicholson says, "Let me make it easy for you. I'll have the chicken salad sandwich on wheat bread. Hold the mayonnaise. Hold the lettuce. Hold the chicken salad. Toast the bread." That's it: curriculum guidelines and menus, be damned. Work with the ingredients you've got, adapting them to suit your needs and the needs of your students.

Since you're untenured, Ms. Class does recommend you take a realistic view and, like Jack Nicholson, strip the curriculum to meet your needs. Figure out what you must do to satisfy the administrator. Probably you should have the kids memorize their math facts. Administrators have a way of zeroing in on the obvious. But that need not take up much of your math time. Once you've done the obvious, you'll have plenty of time left for what matters.

CUSTODIAL TIME ON TASK

Dear Ms. Class:

Recently while working late at school I spotted the custodian at the end of the hall—in his underwear. I ducked into a restroom and hid there for ten minutes. Then I dashed out of the building. I don't think he saw me. I frequently work late, and I don't want any more incidents. I don't feel comfortable asking the man to wear more clothes, but I don't want to cause him trouble by getting the principal involved. Any advice?

— Laramie, WY

Dear Laramie:

Your dilemma causes Ms. Class to rescind a two-decade-long principle: never argue with custodians and secretaries. You seem to have three choices:

1. Leave an anonymous note indicating he's been observed "underdressed."

2. Let the principal sort things out. Getting paid one and a half times your salary means he can correct and chastise custodians and secretaries at will.

3. Best of all, go home on time, leaving the custodian to dress and undress as he wishes. Ms. Class wonders why you work late so often. Getting out of the building on time is definitely your best option.

Dear Ms. Class:

How does one go about getting the custodian to clean the room—without antagonizing him?

— Santa Fe, NM

Dear Santa Fe:

You are up against custodial eminent domain. The National Standards for Custodians sets specific guidelines:

- Empty trash cans on the second Thursday following the second Tuesday of every third month, whether they need it or not.
- Leave floors alone until they pass the custodial litmus test, that is, until they change color.
- Don't dust or mop. Wait a few years and get a snow blower.
- When the toilets get so dirty they don't flush, apply for a transfer to another school.

Dear Ms. Class:

Enough about negligent custodians. I'll tell you about an outstanding one. For six years, he's coped with my mess without a word of complaint. Unasked, he helps me clean up papier-mâché overflow—and then comes back to tell the kids how much he likes their sculptures. When a child gets sick, we ask for Joe because we know he will comfort the child as well as clean up the mess. If I were a better-organized person and one less inclined to launch these eight-year-olds into ambitious projects, Joe's job would be a lot easier. But he smiles and he cleans. He says he's going to get his revenge by making sure his grandson gets into this class.

— Tucson, AZ

Dear Tucson:

Ms. Class is grateful for your letter. Too often we take the time to write only when we have a complaint. You have reminded us all to scatter a few roses occasionally. Ms. Class hopes you share your letter with Joe and that you remind students to write him a thank-you note from time to time. Ms. Class doesn't know if there is such a thing as Custodian's Day. If there isn't, your class could invent it. What fun! Please send Ms. Class an invitation.

DEPARTMENT OF EDUCATION BUNGEE JUMPING

Dear Ms. Class:

I wonder why politicians choose lawyers to head the U. S. Department of Education. Why not appoint an educator?

— Provo, UT

Dear Provo:

Ms. Class appreciates your point, but the Ed.D.'s she knows don't know any more about schools than lawyers do.

Scottish education reformer A. S. Neill says the real problem with education departments is that, like all departments, they lack a sense of humor. "And it is humor that makes a man decent and kind and human."

DISADVANTAGED MAPPING

Dear Ms. Class:

I'm regarded as a good disciplinarian. If I ever send one of my sixth graders to the office, I regard it as a personal failure. But this year I have a disadvantaged student who is out of control. I've tried everything from alternative curriculum to bribery. Nothing works. Can you offer some advice for dealing with disadvantaged students?

— Brooklyn, NY

Dear Brooklyn:

Although Ms. Class respects your willingness to accept responsibility and not try to push problems off on someone else, she laments your use of the term *disadvantaged student*. To use such a term is to hide behind a euphemism. Ms. Class wonders if you mean a child who is poor, a child of an ethnicity different from your own, a child who cannot read, or perhaps something else.

Although Ms. Class does not employ vulgarisms herself, she admires the honesty of James Herndon, a longtime seventh-grade teacher and author of *The Way It 'Spozed to Be.* Mr. Herndon describes his most difficult student not as disadvantaged but as "a mean son of a bitch, no matter how he got that way."

How old is your troublesome student? Don Marquis recommended, "If a child shows himself incorrigible, he should be decently and quietly beheaded at the age of twelve."

Of course Ms. Class doesn't call her students by vulgarities; nor does she behead them. But when the day is long and the twelve-year-olds obstreperous, retreating to a delicious moment of daydreaming about the guillotine is much more satisfying than calling them "disadvantaged."

DISCIPLINE OWNERSHIP

Dear Ms. Class:

I have completed a course in assertive discipline, and I just want to share with everyone how wonderful this course is. For the first time in my seven years of teaching, I have solved the problem of classroom control with my active bunch of fifth graders.

— Boise, ID

Dear Boise:

Please note that no one ever takes advantage of Ms. Class without her consent, not even a ten-year-old.

Assertive discipline is as attractive and easy as all truly great swindles are. Ms. Class begs you to consider that classroom control differs from stockyard control. Yes, in the short term, assertive discipline works. So do cattle prods.

Dear Ms. Class:

We are all concerned with the terrible behavior of children in our grades-four-to-six school. The language in the hallways is incredible. I find it hard to believe that such young children know these words. I'm not sure I know all the words they seem to know. These kids are loud and disrespectful and don't seem to care about anything but themselves. I hate to say this, but these kids are rotten people.

We have a schoolwide behavior system of rewards and punishments. This keeps control in the classrooms, but the hallways and cafeteria are a disaster.

— Milwaukee, WI

Dear Milwaukee:

Ms. Class understands your distress with impolite language. Gone are the days when children limited themselves to such epithets as "booger face" and "maggot breath." Nonetheless, Ms. Class cautions you not to confuse good behavior with good character. Stimulus-response programs such as the one you mention can produce specific, short-term good behavior. They have nothing to do with building character.

It is, of course, tempting for schools to prize docility—honoring the child who does what is wanted without even having to be told. But schools need to prize other qualities too. Ms. Class commends to you, dear teacher, the advice of Harlem educator Ned O'Gorman. In *The Wilderness and the Laurel Tree* Mr. O'Gorman says that teachers should "praise arrogance, anger, and stubbornness, rather than docility, mildness, and passivity."

If your prefer to reflect on the lessons of history, consider Kropotkin's comment on the Russian Revolution: "The hopeless don't revolt, because revolution is an act of hope."

In any case, just remember: you cannot nominate students to the Federal Relocation Program.

Dear Ms. Class:

I am a new teacher. My principal says that the most important thing I can do is learn how to get discipline in my classroom. He says consistency is vital for teachers, and he has given me a behavioral checklist to help me achieve consistency. I worry that I seem to spend more time on the checklist than on the curriculum. Can you give me advice on how to keep control and still have time to teach?

— Pierre, SD

Dear Pierre:

The reason administrative positions require a special certification is so prospective principals can learn to make perfect and impossible statements about discipline. Contrary to what they learn in their courses, conformity is not one of the ten commandments. Neither is consistency. And inconsistency isn't one of the seven deadly sins, either. When Sam Pickering, the model for the teacher in *Dead Poets Society,* heard a school psychologist say to kindergarten parents, "be consistent. When you make a decision stick to it," he reflected that by the time his son Francis was five he had battled Dad out of decisiveness. "Suddenly, though, I realized that the psychologist got his ideas from a textbook, not from life. Firm decisive parents, I decided, raised quitters, children who taking *no* for *no* buckled under when the going got tough. I, on the other hand, was instilling drive, intensity, persistence, and the great American virtue of stick-to-itiveness. When the going got to no, Francis clamped down, and no matter how I or anyone else shook or twisted, he hung on until yes."

Ms. Class hopes Sam Pickering has convinced you not to worry about consistency. The most important thing you can do is to *teach* your students something. The second most important thing is to encourage them to become risk takers so they can teach themselves. When you get the curriculum right, classroom behavior follows. Contrary to most administrative advice, it doesn't work the other way around.

Dear Ms. Class:

You can't teach children who aren't in control. And you can't get them under control without a clear and consistent discipline code of clear consequences. My school has been operating two years without a discipline policy. A faculty committee came up with a discipline policy of thirty-two items, but the administrators worry our document is an infringement on their authority. They have called for joint meetings—with teachers, parents, and administrators. I worry that we will just spend more time reinventing the wheel—and meanwhile, the kids are out of control.

— White Plains, NY

Dear White Plains:

Ms. Class wonders why, when there were only ten commandments, a school needs a thirty-two-item discipline code.

There are two issues involved here. First, calling for more meetings is the administrative ploy for tabling the issue. If enough meetings are held, the meetings become more important than the problem.

Second, if and when you get it, a thirty-two-item discipline code isn't going to make you as happy as you hope. What you are looking for is a code of justice: namely to punish the guilty. But as the great jurist Clarence Darrow pointed out, "There is no such thing as justice—in or out of court." To count on thirty-two tenets bringing justice to your schoolroom is to doom yourself to disappointment.

Dear Ms. Class:

I am interested in learning about innovative classroom management systems such as congruent control. Please help me!

— Canton, OH

Dear Canton:

Ms. Class wonders if you mean discipline. Since you seem to want to be up-to-date, here are some words you can punch into a computer search:

assertive discipline
behavior modification
collaboration
conflict resolution

congruent communication
democratic decision making
influence management
joint decision making
M & M bartering
negotiation
shared decision making
values clarification

The next time you write a discipline referral, you can demonstrate that you are an educationist with modern ideas by using the discipline shuffle board (see below): choose one term from column A, one term from column B, and one term from column C. So your referral might read: Sadie has difficulty with her *collaborative modification parameters*.

If you are looking for a career change, design workshop topics using the same method, billing yourself, for example, as an *interpersonal motivational clarification facilitator*.

A	B	C
values	status	device
conflict	problem	management
interpersonal	motivation(al)	resolution
behavioral	cooperation	mechanism
collaborative	decision	orientation
hostility	negotiation	parameter
democratic	relations	process
joint	movement	plan
developmental	modification	goal
congruent	decision	area
sequential	role	clarification
experimental	influencing	closure
viable	demonstrable	ramification

Dear Ms. Class:
    Even though I'm a principal, I find myself occasionally enjoying your humor. I do wonder, however, how long you'd keep smiling if you had to deal with the ridiculous "discipline problems" teachers send to my office. One teacher sends students to me when they show up to class without a pencil. Another sends them if they don't bring in homework. If students run in the hall, mutter a "shit" or "goddamn," or chew gum in class, they end up in my office.

— Santa Rosa, CA

Dear Santa Rosa:

Ms. Class suggests this modest proposal: ask teachers to write a five-hundred-word essay on why the principal needs to see each discipline referral. This will either cut down on discipline problems or improve faculty writing.

Dear Ms. Class:

This is my first year of teaching. My class embarrasses me every time we have a fire drill. They talk, poke, and in general create a disturbance. Please help me.

— Bismarck, ND

Dear Bismarck:

Every untenured teacher thinks other classes behave better than hers, particularly during fire drills, when every sneeze becomes so noticeable in a sea of silence. Although Ms. Class in no way wishes to diminish the importance of orderly fire drills, she begs you to stop looking in the mirror and chanting, "Mirror, Mirror, on the wall, who has the quietest fire drill line of all?" Ms. Class suspects you are being unnecessarily hard on yourself and your students. It sounds as though you are expending too much energy looking over your shoulder at other teachers' classes. Try inviting a member of the fire department to talk to your class on the importance of fire drills. If you are still worried, ask for a few tips from a teacher whose students' fire drill deportment you admire. You'll make that teacher's day. Teachers love giving advice.

Dear Ms. Class:

I have watched you skirt and scramble the discipline issue, and I wonder why. The truth is simple: schools should take a lesson from the military. Institute dress codes, behavior codes, learning expectations, and standards. Kick out troublemakers.

— Wheatland, CA

Dear Wheatland:

The truth is never pure and rarely simple. Ms. Class is relieved you don't advocate executing troublemakers.

Ms. Class's own second-grade teacher tied children to their desks if they were prone to wandering. She wound long, thick ropes round and round the child and the chair. Children who talked had their mouths taped shut with great gobs of tape. Ms. Class, who as you might suspect was talkative, recalls being glad her father was president of the board of education when she was in second grade.

DRESS CODE HIGH GEAR

Dear Ms. Class:

What do you think about bralessness? Not only does my department chair jiggle when she walks, her nipples are visible through the thin tops she wears. Since I teach eighth graders, she causes a disruption whenever she comes into the room. What can I do?

— Troy, NY

Dear Troy:

Since Ms. Class subscribes to the notion that clothes make the man (or woman), she suggests you spearhead a drive for a dress code for adults who work in your school. A neat, navy blue uniform with crisp white shirt would raise the professionalism of the staff and the grade point average of the student body. Ms. Class does not advocate that untenured faculty be forced to wear beanies, but administrators will probably want to be singled out by chevrons or some other heraldic device.

Dear Ms. Class:

Some teachers in our school have taken to wearing nose rings to school. It seems odd to me. What do you think?

— Long Beach, CA

Dear Long Beach:

Nobody over age twenty-one ought to wear a nose ring unless he/she meets two qualifications:

1. He/she carries a passport from an Eastern Hemispheric nation.

2. He/she carries papers proving royal descent.

Dear Ms. Class:

I teach in a very troubled district. Name an educational crisis, and we have it. If my school has a pedagogical policy on anything, I'm not aware of it, but recently the board of education passed a dress code policy. They define "wearing head coverings in the school building" as "misbehavior which impedes orderly class-room procedure." The effect is now we just have one more thing to get into a hassle with students about.

— Chicago, IL

Dear Chicago:

One could wish, couldn't one, that school boards would worry more about what's going on in the head rather than what sits atop it. If a school board wants to tackle the troublesome issue of appropriate dress for en-gaging in academic endeavor, then the insistence on bare heads seems a rather timid gesture. What are board members' thoughts on bare midriffs, bare chests, bare legs above the knee?

Ms. Class worries about equity. If a girl can decorate her head with scarves, wigs, hairpieces, and braids and bangles in the manner of an African tribeswoman, why then cannot a boy decorate his head with a nylon stocking? Are sweatbands permitted? At what point does a wide sweatband become a small hat?

Ms. Class does not wish to pursue this issue to the point of giddiness, but she recalls her own teaching days when "dungarees" were banned from the classroom. When the dungaree memo appeared, teachers rushed to their dictionaries and then pretended to watch for boys wearing pants of "a heavy coarse durable cotton twill woven from colored yarn." A vice principal tried to clarify the issue. "The real issue is cuffs. Pants must have cuffs." In practice, most teachers avoided the issue by looking at boys only from the neck up. Ms. Class suspects that if the head-covering rule makes it off the school board table, teachers in your school will start looking at students from the forehead down.

Ms. Class believes that the essence of teaching has not changed in the past twenty years: the essence of teaching is knowing what to ignore.

DRUG AWARENESS 1

Dear Ms. Class:

One of our teachers might be taking drugs. Every lunchtime, he sits alone in his car and gets the windows fogged up with smoke. A colleague and I think he's smoking pot because he acts so goofy sometimes. We wonder what our legal obligations are. A teacher is required to report possible drug abuse on the part of students. Does this apply to staff? On the one hand, we don't want drug addicts teaching in this school. On the other hand, we don't want to get sued. What should we do?

— Topeka, KS

Dear Topeka:

Nothing. If sitting in a car—or acting goofy—were against the law, we'd have a critical teacher shortage.

DRUG AWARENESS 2

Dear Ms. Class:

After a drug awareness program put on by our local police department, one of my fifth-grade students wrote me that her mother and her mother's boyfriend smoke pot. Although the girl is always neat and appears well fed, her previous notes to me indicate that she worries about the abusive nature of her mother's relationship with this man. In addition to using drugs, the couple also drink a lot, fight a lot, and neglect the four children. I feel it is my responsibility to inform the authorities. I want to get some help for these children. Also, in my state if a teacher does not turn in known drug abusers she can be fined and her license revoked.

Some of my colleagues insist that I'm overreacting and this is none of my business. What do you think?

— Fresno, CA

Dear Fresno:

First of all, Ms. Class thinks you should stop encouraging children to write their family's personal business in their notes to you. Children need to learn the difference between personal and public discourse. School is a place for public discourse, not a place for children to write about their parents' sexual relationships or drinking patterns.

Second, you do not have any evidence—other than the girl's say-so— that there is drug or alcohol or spousal abuse in the family. What to adults is a disagreement may be very scary to a child. Ms. Class is not suggesting that you ignore possible abuse. Ask the school nurse to contact the mother. The family may indeed have a problem. But the real problem may well be an unhappy little girl who wants attention, perhaps a child who needs professional counseling, not police interrogation. In any case, you should definitely turn in your police badge and stop using a classroom note exchange as an excuse to probe intimate family matters.

EASY-READER IMPACT STATEMENT

Dear Ms. Class:

Although I believe in heterogeneous grouping, I also want my students to have the experience of sharing a piece of great literature. My school has class sets of ten great classics in easy-to-read editions: *Gulliver's Travels, Moby Dick, Oliver Twist, Ivanhoe, Treasure Island, Tom Sawyer, The Three Musketeers, Don Quixote, Robinson Crusoe,* and *Julius Caesar.* Which would you recommend for fifth graders?

— Little Rock, AR

Dear Little Rock:

None. Ms. Class entreats you to abandon this idea. All classics cannot be made accessible to all readers. In an easy-to-read edition, *Moby Dick*, for example, becomes a fish story. Please consider that a reader has to earn *Moby Dick*. No one under forty should attempt this masterwork.

If Moses hadn't been in a hurry he would have received the eleventh commandment: *Children shall not be force-fed books written for adults.* None of the books you mention were written for fifth graders. Ms. Class recommends choosing a good book that was written for fifth graders. Your librarian can help you. For starters, Ms. Class recommends these golden oldies, which are readily available—and wonderful: *Incident at Hawk's Hill*, by Allan Eckert; *The Great Gilly Hopkins*, by Katherine Paterson; *The Pinballs*, by Betsy Byars; *From the Mixed-Up Files of Mrs. Basil E. Frankweiler*, by E. L. Konigsburg; *The Broccoli Tapes*, by Jan Slepian. These books are so good that not only has Ms. Class read them several times, her husband has even read them.

EDUCATE: VERB FORMS

Dear Ms. Class:

The woman who teaches next door lets her students walk all over her. She's a nice person and means well, but she can't control her students. How can I help her?

— Muncie, IN

Dear Muncie:

Try putting things in perspective. You think your colleague lacks control; maybe she thinks you are uptight. It all depends on where one is standing, doesn't it?

Think about these educational verb forms:

- I am educated; you put in your time; he squeaked by on a football scholarship.

- I've considered all options; you've changed your mind; he's gone back on his word.

- I have strong convictions; you're opinionated; he's biased.

- My students collaborate; your students talk a lot; her students walk all over her.

EDUCATION COURSE WHIPLASH

Dear Ms. Class:

My district requires teachers to earn a certain number of graduate credits every five years to maintain their teaching credentials. I don't have a problem with that.

The problem is the content of the courses. The professors offer grandiose and outrageous plans for changing the world. They lecture us about the oppressive capitalistic class structure, about our duty to choose literature that supports a nonsexist, nonracist, proabortion, egalitarian social structure. Pardon me, but I'd just like a little advice on teaching ninth graders. I wouldn't dare admit I'm a Republican who owns stock in the Exxon Corporation and thinks abortion is wrong. I don't bring my politics or religious views into my classroom. I don't think they identify who I am as a teacher, and I resent professors who insist they do (though I'd never be stupid enough to reveal my politics or my stock portfolio to them). I apologize for this diatribe, but I'm really ticked off. Here's my short question: do you think abortion, right or wrong, has any place in English class?

— Lansing, MI

Dear Lansing:

Ms. Class is herself a private person. She is distressed by the rigid stances taken in the name of diversity and tolerance. She agrees that teaching abortion rights in your English class is as inappropriate as teaching fetal rights. The irony is that teachers don't have as much influence on their students as your professors seem to think they do. Ninth graders couldn't care less whether their teachers are Republicans, Democrats, Socialists, or Rosacrucians. Perhaps it's just as well.

Dear Ms. Class:

I have been teaching for three months. My university training has prepared me in reader response, cooperative learning, and authentic assessment. But I don't know a thing about the nitty-gritty of day-to-day classroom survival. I wonder why education courses don't provide prospective teachers with the reality of teaching in inner-city schools (such as, "Always walk on the staircase in pairs").

— Newark, NJ

Dear Newark:

Ms. Class knows what you mean. She has always had ambitions to teach a course on basic classroom survival skills. She's not talking about *Milk Carton Creativity* or *Macaroni Math*. Schools of education already offer an extensive range of such courses. What Ms. Class is advocating is: How to Make a Three-Prong Plug Go Into a Two-Plug Socket; How to Build Bookshelves out of Boards and Garbage Cans; How to Clean the Fish Tank and Regenerate the Filter (Not to Mention the Fish). Fledgling teachers need a catalog of possible responses for a variety of occasions:

- The first time you're called a white m-f.
- The first time you're called honey.

- The first time your principal appears for an unscheduled observation and you, recovering from a late night, have just told the students they can listen to rap.
- The second time your principal appears for an unscheduled observation and you, needing to straighten out your checkbook, have just told the students they can listen to rap.
- The first time a student asks you out.
- The first time your principal asks you out.

And so on.

The reason no such course exists is that no Ed.D. could teach it and universities are careful about protecting their territorial rights. They are afraid the walls would crumble if they invited a teacher in to teach a course—and bring a whiff of reality into the ivied halls.

Dear Ms. Class:

I don't ordinarily read your work but I happened to come across your intemperate attack on college education courses. I would entreat you to reconsider your position. You do a disservice to the profession when you demean courses that call on the highest ideals of human psychology, courses designed to change the hearts and minds of future educators. It would be easy to give teachers what they want—cute projects they can do on Monday. Instead, we remain steadfast in our determination to guide them to higher principles. Future teachers would be better served by your supporting our efforts rather than attacking them.

— Los Angeles, CA

Dear Los Angeles:

Ms. Class does not believe that the English novelist John Galsworthy ever took an education course, but he pointed out that idealism increases in direct proportion to one's distance from the problem. American newspaperman and wit H. L. Mencken is a puzzlement. His biographies do not indicate that he studied to be a teacher, but surely anyone who could say that an idealist is "one who, noticing that a rose smells better than a cabbage, concludes that it will also make better soup" has met a few Ed.D.'s.

EFFECTIVENESS ERECTIONS

Dear Ms. Class:

I keep hearing a lot about teacher effectiveness. I'd like to receive training. Can you provide information?

— Indianapolis, IN

Dear Indianapolis:

No. Effectiveness is one of those snake-oil terms borrowed from entrepreneurs traveling the consultancy circles. If you're looking for a guarantee that you will accomplish what you set out to accomplish, then sign up to bag groceries or get elected to Congress. A teacher who offers warranties is either simple-minded or sneaky.

A teacher who wants to become more thoughtful about her craft will never go wrong by rereading John Dewey, Sylvia Ashton-Warner, John Holt, Frank Smith, and James Herndon. These educators provide lasting landmarks to guide us no matter how many hot-dog stands of teacher effectiveness are erected along the way.

Dear Ms. Class:

Your romantic pronouncements do not contravene the fact that teachers can and should be evaluated for effectiveness. An effective teacher should offer lessons that instruct; an effective teacher should create an ordered atmosphere in which learning can and will occur. Through observing effective teachers, researchers have developed optimum strategies by which teachers can reach peak performance. There is no mystery to it. These strategies can be taught and they can be learned and implemented in classrooms.

— Madison, WI

Dear Madison:

People who want to talk about and even evaluate teaching should take a page out of hard-boiled detective fiction writer Raymond Chandler. He said of writing, "If the stuff doesn't vibrate, the hell with it. I don't care how ingenious the plot is, it seems to me to mean nothing unless the prose has that glimmer of magic."

Ms. Class feels the same way about teaching. She wants to see that glimmer of magic in the classroom, wants to see humor and caring and tolerance and intelligence. If she sees that, she doesn't worry about optimum strategies, peak performance, and effectiveness, which sound more like something out of an ad agency account rep sales meeting than a third-grade classroom.

E-MAIL DEBT CEILING

Dear Ms. Class:

Our principal is gung ho for technology. She wrote a special grant so that our staff can network. There is now a computer on every teacher's desk. The principal wants us to communicate via E-mail. If we try to ask her a question or make a comment face-to-face, she brushes us aside, saying, "Put it on E-mail!"

She's actually keeping track of the number of entries each of us makes, sending out a monthly report—with a copy to the superintendent. She is talking about making cross-tabulations of interdepartmental mail. The principal sends us daily reminders about the "power and creative insight" that result from pushing keys on the computer.

She hasn't told us when we are supposed to find time for all this communication. Anyway, from what I've seen so far, it isn't communication; it's just typing.

— Philadelphia, PA

Dear Philadelphia:

Ms. Class hopes that one benefit is a reduction in memos clogging your mailbox. Save a tree. But Ms. Class confesses to being bemused by the number of people whose letter-writing output is limited to signing a pre-printed birthday card but who are enthralled by the idea of E-mail. Ms. Class wonders if your principal might better spend her time figuring out what prevents your faculty from talking to each other face-to-face.

EMPOWERMENT EUPHORIA

Dear Ms. Class:

My district is offering an inservice course in teacher empowerment. I am confused by the term. I thought teachers sought greater power over their working lives, meaning salary and working conditions, through their unions. The term empowerment, though, seems more mystical, and certainly the people talking about it are not union types. I'm not sure what the agenda is or where the power is. What does empowerment have to do with power or with the working lives of teachers?

— Kansas City, KS

Dear Kansas City:

Not a thing. If you wonder if you need a haircut, you don't ask the hairdresser; you look in a mirror. If you wonder if you have power, you don't ask your board of education; you look at your students.

Empowerment workshops are the result of both professional ennui and entrepreneurial greed. When people who have become bored by children and curriculum hold endless meetings about restructuring their lives, they hire a consulting empowerist who is out to line his pockets. Ostentatious rhetoric is invariably the result. Sometimes empowerment workshops are initiated by administrators as an effective means of containing teacher autonomy. In either case, teacher empowerment inservice ends up being nothing more than smoke and mirrors.

Don't confuse empowerment with job satisfaction. If you are looking for job satisfaction, consider Winnie-the-Pooh's advice: "Poetry and Hums aren't things which you get, they're things which get *you*. And all you can do is go where they can find you."

Dear Ms. Class:

Don't you think teachers would be more effective in the classroom if they had more clout in the community? And the way to get clout is to get better salaries.

— San Jose, CA

Dear San Jose:

Get serious. With ballplayers and movie starlets pulling down contracts in the millions, teachers are never going to have enough money to earn clout in the community. Besides, we already have unlimited power in the classroom: power to wound or elate, power to be cruel or kind, power to encourage or deflate. The list is limitless as well as very very scary. In the classroom, Ms. Class is ever haunted by the possibility of behaving badly. Ms. Class is not waiting for any committee to give her more power. In Emerson's words, "We should not postpone and refer and wish, but do broad justice where we are."

ENEMIES ACCOMMODATION

Dear Ms. Class:

I wonder how I can manage to work every day with people I positively dislike. I mean, I dislike everything about these two teachers—from the way they chew gum to the way they treat children.

— Yonkers, NY

Dear Yonkers:

Although Ms. Class acknowledges there is no excuse for an adult to chew gum below thirty-two thousand feet, she cautions you to get a grip on yourself: either find some small quality in these teachers you can tolerate and cultivate or ask for a transfer. Petty annoyances will erode your soul. Remember, you can't change them; you can only change yourself. If you are determined to stay in your present school, then keep in mind that teaching well is the best revenge.

On the other hand, if you are an admirer of the Romantic poets, you may want to cultivate your dislike. Lord Byron said that hatred is "by far the longest pleasure."

ENTERTAINMENT INTERFACE

Dear Ms. Class:

I volunteered to organize the faculty Christmas party. I wonder if you have any advice about feeding eighty people. How long should the party last?

— Tulsa, OK

Dear Tulsa:

You provide Ms. Class with one more definition of an optimist. An optimist is someone who thinks a faculty party can be organized.

Nonetheless, here are some tips for reducing the inevitable mayhem that results when teachers are near free food and liquor. People at a faculty party eat sixty percent more than they eat at home or in a restaurant where they are paying for it. They drink two-hundred-eighty percent more. The party is over when the liquor is.

If the party is potluck, teachers will contribute sixty-four bags of potato chips, four lime Jell-O molds in which marshmallows, shredded carrots, and anchovies have reached an uneasy truce, two jars of pickles, and one chicken-liver-and-turnip casserole blanketed with melted cheese. Nine people won't bring anything. *Bon Apétit!*

Dear Ms. Class:

Why do you sneer at teachers? You think real teachers don't make quiche? I doubt that teachers are any more likely to serve Jell-O than doctors or lawyers.

— Poughkeepsie, NY

Dear Poughkeepsie:

Ms. Class was not sneering. *Au contraire.* One of the Jell-O molds at her last faculty Christmas party was equal parts lime Jell-O and vodka. Hang around teachers long enough and you learn that conventional format often disguises fiendish subtlety and surprise.

And where but at a faculty party could you find the clever idea of lining the bottoms of paper plates with duct tape to prevent baked bean melt-through?

If you want to hear about the weird food some people eat, then consider this: people who visited the Vidalia restaurant in Washington, D. C., during the summer of 1994 consumed ten gallons of onion ice cream. Ms. Class does not know how many were teachers.

EQUIPMENT IMPERATIVE

Dear Ms. Class:

I wonder why no equipment in schools works.

— San Antonio, TX

Dear San Antonio:

That is a question that has plagued educators for millions of years. Ms. Class has just one piece of advice: if you want to experience some degree of peace and quiet and sociability during your planning period, never admit that you know how to unjam the paper, replenish the fluid, change the fuses, or otherwise rejuvenate anything that plugs into the wall.

Other universal constants:

- One kick gets it functioning. A second kick cancels the first.

- Pencil sharpeners don't.

- The extension cord is always four and a half inches too short.

- Only custodians know how to work the multiple-choice-test scanners, which is why, in April, the cruelest month of standardized tests, custodians across the country are granted the homage ordinarily reserved for visiting royalty.

- School tape sticks only to itself.

EQUITY SOFTSHOE

Dear Ms. Class:

I'm tired of all the red tape about equality. We couldn't hire an excellent male candidate for curriculum coordinator because, according to some guidelines, our female administrators are underrepresented. Isn't this equality run amok?

— Omaha, NE

Dear Omaha:

Equity is not when a woman of superior ability has the same chance for promotion as a man. Equity is when a female whose only qualification is having coached a winning basketball team is named principal.

ERROR-OF-THEIR-WAYS WITNESS PROTECTION PROGRAM

Dear Ms. Class:

I hope you can help me with a problem. I teach second grade, and the other second-grade teacher in the building hands out math worksheets for her students to color. Since students choose colors according to math answers, all the results are identical. My colleague hangs up these mass-produced "pictures" in the hallway. I am embarrassed for visitors to see this. How can I convince my colleague these productions are an abomination and that only examples of children's individual creativity should be on display?

— Taos, NM

Dear Taos:

Ms. Class would remind you that pointing out the errors of others should be left to the experts: God, their mothers, and Ms. Class.

Dear Ms. Class:

A colleague of mine of whom I am very fond mispronounces "beautiful" (be-oo-tee-ful) and "library" (li-bary). It grates on my nerves like a fingernail on the chalkboard. I feel I should correct her but wonder about the best way to do it.

— White Plains, NY

Dear White Plains:

Although Ms. Class herself has made a vocation of correcting people for their own good and although Ms. Class will confess to enjoying the wicked satisfaction of revealing her own superior knowledge to the world, she would caution you that she corrects only upon request. She does not search out error like a pig foraging truffles or a chimpanzee picking fleas from a companion's pelt. If your friend asks you how to pronounce any word, then by all means tell her. If she fails to ask the question, dear teacher, you must not offer the answer.

Dear Ms. Class:

The teacher next door is the Jesse James of sarcasm. He shoots barbs across the room and leaves no one standing. I figure teachers can take it, but I wonder how we can toughen up students to withstand this guy's barbs. I wonder if you have children and how your own children adapt to your sometimes wicked tongue.

— Casper, WY

Dear Casper:

Ms. Class, who realizes she would never be mistaken for Pollyanna, believes sarcasm, particularly when directed toward children, is the ninth deadly sin, whether those children are one's own or merely left temporarily in one's care. Ms. Class herself is occasionally acerbic but never sarcastic with children and rarely with adults.

One of the ironies of teaching is that we find it so easy to correct students but so impossible to confront our colleagues. Invite this caustic colleague for a cup of coffee after school. Tell him the acid tongue distresses you. You can invite a third colleague as moral support. Be supportive. As you assuredly do with children, find something positive in your colleague's classroom deportment before hitting him with the negative.

EXAMINATION INTERACTION

Dear Ms. Class:

My department chair and principal are pressuring me to raise my grades. I say if students would do the work they would pass the course. If sixty percent received failing marks, it is because they did not meet my standards. In a world that has gone to the dogs, I feel it is imperative that a teacher not compromise his standards.

— Iowa Falls, IA

Dear Iowa Falls:

Consider this: in the eighteenth century, professors of medicine, the people responsible for teaching—and examining—students, were paid directly by their students. Students paid only if they passed the examinations.

Consider this: how would you feel if every teacher's SAT scores were posted in the faculty room? Some years back, *Esquire* magazine contacted prominent writers and lawyers and other people acknowledged as leaders in their field and asked them if they'd take the SAT exam again—and make their scores public. All refused. Being an adult means you don't have to be humiliated by exams. Should being a child mean you do?

EXCUSE SCANNER

Dear Ms. Class:

My principal doesn't seem to be able to say no. He always disguises refusals by claiming someone—or something—else is responsible. His favorite scapegoats are federal guidelines, the board of education, right-wing pressure groups, and the weather. It drives me crazy. How can I make him own up to his own decisions?

— New Haven, CT

Dear New Haven:

Ms. Class recommends a different approach. You can't beat him, so why not join him? Ms. Class suggests compiling an excuse reference guide. Here are a few universal denials to help you get started. Tell your principal to check whichever one applies for each occasion.

We tried that before and it didn't work.
We've never done it that way.
The computer has to do it that way.
The computer can't do it that way.
He must not have eaten breakfast.
He must have had sugar for lunch.
She's just like her mother.

She's just like her father.
It's too cold.
It's too hot.
It must be the plug.
    the batteries.
    the solenoid.
    the hard drive.
    the software.
    a full moon.
    PMS.
    other hormones, itches, glands.
I must have dialed the wrong number.
It must have gotten lost in the mail.
You know those guys in Washington.
    at State Ed.
    in the Central Office.
    at City Hall.

EXIT PROGRAM FACILITATOR TRACKING

Dear Ms. Class:

    I was just appointed to a new position, exit program facilitator. I was told this appointment would put me on the administrative track, but I'm still being paid on the teacher salary schedule. What can I do about this inequity?

                 — Knoxville, TN

Dear Knoxville:

    What you can do is explain to Ms. Class just what it is you do. Hold the door for students who have been suspended?

    Ms. Class is sorry you didn't get a raise, but in a bureaucracy, getting a fancy title and a telephone is considered the next best thing. Of course, if they didn't give you a telephone, then you definitely have grounds for complaint.

EXPERIENCE BEST-/WORST-CASE SCENARIOS

Dear Ms. Class:

    I don't want to sound obnoxious, but I would like to ask you a personal question. I've noticed that on occasion you refer to your twenty-plus years of teaching experience as a badge of honor, as a way to establish your authority, and as a way to deflect any possible criticism. My question is this: do you think you are as good a teacher as you were, say, fifteen years ago?

— Hinesburg, VT

Dear Hinesburg:

My oh my, you New Englanders don't beat around the bush do you? Ms. Class has everything she had twenty-three years ago; it just hangs lower and runs slower.

EXPERTISE CONSTRUCTIVISM

Dear Ms. Class:

After eight years of teaching mathematics in the "traditional" way, I have transformed my instruction. I did this by reading books and attending workshops. I'd like to share my newfound expertise with colleagues and wonder how I should go about giving workshops in my district.

— Ogden, UT

Dear Ogden:

Ms. Class would congratulate you for your dedication. Having said that, she warns you against assuming a self-congratulatory tone. Ms. Class recommends that you start small. Take the first step in spreading the good word about changes in mathematics instruction by talking with a few colleagues. How about giving one colleague the gift of a set of tangram puzzles? Then offer to teach a class lesson.

And remember: teachers are practitioners, not experts. An expert is someone who knows more and more about less and less.

EXTRACURRICULAR ACTIVITIES COST STUDY

Dear Ms. Class:

Another junior high teacher and I have both applied for the job of cheerleader supervisor. This job includes going along on the bus for out-of-town games. We both need the extra money the job pays, but I'm worried about what trying to get this job has done to our relationship. We used to be friends. Now we hardly speak.

— Narragansett, RI

Dear Narragansett:

Ladies, ladies. Please think about what you are doing. You are risking a friendship over the chance to ride on a school bus with a bunch of twelve-year-olds.

FACILITATOR RELIABILITY EXCLUSION ZONE

Dear Ms. Class:

Please help me settle a faculty-room dispute. Just when is a teacher a facilitator?

— Cucamonga, CA

Dear Cucamonga:

When he or she is trying to show off.

Dear Ms. Class:

I am annoyed and insulted by your snide disparagement of the term *facilitator*. This is a term that helps remind professional educators that their role is to ease the knowledge acquisition process, not to dictate it. We need to show students that there is not a power hierarchy in the classroom, no artificial division between teachers and learners. We need to show them we are all learners together.

— Alexandria, VA

Dear Alexandria:

Ms. Class has a one-word answer: hogwash.

She also has a longer answer. Just because a word has five syllables doesn't mean it's worth anything. "Don't used rotted names," warned poet Wallace Stevens. *Facilitator* reeks with fetidness. Ms. Class comes perilously close to losing her aplomb when she is forced into the presence of this pretentious nastiness, because teaching means so much to her. And the really great vocabulary of teaching consists of one-syllable words: *teach, learn, care, hope, trust, faith, help, read,* and *write*.

FACT AND FICTION DESTABILIZATION INDICATORS

Dear Ms. Class:

I think it is important for first graders to understand that I do not tolerate lying. My problem is that often parents don't want to believe their children tell lies. What can I do?

— St. Augustine, FL

Dear St. Augustine:

Above all else, maintain an attitude of humility about what you know for a fact. Case in point: when Olympic decathlon star Bob Mathias was in first grade, his teacher refused to believe him when he said there was a new baby in their family. Bob's mother had been to school the week before, and the teacher knew for a fact that she wasn't nine-months pregnant. The teacher persisted, and so did Bob. Determined to convince his teacher, Bob put the newly adopted baby on a pillow in his wagon and took her to school for show and tell.

Dear Ms. Class:

How can teachers expect students to tell the truth when they fill their days with made-up stories? My first grader's teacher reads fairy tales, Dr. Seuss, Sendak, and other fantasies to the children. My second grader just sat through three weeks of hearing *Charlotte's Web* read aloud. Now he goes around the house looking for spiders, expecting them to talk. He'd be better off hearing about the lives of great Americans, about the solar system, and about other facts in the real world. I want my children to understand the difference between fact and fiction. I send them to school to learn important information so they can will be successful in life. Why don't the teachers stick to facts?

— Hartford, CT

Dear Hartford:

Wallace Stevens was a Hartford insurance lawyer; you can't get much more factual than that. But he was also an extraordinary poet, and he wrote that "the purpose of poetry is to help people live their lives." In *Advice to a Young Scientist,* Nobel-laureate scientist Peter Medawar pointed out that "no new truth will declare its self from inside a heap of facts."

You should thank your lucky stars that your children's teachers are showing them how to look beyond the reach of their noses, extending their perceptions of reality. All the world's great thinkers confirm that myths tell us who we are. Myths and other fictions warn us of our interior monsters. They also show us our heroism, which can free us from those monsters.

Dear Ms. Class:

I'd sure like to know where you get the facts to back up your outrageous claims.

— Independence, MO

Dear Independence:

Ms. Class makes them up, of course. Making things up is much more creative and stimulating than trying to remember facts. Ms. Class agrees with Don Quixote that facts are the enemy of truth. Besides, you'd have to pay a lot more for a book filled with facts.

FACULTY FRACTALS

Dear Ms. Class:

I attended a fascinating workshop on creative visualization and would like to try it at our school. What do you think my chances are of getting other faculty members involved?

— Washington, DC

Dear DC:

When Ms. Class embarked on the advice business, she knew that one day it would break her heart. She can report that your chances are that fifteen percent of the faculty will try anything.

FACULTY MEETING FOCI

Dear Ms. Class:

I wonder why I sit through faculty meetings in a stupor. Later I think of things I could have said and should have said. But during the meeting these things just don't occur to me. Nothing occurs to me but trying to remain upright.

— Fargo, ND

Dear Fargo:

You are describing a condition known as teacher torpor, character-ized by listlessness, lack of muscular support, and intermittent brainwave shutdown. There are two remedies:

Alcoholic: Take two gin and tonics, and relief will be immediate.
Nonalcoholic: Read a detective novel, an antidote to many irritations.

Please remember this great teaching axiom: only dull people are at their best during faculty meetings.

Dear Ms. Class:

Is it proper for a teacher to knit during a faculty meeting?

— Battle Creek, MI

Dear Battle Creek:

Certainly. One should have something to occupy her mind. Ms. Class knit her way through graduate school and ended up with an M.A. in medieval literature and sixteen sweaters.

For faculty members who don't knit, Ms. Class recommends Etch-a-Sketch and liquid embroidery.

FACULTY ROOM PIT STOP

Dear Ms. Class:

I'm a new teacher. I go to the faculty room every chance I get and try to make friends with my new colleagues. They have not offered a warm welcome. They are quite cliquish and make no effort to include me in their conversations.

— Paducah, KY

Dear Paducah:

Ms. Class wonders how a new teacher finds time for loitering in the faculty room. Ms. Class wonders if your teacher-training courses did not warn you that faculty rooms are the last bastion of the desperate and the dissolute. Change your tactics at once. Try cultivating friendships one teacher at a time. Invite a teacher into your classroom for a cup of coffee (you could bring a thermos of decent coffee as a lure), and ask him or her for some advice on a specific problem. You will form an immediate bond. No teacher can resist giving advice.

Dear Ms. Class:

I can't seem to go into the faculty room without sinking into a pedagogical funk. I don't go often, but I feel I should occasionally make a gesture toward sociability. What bothers me is that someone always makes some proclamation that drives me crazy—something about the basal being better than trade books, the joys of assertive discipline, or whatever. I know I'm not going to convert anybody; I don't even want to try. I just want to be able to say something. Any ideas?

— Daytona Beach, FL

Dear Daytona Beach:

H. L. Mencken had the right idea. His favorite form letter went as follows:

Dear Sir or Madam:
You may be right.
    Yours truly,

Ms. Class regards this as the perfect faculty room riposte. It may not win your argument, but it is guaranteed to leave your antagonist speechless.

Dear Ms. Class:
Can you give me some advice on how to get a reading club started in the faculty room? My idea is that we'd all read the same professional book—and talk about it.

— Baton Rouge, LA

Dear Baton Rouge:
Your attempt is laudable, but you must realize that most faculty-room talk is a combination of that old TV show *Queen for a Day*, where housewives competed to see who was the most miserable, *Let's Make a Deal*, where contestants match their knowledge of the best bargains at K-Mart, and *Geraldo*, where people vie to come up with the most bizarre story of family perversion.
My advice is to move your reading group out of the faculty room and into a bar, where the atmosphere is calmer.

Dear Ms. Class:
I was disturbed by your suggestion that intelligent conversation cannot take place in the faculty room. Don't you think a group of educated people could agree on some conversational taboos?

— Beaumont, TX

Dear Beaumont:
No. Faculty-room conversationalists have no shame. No topic is taboo: money, surgery, incest, illegitimacy, gambling odds, and cute pet tricks.

Dear Ms. Class:
I know this will sound naive, but I wonder if teaching can ever be a profession until it provides teachers with a clean, well-lighted place in which to work—in other words offices for teachers. The faculty rooms of every school I've been in are a disgrace.

— Springfield, MA

Dear Springfield:
Yes, it is Ms. Class's experience, too, that teachers have to work in dirty, poorly lighted places. Ms. Class's worst experience was in an old brick school building in center city. The student lavatories were unspeakable, which is why they used the faculty facilities. The faculty lavatories were so filthy Ms. Class used her lunch break to dash over to a department store and pay twenty-five cents for admittance into a toilet stall. The building was finally condemned and the school moved. Then the building was completely overhauled, with carpeted offices, air conditioning, and other amenities for the superintendent and board of education.

Recently, Ms. Class was in a bright, clean faculty room in California. She witnessed the principal cleaning up the place in the middle of the day. He looked a bit abashed to be caught in the act but defended himself by explaining, "Teachers should have a clean place to come to." He's new at the job. Ms. Class wonders if his good example will influence his teachers to clean up after themselves or if he'll finally abandon the idea of maintaining sanitary standards.

FAILURE PARADIGMS

Dear Ms. Class:

I'm driving myself crazy by trying to make individual final exams. I just can't stand the thought of kids failing, and there is no way they can all pass the same test.

— Salem, OR

Dear Salem:

The pat answer these days would be to recommend that you switch to portfolios, encouraging students to display their best work. Ms. Class finds that concept laudable, but she would like to point out that you can't eliminate failure for children. You shouldn't even want to. School should be a place where it's okay to make mistakes. School should even be a place to find out what you're good at and what you're not good at. Think about this: Robert E. Lee failed to get into West Point the first time he applied; so did Pershing and MacArthur. Eisenhower took an extra year of high school to make it. Patton took three years to get in and five years to get out.

Edgar Allan Poe got in but was kicked out. Ms. Class tried to verify the rumor that he was kicked out for appearing naked for inspection on the parade grounds, but officials at West Point did not answer her letter of inquiry. Ms. Class realizes that Mr. Poe's state of undress has nothing to do with your question, but it would make a good story for the faculty room, surely more interesting than final exams.

Dear Ms. Class:

What about teacher failure? How do you suggest dealing with that?

— Hoboken, NJ

Dear Hoboken:

If at first you don't succeed, destroy all evidence that you tried.

FIELD TRIP FRENZY

Dear Ms. Class:
Our school has received special funds for field trips. I wonder if you have any recommendations.
— Portland, ME

Dear Portland:
Ms. Class's religious principles prevent her from taking field trips, but she found out a lot about field trips before she became a convert. It is a fact that the field trip was invented in 1673 by a Puritan principal who worried that teachers might be too comfortable. Ms. Class advises, dear teacher, that you read the small print in your health insurance benefits and exclusions before stepping outside the schoolhouse door. Of all the rituals practiced in schools, the field trip is by far the most revolting. Before agreeing to schedule field trips so frequently, consider the following:

1. Field trips cause rain.
2. Field trips were invented by people whose bladders required emptying only once every twenty-four hours.
3. The most disruptive students are never absent on field trip days.
4. The sixth law of relativity states that time moves slower on a school bus.
5. No field trip should be scheduled for any day with a "y" in it.

FREE-PERIOD COUNTDOWN

Dear Ms. Class:
Our board of education is looking for ways of saving money and is threatening to take away our free period. I teach ninth- and tenth-grade English. I already have a hundred thirty students. I don't know how I would manage thirty more. Any advice?
— Fresno, CA

Dear Fresno:
Bite your tongue, dear teacher. No wonder you are taken advantage of; you are committing professional suicide by referring to your fifty-minute professional-service period as a free period. This interval during the teacher's day when someone else is using her classroom leaves the teacher "free" to plan lessons; tutor students who need extra help; prepare study make-up packets for students whose families are leaving for Disney World; balance book club accounts; contact parents who are too busy to come to parent conferences; contact parents who've asked to be notified every time

their children fail to bring homework; call a volunteer to ask if she can come an hour earlier this week; meet with the nurse to secure snake venom prior to a science project; hold conferences about student welfare with the counselor, psychologist, truant officer, social worker, probation officer, principal, and anyone else who will listen; plan curriculum with colleagues; argue with the custodian, secretary, bus driver, and assistant principal; give and get advice from the hall monitors; check the Dow Jones average, the winning lottery numbers, and the trifecta results. Hope springs eternal.

FRUITCAKE MOBILIZATION

Dear Ms. Class:

I have suggested several times to an old friend that maybe it's time we stop exchanging Christmas gifts. The reason I want to stop is she's so cheap. Last year she gave me a fruitcake. I'm sure a student gave it to her. What am I going to do with a fruitcake? My cat won't eat it. My fourth graders won't eat it. I don't know the EPA guidelines for toxic waste removal. How can I put a stop to this?

— Brewer, ME

Dear Brewer:

Nobody eats fruitcake. That same fruitcake has been passing from house to house since 1692, when it was manufactured in a fit of Puritan *joie de vivre.*

Assume your friend has started a tradition—exchanging student gifts. This year you can give her the musical toilet paper roll one of your students gave you five years ago (*see also* "presents").

FUNDING VARIANCE

Dear Ms. Class:

My junior high school has actually received federal funds to improve reading scores through after-school track and field events. I have nothing against sports, but I think the only way you get better at reading is by reading.

— Chicago, IL

Dear Chicago:

If someone will fund it, someone will do it. Ms. Class is surprised no one has come up with the idea of improving the reading scores of first graders through midnight basketball.

As long as federal funds pay for it, the program will be judged a success.

GIFTED AND TALENTED CYBERSPACE

Dear Ms. Class:
I have mixed feelings about the pressure parents in our district are putting on school officials to start a gifted and talented program. I wonder what your opinions are.

— Macon, GA

Dear Macon:
Ms. Class will refrain from bringing up the Lake Wobegon effect. Ms. Class worries that many exceptional children are just given more of the same. When they finish the regular class work, more is piled on. On the other hand, Ms. Class considers asking gifted and talented children to sit around brainstorming the possible uses of a paper clip, coat hanger, or brick, a class-two felony.

Dear Ms. Class:
The alternative to establishing a program for gifted children is to accelerate these children. From my viewpoint, this is a very poor substitute. Kids who are intellectually advanced are not necessarily socially ahead of their years.

— Helena, MT

Dear Helena:
Ms. Class is opposed to children's skipping grades—for the very reason you mention. But that doesn't mean they can't profit from working with older—and younger—children on occasional projects. Ms. Class hates to see bright children "punished" by piling on "more of the same." She'll let Greg make his own case. Greg, a precocious first grader, was sent to the library to do research and report back to his class. The librarian gave him the *Precyclopedia* and showed him how to use it. When she went back to check, he was just sitting there holding the book and staring at the wall. She asked if he had a problem. Greg looked at her and said, "Just because I can read doesn't mean I'm the type of kid who wants to sit here and read all these pages."

The librarian sent Greg to Ms. Class, who was running an open remedial reading classroom. Though funded by Chapter I, it was not called remedial reading by anyone in the school and all children who could persuade their teachers to let them out could come. Ms. Class found it interesting that habitués of the place were the very bright and the very slow.

Greg pretty much camped out in the reading room. He loved all the science experiments available and was capable of independent work. When Ms. Class worried that Greg was a solemn little old man and didn't know how to play, she asked her physicist husband to come in and play trains with him. They set up a windup train and figured out the influence of weight on distance and speed.

There were usually thirty or more children in the room, so apart from the one physics project, Greg did not get a lot of special attention. Ms. Class found he needed just a nudge here or there to keep him spreading his wings. He spent a good part of the year working with remedial readers—in his own unique way. When a group of kids decided to put on a play, Greg nominated himself as the director. The cast of fifth graders did not seem to mind being bossed around by this talented first grader.

GLUE TRANSACTIONS GROWTH OPPORTUNITIES

Dear Ms. Class:

My second graders love to paint Elmer's Glue-All over their fingers, let it dry, and then peel off these ugly strips. They squeal that they are peeling off their skin. How can I convince them this is expensive as well as unhealthy and nasty?

— Tuscumbia, AL

Dear Tuscumbia:

Your query has sent Ms. Class into a reverie that must be the schoolhouse equivalent of Proust's recollection of the *petites madeleines.* For once, instead of answering questions, Ms. Class would like to ask one. She hopes some dear reader can tell her: whatever happened to all those huge jars of library paste that once graced every classroom? There must be millions of empty—or dried up—library paste jars in landfills across the country.

Ms. Class seldom suffers from fits of nostalgia, but does any child today stick a finger into a bottle of Elmer's Glue-All and then lick that finger? Ms. Class tries to avoid such culturally biased and judgmental terms such as *deprived* and *disadvantaged,* but peeling nasty dry scabs of glue seems like a poor substitute for the cool, sweet, moist lumps of paste on the tongue.

GOLD STARS IMPACT STATEMENT

Dear Ms. Class:
    I know you're against gold stars, stickers, and other rewards, but I don't know why. My second graders love stickers.

— Honolulu, HI

Dear Honolulu:
    The noted psychiatrist Abraham Maslow pointed out that if the only tool you have is a hammer, you treat everything like a nail. That's one reason why gold stars, behavior checklists, and other incentives are so dangerous. For the other reasons, having to do with the purposes of education and the harmful effects of equating learning to dangling a carrot in front of a jackass, send Ms. Class a ream of paper and a self-addressed, stamped carton (affixed with $9.86 postage).

Dear Ms. Class:
    My students love stickers and stars.

— Bayard, NE

Dear Bayard:
    Of course students love them. Children love terminator toys, not items advertised in the Metropolitan Museum catalog. That doesn't mean we are obliged to give them what they want.

GRAMMAR RISK TAKING

Dear Ms. Class:
    You should be ashamed of yourself for popularizing ignorance in your attacks on such grammar essentials as apostrophes and gerunds. What this country needs is a return to Latin instruction.

— Houston, TX

Dear Houston:
    Ms. Class realizes it would be futile to indulge herself by demonstrating that she knows how to diagram a sentence. Nonetheless, Ms. Class assumes you know that murder is more common among grammarians than among members of any other profession.
    Contrary to faculty-room rumor, uncorrected grammar does not cause fat deposit buildup. Ms. Class wonders if you delay going to the grocery store until you've run your shopping list through the computer spellcheck.

HALL DUTY HANGOVER

Dear Ms. Class:

My principal preaches at us to "be professional" but at the same time requires us to engage in such menial practices as hall duty, yard duty, bus duty. He'd really like us to take over toilet-cleaning duty, but he doesn't quite have the nerve. At the last faculty meeting he read aloud sections of an article about teachers and students cleaning toilets in Japan.

— White Plains, NY

Dear White Plains:

Ms. Class knows what you're talking about, but she thinks hall duty need not be degrading. If you treat it right, it can be a relaxing part of the day. For several years Ms. Class was assigned to hall duty outside the seventh-grade boys' lavatory. This meant she was supposed to stop kids from running in the halls and smoking in or messing up the lavatory. Although she did stop runners, she spent most of this duty period writing letters to her students, a pleasant way to spend the fifty minutes.

Ms. Class confesses she never entered the boys lavatory to interrupt thirteen-year-olds either in their secret smoking or their peeing wars—you know, shredding toilet paper with their forceful spray. Ms. Class heard about these feats from the men who had hall duty. She had no desire to see it for herself.

Was Ms. Class neglecting her duty? Maybe so. But seventh grade is such a tough year: a year of pimples, rejection, hurt, and weirdness. Minds trying to control bodies that operate in some sort of zero-gravity zone, minds worrying that those bodies might never catch up to the girls in height. She rather hated to disrupt the guys' one pleasure, one she considered less offensive than their belching contests. She reminds herself that a large part of teaching is knowing what to ignore.

HALLOWEEN HYSTERIA

Dear Ms. Class:

I have read that some religious groups are objecting to Halloween festivities in the school—on the grounds that it is a pagan holiday that encourages worship of witches. Should I outlaw Halloween?

— Yuma, AZ

Dear Yuma:

Even if you wanted to, you couldn't do it. Children don't get a vote, but adults love Halloween at least as much as children, and the adults who love Halloween far outnumber the loudmouths who don't. If any administrator express nervousness about Halloween, point out that in the real world Halloween is a hot item. Halloween books and cards are outsold only by Christmas items. Religious fanatics have trouble influencing events in the real world so they put all their efforts into causing trouble in school.

Ms. Class predicts that Halloween is here to stay. After all, Halloween is not simply one day; it is the span connecting summer and the eating season, that period from Thanksgiving to New Year's. A teacher may wish to maintain her decorum by agreeing to dress up in silly gear only on October 31, but that doesn't prevent her from reading Halloween poems and stories aloud for the preceding thirty days.

HALLWAY HEGEMONY

Dear Ms. Class:

I wonder why architects don't design schools with wider hallways. Our school is one long traffic jam during the five minutes between classes. How do other schools manage this?

— Danbury, CT

Dear Danbury:

They don't. You will better understand the problem if you consider the laws of school design:

First law: architects don't know any children.

Second law: architects were never children themselves but sprang fully grown from a drafting table in the subway labyrinth where *Return to the Planet of the Apes* was filmed.

Third law: architects don't consult with the two groups of professionals who know how schools work and where kids will create traffic jams and bottlenecks, become nuisances, engage in dangerous and/or illegal activities—teachers and custodians.

Fourth law: architects sign a blood oath that no hallway shall ever be the shortest distance between two points.

Fifth law: architects' favorite formula is T > H (traffic increases to overflow all hall space available).

HANDICAPPING HEURISTICS

Dear Ms. Class:

I am sure you had no wish to be offensive, but referring to children as "handi-capped" is wrong as well as offensive. Although you may be temporarily abled at the present time, all people are differently abled; that is to say we all have different strengths and weaknesses. For the sake of our students' ability to encounter and appreciate the great variety of abilities in the real world, we need to welcome all children into all classrooms.

— Milpitas, CA

Dear Milpitas:

You may be right. But you know and Ms. Class knows that banning one word and coining another does not change the fact that some people are less able than others. Ms. Class has not noticed the real world opening up its offices and factories to people who suffer from severe handicapping conditions such as, to use a now-forbidden term, retardation. Ms. Class *has* noticed that no one asks eight-year-olds how they feel sharing a classroom with children whose disabilities are harrowing.

The sensitivities of "normal" children is one issue. The other issue is the sensitivities of handicapped children. Placing mentally and emotionally handicapped children in regular classrooms is hard on those children. No matter how nurturing the teacher tries to be, the hard fact is that the real world outside the classroom is not kind. Michael Dorris, author of the heartbreaking book *The Broken Cord,* notes that in all the years his son Adam went to regular school and everybody pretended he was a regular boy, no child ever phoned Adam after school; no child ever invited him to a party.

Ms. Class has written on this topic a number of times, and every time she does she is attacked by professors of special education and thanked by parents of handicapped children.

HOMEWORK STRESS MANAGEMENT

Dear Ms. Class:

I notice that most of your letters are from teachers, but I hope you will be willing to give a parent some advice. Teachers in my children's school seem to be waging a contest over who can assign the most homework. I don't want to give that old excuse that I am a working mother. I can't imagine any parent wants to spend three hours a night standing over their fourth and seventh graders to make sure all the tedious pages of homework are completed. Forcing a ten-year-old to work out forty nasty subtraction problems, where the last three numbers on top are zeros, seems excessive to me. What can I do to aid and comfort my children that won't offend and alienate their teachers?

— Eau Claire, WI

Dear Eau Claire:

There are two ways to proceed:

1. *Quiet Subversion:* After checking that your ten-year-old does indeed understand how to subtract from zero, hand him/her a calculator.

2. *Open Rebellion:* Talk to other parents, form a committee, and meet with the teachers. Go with a list of the other valuable activities you have planned to do with your children in the evening hours: take a walk, read a book, go to Scouts, and so on.

Parental pressure probably caused the homework escalation; parental pressure can also deflate it. Do you think teachers like checking homework? You just might discover that teachers are as anxious to de-escalate homework production as you are.

Dear Ms. Class:

I am a teacher writing to you as a parent. Our school has a policy that homework *must* be given four nights a week. I confess that I get busy and don't always give the most inspiring or worthwhile homework, but I never stoop to the level of my son's teacher. She gives nothing but drill sheets. I don't see why an excellent reader should waste his time circling long vowels. Any advice?

— Durant, OK

Dear Durant:

There are two ways to proceed:

1. *Open Rebellion:* Talk to your colleague. Explain that you'd rather your son spend his precious evening hours reading vowels than circling them. Offer to write a note certifying that he has read thirty minutes (or some time period you and the teacher agree on) in lieu of the dreaded worksheet.

2. *Quiet Subversion:* Follow Frank Smith's advice. Explain to your son that some school tasks are useless. Explain that his teacher assigns the worksheet because it is a school rule and that your son must do it because it is a school rule. Smith points out that children can accept such make-work piffle. The only time it does them any harm is when we insist on pretending that it is worthwhile.

HOPELESS SITUATION ASSET ALLOCATION

Dear Ms. Class:

My students come from a huge inner-city housing project. They are surrounded by drug dealing, prostitution, gang warfare, thievery, and death. How can I be expected to teach them to read and do math?

— Brooklyn, NY

Dear Brooklyn:

What you need to remember is that for many of your students school is an oasis of relative calm, order, and predictability. You cannot protect them from drugs, disease, and violence. What you can do is teach them.

One of the hardest things about being a teacher is you so seldom know of the positive effects you have. Ms. Class can only tell you that she recently heard from Shari, one of the most incorrigible of her seventh graders, a girl who dropped out of ninth grade some ten years ago. Shari wrote Ms. Class recently because she wanted her teacher to know that she takes her children to the library every week, that she can't wait until they are old enough for her to read them some of the same books Ms. Class read to her.

Ms. Class tells you with tears in her eyes that Shari's listing of the names of those books and authors that continue to enrich her life makes Ms. Class proud to be a teacher.

Ms. Class is not given to handing out absolutes, but please remember these two difficult truths of teaching:

1. No matter how much you do, you'll feel it's not enough.

2. Just because you can only do a little is no excuse to do nothing.

HOW-TO BOOKS CALL-WAITING

Dear Ms. Class:

Over the years, I know I've spent several thousand dollars on how-to books. I find cute lessons that give a boost to me and to the children. My problem is I never seem to make these lessons an ongoing part of my curriculum. Instead, I buy a new how-to book and try its lessons—once. Then I buy another book. How can I stop this cycle?

— Beaverton, OR

Dear Beaverton:

Reading those how-to activity books is rather like eating Twinkies. They're popular, synthetic, and soft at the center. You keep on moving on to new ones because the ones you've tried don't sustain you. Ms. Class does not believe there is anything inherently wrong with a blackline master, but twenty-plus years spent hanging around schools has shown her that there are more ways to do something wrong than there are to do it right.

Your problem may be not in those how-to books but in job dissatisfaction. Take a look at what you're doing. A close look. Try making a list of what gives you satisfaction and what doesn't. Trust your own instincts. Build on those things that give satisfaction. Talk to your students. Ask them for suggestions on improving the class. You'll be surprised at the good ideas they have (and you probably won't be surprised at the loony things they come up with). When you get restless, pick up a joke book instead of a how-to book.

HYPERACTIVITY ACCOMMODATION

Dear Ms. Class:
How can you tell if someone is hyperactive?

— Coeur d'Alene, ID

Dear Coeur d'Alene:

- A hyperactive parent inquires how his child is doing more than twice a year.
- A hyperactive teacher keeps her dittos in alphabetical order and files the weekly lunch menus chronologically. No kidding. She can tell you what was served in the cafeteria on the third Wednesday in October, 1973.
- A hyperactive administrator washes the coffee pot and the cups in the faculty room.
- A hyperactive custodian has never been found.
- A hyperactive student is never absent.

Dear Ms. Class:
What's the latest word on sugar and hyperactivity?

— Independence, MO

Dear Independence:

Research is not complete on the effects of sugar on teachers' hyperactivity. One teacher of Ms. Class's acquaintance, not content with Oreos and Twinkies, eats dry brownie mix right out of the box. Ms. Class admits she admires the efficiency. No dishes to wash. This teacher has had a brownie-mix lunch for fifteen years and has not been convicted of a felony.

IMMATURITY CORRELATION INDEX

Dear Ms. Class:

I teach a class of immature third graders who can't sit still. I have never seen eight-year-olds who act so childish. What can I do?

— Belknap, NH

Dear Belknap:

Ms. Class would remind you that it is the right of children to be childish.

Dear Ms. Class:

My principal means well. He wants to create a feeling of excitement for reading in the school. So he's agreed to eat lunch in his pajamas while sitting on the school roof if fifth graders read a thousand books. He actually hopes this stunt will get public attention. He thinks it will convince the public we are devoted to reading. I think it will convince the public we are clowns. Please withhold my city. I don't want people outside our county to know what fools work here.

— Anonymous

Dear Anonymous:

Ms. Class would remind you that it is the right of principals to be childish.

You may find some perverse consolation in knowing that this principal-on-the-rooftop reading incentive has taken place in at least half a dozen schools around the country.

IMMEDIATE FEEDBACK TRANSMISSION

Dear Ms. Class:

I have taught remedial reading for twelve years. I actually manage to get children to test out of the program. Now the administrator has decided that what remedial students need is immediate and impartial feedback. The computers have already arrived, and I have been ordered to code every book I use to a list of skills in the computer management system, so I can keep track of the students' skills, rather like a handicapper figuring the odds.

I have to admit that my students do have trouble with delayed gratification, and I wonder if there is research supporting immediate feedback.

— Atlanta, GA

Dear Atlanta:

Certainly. There is research supporting anything you can imagine. But what you must remember here is that the notion of immediate feedback was invented for profit, not pedagogy. Ms. Class is wary of any program that encourages ideological indolence, offering streamlined, easy-use, iron-on mechanized lessons to replace sloppy, inefficient human contact with students. You can't snuggle up to a cathode ray tube or a transistor, and Ms. Class is sure she doesn't have to tell you that a lot of children need snuggling even more than they need consonant blends.

Ms. Class is also wary of any program predicated on the notions that learning is sequential and that children learn what teachers teach.

INDIVIDUALIZED INSTRUCTION FLOTATION DEVICE

Dear Ms. Class:

I am trying to implement individualized instruction in my fifth-grade classroom. Where do I start?

— Austin, TX

Dear Austin:

Ms. Class appreciates your candor in not claiming you already "do" individualized instruction. Everyone seems to be in favor of individualized instruction. The actual, practical, in-classroom meaning of this term is obscure but tantalizing.

Ms. Class suggests that you begin individualization by allowing your fifth graders to choose their own books for reading time. Don't decide ahead of time that everybody will be in a discussion group or that everybody will keep a reading log or a vocabulary notebook. Just let them choose books and then base what happens next on what you observe about their choices and their willingness (or lack thereof) to sit with a book.

A classroom with two five-member discussion groups, three sets of buddy readers, seven children reading silently, and two children listening to books on tapes is more individualized than one with twenty-five children simultaneously recording their "If I were Laura" statements in reading journals.

IQ TEST RECIPROCITY

Dear Ms. Class:

I wonder why there is so much controversy over IQ tests. Don't we need to know what students are capable of doing?

— San Antonio, TX

Dear San Antonio:

IQ tests are the brussels sprouts of education, unattractive no matter how they are presented. Ms. Class does wonder why a school district spends so much time and money to test the intelligence of its students and then insists on offering all of them the same curriculum. Ms. Class also wonders why we spend monies testing the intelligence of students but continue to ignore the intelligence of persons running the schools.

INSERVICE INPUT

Dear Ms. Class:

Our district mandates four days a year for inservice training. They usually end up being days when publishers' representatives are invited in to promote their products. I wonder what you think of this type of teacher training.

— Dade County, FL

Dear Dade County:

People in charge of inservice training need to recognize the difference between an infomercial and staff development. At best, a presentation offered by a publisher can be interesting and informative. At worst, it has about as much value as a sprained ankle. Inviting publishers' representatives into the schools is rather like asking the fox to guard the chicken coop. You need to remember that the job of the publishers' representatives is to sell products. Regardless of what they may say, their job is not to educate teachers.

INTERCOM OUTPUT

Dear Ms. Class:

Intercom announcements interrupt my class at least half a dozen times a day. This is bad enough, but most of the time the sound is so distorted, I can't even understand what is being said. So we get interrupted and then we waste another ten minutes trying to decipher the message.

— Bakersfield, CA

Dear Bakersfield:

You must teach in a large school. Ms. Class's three-year, fifty-state (plus Guam and Puerto Rico) intercom research shows that the bigger the school, the more garbled the message. The corollary to this principle is: the bigger the audience, the worse the public address system.

Intercoms are proof that invention is the mother of necessity.

JARGON AUTHENTICIZATION ANXIETY ATTACK

Dear Ms. Class:

My critical analysis of your increasingly visible public discourse reveals a failure to facilitate transitionalization into alternative ways of knowing the politicized implications of the commonalities of the individualized gendered, raced, and classed teacher and student voice in the authenticized context of historicalized critical pedagogy. This gendered, raced, and classed omission of the authentic knowledge base implicates you as an imperialist participant in the retrograde authority structure. If oppositionalist divisions are to achieve a transitionalization and ultimate dismantling of the oppressive mythical norm of institutionalized racism, sexism, classism, and temporary ablism, then your failure to contextualize authentic strategies further marginalizes the struggle for empowerment.

— Alexandria, VA

Dear Alexandria:

You may be right, but such language is the last refuge of the desperate. Why not speak your mind? Why not simply say you think Ms. Class is an idiot—and a bigot to boot? Ms. Class has no patience with people who cover up their intentions with verbiage. Ms. Class suspects you might be inclined to call a shoplifter a "nontraditional shopper."

Dear Ms. Class:

Obviously, the jargonaut who wrote you was at the extreme end of language pomposity. But you do your usual thing of ignoring the real issue for the sake of a witty answer. Every trade has its specialized vocabulary. Every trade needs the code words that are actually handy shortcut signals to other members of the fraternity. In such cases, jargon facilitates communication.

— Urbana, IL

Dear Urbana:

You present the standard argument for jargon. Ms. Class likes hardware stores because the people there cheerfully abandon their arcane language when someone comes in asking for a gizmo or a whatzit. Harvard psychiatrist and MacArthur genius award winner Robert Coles says that "when the heart dies, we slip into wordy and doctrinaire caricatures of life. Our journals, our habits of talk, become cluttered with jargon or the trivial. There are negative cathects, libido quanta, presymbiotic, normalaustic phases of mother-infant unity." Coles observes that such dross is excused as a shortcut to understanding a complicated message by those versed in the trade, "but the real test is whether we best understand by this strange proliferation of language the worries, fears, or loves in individual people." Coles concludes that "as the words grow longer and the concepts more intricate and tedious, human sorrows and temptations disappear."

Strong, sensible words bring us close to the reality of the moment. Case in point: Ms. Class has been sailing as First Mate on Lake Champlain, surely the mostly beautiful lake in the world, for some twenty years. When the waters are quiet and the sailing routine to the point of dullness, Ms. Class's husband likes to refer to halyards and cleats and jibs and the area in the boat abaft the thwarts. But when the wind picks up to thirty knots and thunderclouds threaten, he doesn't take any chances. He abandons the esoteric code words and yells, "Let go of the rope!"

JOURNAL JINGOISM

Dear Ms. Class:

The other members of our second-grade team insist that journaling should become the standard component of the writing curriculum, and to that end they want our students to keep six separate journals: Math Journal, Social Studies Journal, Literature Journal, Science Journal, Vocabulary Journal, and an All About Me Journal. I encourage my students to write a lot, but I think the idea of seven-year-olds keeping a journal is developmentally unsound. Am I missing something?

— San Antonio, TX

Dear San Antonio:

Ms. Class confesses she detests the coinage *journaling*—an abomination to the eye and ear. But if your team runs out of ideas, Ms. Class has seen published strategies for students to keep soap opera-watching journals, though second grade is perhaps a bit young.

Of course, asking seven-year-olds to write in a notebook they call a journal doesn't mean they are keeping a journal. Beatrix Potter and Louisa May Alcott were both inveterate journal keepers. Potter began hers at age fourteen. Alcott was precocious and began hers at eleven. Ms. Class does not know of any seven-year-olds—or forty-seven-year-olds—who managed to juggle six journals simultaneously. Who would want to? Only in schools do we see journals running rampant.

More to the point is the misapprehension of what a journal is all about. In *Double Discovery* Jessamyn West comments on the distinction between journal keepers and letter writers. "Letters tell you what the writer thinks of the recipient; journals tell you who the writer is." Journals, then, are more internal, letters more external; journals are introspective; letters are social. Robert Louis Stevenson, so open and faithful to a lifetime of letter writing, was no fan of Thoreau, who lived his life talking to himself and filling fourteen volumes of journals. Virginia Woolf was both an inveterate letter writer and journal keeper. And she committed suicide.

Laura Ingalls Wilder paid five cents for a little memorandum book with blue lines when she and Almanzo and their seven-year-old daughter Rose left their drought-stricken farm in South Dakota and traveled to a new farm and a new beginning in the Ozarks. Laura kept careful notes of the details and incidents of her new life, but the result is curiously voiceless. Twenty-one years later, when Laura took a trip to San Francisco, the letters she wrote home to Almanzo were filled with voice and life. Ms. Class sees these letters as her warm-up for the *Little House* books.

Ms. Class knows that she will receive a torrent of angry mail if she dares to suggest that it is wrong to ask second graders to be introspective. Nonetheless, your team would do well to think long and hard about the differences between journals and letters. What seven-year-old can figure out the purpose of a journal? And what seven-year-old can resist the lure of the letter?

JUSTICE JUGGERNAUT

Dear Ms. Class:

It really bothers me that teachers—good, bad, and indifferent—all get the same salaries. I believe in merit, in people who do a better job getting a better salary.

— Des Moines, IA

Dear Des Moines:

Be careful of what you wish for. Just ask yourself: who would be deciding merit? your principal? your school board?

Stop worrying about whether the teacher next door puts in as many hours as you do or whether her bulletin boards are as clever. Think instead about an airplane trip. No two people on that plane have paid the same price for a seat. In Erma Bombeck's words, some travelers are on "super savers where they travel on Tuesday morning only during the months when oysters are in season if they buy their tickets at high tide on the day they were born." Please think about this, Des Moines: a teacher merit pay schedule makes the airline ticket pricing scheme look rational.

Dear Ms. Class:
    Your point about merit pay is well taken, but surely there is some way to reward meritorious teachers.
                                                                    — Atlanta, GA

Dear Atlanta:
    Nope. And if you persist in this course, surely you will go mad. Men are paid millions of dollars to chase little white balls, and what's the good of that? A teacher shouldn't be discouraged by the professional injustice that surrounds her working day, but it's okay if she learns how to get even occasionally. It's this very desire that prompted Ms. Class to become a writer.

JUVENILE DELINQUENT RESEARCH BASE

Dear Ms. Class:
    The star quarterback of our championship football team was picked up at a drinking party. That in itself is a violation of the team's code, supposedly punishable by dismissal. Even worse, the party attendees are implicated in crime. I suppose it could be construed as malicious mischief—they went around town letting air out of teachers' tires. Three of them (not the quarterback) were caught and implicated the others (including the quarterback). The case has been "postponed" until after the state championships and the quarterback is still on the team. The school board's official statement is "to discuss a case before the courts act on it would be improper." Their unofficial attitude is just like the principal's and the coach's: "Boys will be boys."
    The really outrageous thing is that this is not the first time everybody has looked the other way when this juvenile delinquent has gotten into trouble. For years they've regarded his antisocial behavior as "highjinks." I am disgusted that the school refuses to take its proper role as moral guide to all students.
                                                                    — Abilene, KS

Dear Abilene:

Although it breaks Ms. Class's heart to say this, she must inform you that you are fighting against hallowed tradition. From Billy the Kid to Bonnie and Clyde to D. B. Cooper to Bernard Goetz, America has celebrated juvenile delinquents—even when they were no longer quite juvenile. They are a part of our national heritage. Especially if they have a good hook shot or can switch hit.

Nonetheless, Ms. Class begs you not to despair. One good teacher in twelve years of schooling can sometimes transform a delinquent. Even a football player.

KISS-AND-TELL LAND MINE

Dear Ms. Class:

I've known my principal since we were in college. If truth were known, his term papers were more mine than his. Early in our careers, we taught in the same building. Now, ten years later, we meet again, but I'm still a teacher and he's a new principal. Suddenly he has become an alien being. He's rarely available to solve problems, and when I can find him he acts as though we have no common past, as though I should suddenly believe he's my superior. The other day he reminded me to call him "Mister" during the school day. I'm having a tough time adjusting.

— Helena, MT

Dear Helena:

Just remember this universal truth: it may be easier for a camel to pass through the eye of a needle than for a teacher to find a principal when she needs one, but a principal will always come around when he needs you.

Ms. Class would advise you to pay heed to the dangers of kiss and tell: stop telling people of your past relationship with your principal; refrain from mentioning that the only thing he passed on his own in college was his eye test. Such information honors neither of you, and forces him to find a way to discredit you.

KNOCK-KNOCK JOKE EXPERIENTIAL RELIABILITY

Dear Ms. Class:

I teach corrective reading and I'm working hard to help my third-grade students learn knock-knock jokes. The federal programs reading implementation coordinator objects, saying we need to concentrate on a skills continuum. Who's right?

— Troy, NY

Dear Troy:

You know, of course, that you are right. You must assure Ms. Class you will continue your good work, or she will have to visit the office of the federal programs reading implementation coordinator and do something desperate. Ms. Class doesn't need to tell you that knock-knock jokes are the rite of passage into third grade. A child isn't a legitimate third grader until he can read and enjoy this important cultural artifact.

Ms. Class just may do her doctoral dissertation on the linguistic power of riddling. If she does, she will send you the underlying skills continuum of the knock-knock joke.

KNOWLEDGE PREDICTORS TAKEOVER BID

Dear Ms. Class:

The longer I teach, the more I question what I know. I wonder what's wrong with me. Other people are so confident. Important principles of pedagogy seem to roll off their tongues.

— Camden, NJ

Dear Camden:

The next time you are listening to one of these silver-tongued orators, just remember three things:

1. It takes a lot longer for a person to say what he thinks than to explain what he knows.

2. In teaching, the more a teacher really knows (as opposed to faking it), the more she knows she doesn't know.

3. The more a teacher knows, the more she forgives, which is why you will maintain your collegial relations with the silver-tongued charlatans.

Scottish school reformer A. S. Neill had a modest proposal that Ms. Class rather likes. She thinks at the very least it would level the playing field of inflated rhetoric. Worried that teachers who work at a subject year after year become expert at it and insisting that novices are better teachers than experts, Neill proposed that teachers take up a new subject at the beginning of every school year. Neill said that after a teacher had taught mathematics, history, drawing, French, German, Latin, chemistry, wood-work, and on and on, "it would be time to retire . . . with a pension or a psychosis."

With the exception of a six-year stint at a middle school, Ms. Class changed schools and tenure areas every two years and can testify that this practice keeps a teacher on her toes.

KNOWLEDGE QUALITY CONTROL

Dear Ms. Class:

Every place I turn I'm bombarded with reports about what kids don't know. Everyone says this is the failure of the schools. I wonder why the people who administer these tests don't ever look at what kids do know.

— Anchorage, AK

Dear Anchorage:

The problem is that much of what self-proclaimed experts think kids should know makes no sense. When Ms. Class taught third grade she was expected to teach her students the difference between metamorphic, igneous, and sedimentary rocks, terms she herself encountered in a college geology course. Third graders like rocks, so Ms. Class muddled through an adapted rock curriculum.

Ms. Class was also supposed to teach her students about the concept of city—from Timbukto to the New York City budget. (No, Ms. Class is not making this up. She has no talent for fiction.) Third graders don't have much patience for budgets, so Ms. Class scrapped the text and read *The Trumpet of the Swan* instead. If anybody asks her students to locate Western Canada and Montana on a map, they'll do fine.

Here's one more report for you to consider. Ms. Class keeps it on her bedside table—as a reminder to be humble about her influence. According to the Center for Science in the Public Interest, eight- to twelve-year-old children can name 4.8 U. S. presidents. These same children can name 5.2 alcoholic beverages. This does make one ponder the respective influences of home and school on our information highways and byways.

Dear Ms. Class:

You could have been fired for ignoring the district social studies curriculum. I believe you should have been fired. What would happen if every teacher abrogated her duty to impart to children the knowledge that people in charge deem important?

— Detroit, MI

Dear Detroit:

Ms. Class has little faith in the people in charge and wishes more teachers would assume personal responsibility for the curriculum they bring to their students. Ms. Class believes that the notion we can make children learn is foolish and dangerous. All a teacher can do is provide experiences from which children can construct their own understanding. That's why Ms. Class refuses to teach the New York City budget to eight-year-olds.

LABELING IMPERATIVES STOCKPILING

Dear Ms. Class:

I recently transferred to a school where the students are divided into groups: top reading, middle reading, low reading; top math, middle math, low math; and so on. I know that some of my students in middle math are better than some students in high math and some are worse than students in low math. I like my colleagues. They work hard for the benefit of students. I wonder if I dare tell them I think this system is crazy.

— Beaufort, SC

Dear Beaufort:

You have observed an important pedagogical principle: no matter how carefully you sort students into homogeneous groups, significant differences will emerge. Please know that students are more different than they are the same. Also please know that students are more the same than they are different. How both these principles can be true is one of the great mysteries—and joys—of teaching.

Many educationists seem to regard the unlabeled student with suspicion. Like an uncollared dog, the unlabeled student is viewed as an untamed beast, something that must be brought under proper control.

Ms. Class looks to the day when administrators catch on to the fact that the way to control teachers is to label them. How many teaching-disabled instructors are there in your building? Who would be eligible to attend accelerated faculty meetings?

Dear Ms. Class:

You can say what you like about students being more the same than they are different, but equality is running amok in my district. My district has delabeled students. You liberals can claim that all children should be dumped in the same classroom melting pot, but as an experienced teacher I know that the emotionally disturbed children coming this fall will poison the soup. I believe in being fair. I will give these children a chance, but this place is already crazy. I can't imagine what will happen when they bring in the certified crazies.

— Albany, NY

Dear Albany:

Ms. Class agrees that the outlook is not bright. But on the matter of labels, she would caution you to consider David Rosenhan's classic study "On Being Sane in Insane Places." A group of people, including a graduate student, three psychologists, a pediatrician, a painter, and a housewife, got themselves admitted to twelve psychiatric wards by claiming to hear voices. Once they were institutionalized, however, these people behaved "normally." They did not impersonate mental patients in any way.

Although a sizable number of patients on the wards quickly caught on to the ruse, no member of the professional staff suspected that anything was amiss. Several "patients" took notes of all that was happening; another conducted therapy sessions with fellow patients. All these actions were interpreted as insane by the professionals. All the pseudopatients were treated as schizophrenics throughout their hospital stays, and all were discharged as insane persons who were temporarily "in remission."

Ms. Class happens to have very strong feelings about the misuses and misapplications of wholesale mainstreaming, but at the same time she is ever humbled by the knowledge that one's observations and teacher savvy are ever colored by what one thought one knew ahead of time.

LAKE WOBEGON EFFECT

Dear Ms. Class:

The parents of one of my third graders want me to hold him back this year. They think this will help him become a star pupil rather than a mediocre one. Craig is in the lowest reading group, but he cheerfully plugs along. Craig is very popular. Things don't come easily to him, but he works hard and he likes school. I don't see any reason to retain him. What do you think?

— Phoenix, AZ

Dear Phoenix:

It sounds as though Craig's parents suffer from a variation of the Lake Wobegon effect: if your children aren't above average this year, then hold them back so they can be above average next year. You must hold firm to your resolution not to hold Craig back. No matter what his parents think, keeping him back will not improve his class ranking. He'd still be in the low reading group.

Instead of concentrating on that reading group, and Ms. Class will go into the reasons for abolishing *that* at another time, help Craig's parents celebrate Craig's strengths. Obviously, one of his strengths is having parents who care. They just need to redirect their energies. Sit down with these caring parents and make a list of Craig's other strengths—interpersonal skills, dependability, loyalty, humor, originality—all the things that count in the real world but are too often given short shrift in school.

If all else fails, cite statistics: of ten children retained, seven do worse the second time around.

LEARNING DISABILITY ETHNOGRAPHY

Dear Ms. Class:

Five "learning disabled" students have been mainstreamed into my classroom. I can't see that they have anything in common. I wonder what the label means.

— Albuquerque, NM

Dear Albuquerque:

Special education, long the stepchild of education, was transmogrified into learning disabilities, which became the umbrella term of the late 1980s. In the 1990s, although children are still given the generic LD term, a large subset of definitions is emerging. Here are selected terms from a five-page "Glossary of Appropriate Terms" developed in one school district to explain the acronyms in the California Master Plan for Special Education:

CH	Communicatively handicapped
DD	Developmentally disabled
EH	Educationally handicapped
EDY	Educationally disadvantaged youth
EMR	Educationally mentally retarded
IWEN	Individual with exceptional needs
LDG	Learning disability group
LEP	Limited English proficiency
LH	Learning handicapped
MH	Multi-handicapped
MR	Mentally retarded
SED	Severely emotionally disturbed
SH	Severely handicapped
SR	Severely retarded
TMR	Trainable mentally retarded

Many officials urge their districts to drop the EH and EMR designations, replacing them with the catchall "learning handicapped." Progressive districts further destigmatize the label, designating students as "differently abled."

As any teacher not debilitated by chalkdust fever knows, changing a label does not change the problem. Ms. Class recommends that you discover the different abilities in your mainstreamed students the same way you discover it in other students—by watching them. This may not be the most efficient method, but it is the best thing we have come up with so far. Please keep in mind: school is the marketplace of possibility, not efficiency.

The one thing you can insist on is that children with severe problems be mainstreamed *after they have demonstrated the academic and social skills needed to profit from regular class placement.* This is the euphemistic way of saying you should fight against placement of children who cannot control their bodily functions or respond appropriately to the calling of the roll.

LEFT-BRAIN DEFICIT CUTTING

Dear Ms. Class:
I find it unfortunate that you seem to disparage all left-brain (linear) thinking.
— Taos, NM

Dear Taos:
Au contraire. Knowing how rare it is, Ms. Class gives her full support to thinking whenever and wherever it occurs and in whatever form.

LESSON PLAN FILIBUSTER

Dear Ms. Class:
I need some help in cutting down the time it takes to write lesson plans. I work on them for several hours each week so I can hand them in on time each Friday morning. So my principal gets these carefully thought out plans, but the twelve-year-olds I teach are so unpredictable that I rarely have time to look at these plans when I'm actually teaching, never mind follow them. The whole process is so frustrating. I work so hard at these plans. How can I find the time and space to use them?
— Cincinnati, OH

Dear Cincinnati:
First Ms. Class will explain the reason for the lesson plan rule. Then she will help you circumvent it.

Those perfect and impossible lesson plans belong to the clean underwear theory of education. You write them in case you are run over by a car
and can't get to a phone to tell your principal whether your class is studying
Eskimos or Egyptians. According to this theory, studied in Art and En-
forcement of Principalship 101, your plans will let the substitute teacher
know what's supposed to happen in your classroom.

But since the substitute won't be able to follow the plans any more than
you can, here's what you should do.

1. Turn your lesson plan book into a diary. Write about what actually
    happened in your classroom during the past week. As you learn to
    record happenings and even reflect on them, your plan book will
    become a source of valuable information and insight in months and
    years to come.

2. Keep a neat and tidy "lesson drawer" in your desk. Fill it with activi-
    ties the substitute and children will enjoy doing together. Resist the
    temptation to use these activities yourself on those days you are
    feeling desperate.

Dear Ms. Class:
Your advice on lesson plans is outrageous. It could get a teacher fired. As a
principal, I think it should get a teacher fired.

— Colorado Springs, CO

Dear Colorado:
Lighten up. Ms. Class endeavors to give teachers ammunition to resist
the frenzied dictums of petty tyrants. The social critic Paul Goodman once
wrote a letter to the New York Commissioner of Education, with a copy to
the governor, on behalf of a teacher who refused to prepare a two-week
lesson plan. Goodman pointed out that "formal preparation of a lesson plan
beyond the next hour or two is not only unrealistic but can be positively
harmful and rigidifying."

What's more, Robert Frost once confessed, "I have never started a poem
yet whose end I knew." How, then, can teachers, the poets of pedagogy, be
expected to predict the ends of lessons a week in advance?

Dear Ms. Class:
Okay, I guess you mean well. But get real. Lesson plans are necessary to the
well-ordered universe of the school. The responsible administrator needs some
indication that the teacher has a plan, that there is some order in the universe of
the classroom, that the teacher is following the district curriculum guidelines.

— Alexandria, VA

Dear Alexandria:

Once in her career Ms. Class did write an honest-to-goodness, official lesson plan. She was miffed that her principal had been to a conference and all of a sudden was whistling in the hallways about individualization. He acted as though he was bringing news of some exotic notion to the faculty.

If Ms. Class has had any method in her teaching career, that method could be termed *individualization*. From the moment a student in her ninth grade in Queens, New York, refused to read *Silas Marner*, she's been sympathetic to a fault to the individual needs of her students. She's learned from them, too. The first year he refused to read it. The next year she refused to teach it.

So Ms. Class resented the suggestion by administrative fiat that she was to prove her understanding of individualization by employing behavioral objectives in her classroom. Although she could not bring herself to write a behavioral objective, Ms. Class did write an individualized plan—laying out in precise detail what she would do with each one of her seventh graders for five days.

She wasn't planning anything special that week. What was unique was that she wrote everything down, something she'd never done. Something no one in her right mind would attempt to do.

Ms. Class spent twenty-six hours writing her lesson plans. She used up half the plan book. Need she note that the principal was not amused? Convinced it was some sort of subtle union plot, he kept muttering things about insubordination.

And that's only the beginning of the story. Having written these beautiful plans, Ms. Class decided to follow them. Her earnest attempts lasted one hour and three minutes. She can be very precise about this time because on Monday at 9:38, Keith's father knocked on the window. She nodded and smiled—and kept on with her plans. But he kept knocking on the pane, gesturing for her to come over. Finally, Ms. Class opened the window, and Keith's father climbed in.

Ms. Class never found out why Keith's father came through the window. Maybe he was just passing by, in the neighborhood, so to speak. Maybe he felt bad about not showing up for parent conferences. Whatever his reason, please be assured that the best laid plans do go awry when somebody's father climbs in through the window.

Even though this was an extraordinary event, Ms. Class knows that teachers encounter a metaphorical climbing-in-the-window just about every day, and that's why it is futile to spend much time on lesson plans.

LETTER-WRITING SCAFFOLDING

Dear Ms. Class:

Our three fourth-grade classes recently visited the state museum. The guide was extremely helpful, and we want to express our appreciation. The problem is this: my two colleagues feel one group letter signed "The Fourth-Grade Class" is sufficient. They say nobody would want to receive eighty-two thank-you letters. I say every child should have the experience of writing such a letter. Who's right?

— Glens Falls, NY

Dear Glens Falls:

Ms. Class wonders why people would want to bring children into a world where no one writes letters. Ms. Class extends her best wishes to anyone who tries to buck the fill-in-the-blank mentality that pervades what we still call culture. No one could receive too many thank-you letters.

LIASONS DANGEROUS

Dear Ms. Class:

A longtime teacher in my school is lesbian. She has told several people that she intends to "come out" by announcing her sexual preferences to her fifth-grade students. I like this teacher, but I think her determination to be open and honest about her sexual orientation will destroy her career—and tear our school apart. I'm concerned about our conservative school board, but I confess that even though I don't consider myself conservative, I'm indignant at the prospect of having to take sides on matters that should remain personal and private. Please do not print the name of our small town.

— Anonymous

Dear Anonymous:

Ms. Class shares your distress. She laments the influence of a tabloid-talk show sensibility that encroaches on our daily lives. Ms. Class knows a teacher who regales her class with tales of weekend encounters with men she meets through the personal ads. Ms. Class would prefer that everyone's intimate relationships remain personal and private. She thinks there must be some area between hiding in the closet and explaining your sex life to ten-year-olds. Of course this means heterosexual as well as homosexual. Ms. Class must admit, however, that she has no practical plan for achieving such a state of public decorum in our current tell-all era.

LIE DETECTOR LIQUIDATION

Dear Ms. Class:

I'm disturbed by the number of lies my fifth graders tell. What can I do about it?

— Dayton, OH

Dear Dayton:

First you should read *John Patrick Norman McHennessy—The Boy Who Was Always Late*, by John Burningham. It's the story of what happens to a boy whose teacher locks him up in a room until he writes, "I must not tell lies" five-hundred times—and what happens to her, too. Come to think of it, some of Ms. Class's favorite books are about liars. Here's a sampling:

> Her name was Poppy Brown, and she was a liar.
> It was the only remarkable thing about her
>
> *The Stonewalkers,* by Vivien Alcock

> I began to use Show and Tell to tell the class funny things
> that had happened to me. When I ran out of true things to tell,
> I started making them up.
> The teacher made me sit down. She said that there was a big difference between Show and Tell and Show and Fib.
> Personally, I don't think teachers like it when their students are funnier than they are.
>
> *Skinnybones,* by Barbara Park

> "Why didn't you tell me that tomorrow was Parents' Conference Day?" asked his mother.
> "Didn't I tell you?" he asked innocently.
> "No, I don't think so."
> "I told you," he said. "You said you couldn't go. You must have forgot."
> "Mrs. Ebbel seems to think it is important for me to be there," said his mother.
> "That's just her job," said Bradley. "The more mothers she sees, the more money she makes."
>
> *There's a Boy in the Girls' Bathroom,* by Louis Sacher

Liar, liar, pants on fire! Ms. Class wonders if your fifth graders tell more than two lies a day. Research shows that adults who keep diaries of the lies they tell admit to about two lies a day in those journals. Ms. Class suspects that because of the delicate nature of their work, the figure for teachers would be higher. She recommends that before instituting an antilying curriculum, you try keeping a journal of the lies you tell in school.

Here's some food for thought: mystery writer Dick Francis observes that the most damaging lies are told by those who believe they're true.

LIFE SKILLS PLURALISM

Dear Ms. Class:

Our elementary school is transforming its curriculum to incorporate practical life skills. We want to prepare our children to enter the real world of the twenty-first century. Do you know of any foundations that might give us funds to help us implement this transformation?

— Providence, RI

Dear Providence:

Since Ms. Class does not believe in practical education, she could not possibly aid and abet your endeavor. Ms. Class believes children have plenty of time once they leave school to become practical: to learn how to cook, clean house, wire a doorbell, and balance a checkbook. In school, children should learn about the power and pattern of great literature, the arts, and numbers, as well as the beauty and wonder of science and the grand mysteries of the universe.

Ms. Class asked her husband, a scientist, if he thinks students should be taught life skills. He said, "Definitely. Everyone should learn CPR."

LITERATURE LESSONS BULL MARKET

Dear Ms. Class:

I agree with you that children should be encouraged to enjoy literature, but I think if a teacher chooses carefully she can find great literature that teaches important lessons. As a second-grade teacher I know I can teach important lessons at the same time I'm encouraging children to enjoy what they read.

— Harrisburg, PA

Dear Harrisburg:

Of course you are right: great literature has important values, but for young readers pleasure must come before moral purpose. Ms. Class entreats you to walk into your classroom with just the book. No study guide. No ulterior motive. Just the book. Ms. Class begs you to do this because she knows what can happen. Ms. Class has in her possession a study guide for Judith Viorst's poignant story *The Tenth Good Thing About Barney*. The student is instructed: "If one of your pets died, how would you say goodbye? Plan a memorial service that would be meaningful to you."

Ms. Class is not making this up. Her imagination is just not up to the task.

LOST OBJECTS RECONFIGURATION

Dear Ms. Class:

I don't blame parents for being annoyed when mittens disappear and lunch boxes self-destruct, but I don't know what I can do about the fact my students can't keep track of their clothing or other possessions.

— Cumberland, MD

Dear Cumberland:

Although humorist Mark Russell thinks the multiple rings of Saturn are composed entirely of lost airline luggage, Ms. Class knows there isn't enough luggage to account for those rings. Ms. Class knows those rings are composed of lost mittens, jackets, and staplers.

Dear Ms. Class:

Although I appreciate the humor of your lost mittens remarks, for me, losing or misplacing things has become a serious problem. It happens so often that I worry that it's the first stages of Alzheimer's. Since it seems to happen more often at school than at home, I also worry that I'm "losing my grip" as a teacher.

— Lincoln, CA

Dear Lincoln:

Nobody loses things as often as Ms. Class, and she has been doing this since the very first day in the classroom when she lost the roll book. She doesn't need to tell you that a teacher is not allowed to lose the roll book, which, as the secretary informed her "is a permanent, legal document." That same secretary refused to let Ms. Class leave the building until the roll book was found (in the nurse's office).

The eminent philosopher-mathematician Alfred North Whitehead is credited with the materials disappearance principle: "Just because you eventually find what you've been looking for doesn't mean it didn't disappear for a while." Ms. Class would only add that you usually don't find it until you've replaced it.

Truth-in-advice-giving disclosure: Ms. Class has special sympathy with people who misplace eyeglasses, keys, test papers, and love letters. Ms. Class herself once misplaced a third grader. Please know there were extenuating circumstances. Ms. Class's students considered it a special privilege to read in a private, dark place. The favored spot was a closet Ms. Class cleaned out for that purpose. Ricky went into the closet early one afternoon. Two hours later school was dismissed and Ms. Class went grocery shopping. With her cart half-filled and while examining boston lettuce, Ms. Class experienced one of those moments of pure terror that Emily Dickinson called "zero at the bone." Leaving the grocery cart in the aisle, Ms. Class drove back to school, raced into the building, and found Ricky sound asleep in the closet. Ms. Class woke him up, drove him home, and never told him he'd been forgotten. Third graders deserve to hold on to as many illusions as possible.

MAILBOX ENVIRONMENTAL IMPACT STATEMENT

Dear Ms. Class:

I wonder how my mailbox can be stuffed in the morning when I clean it out every night, especially considering I leave the building after the secretaries do and get there before they arrive the next morning. Mailbox overload wouldn't be so bad if it weren't for the fact that there always seem to be a few impossible messages such as "Call Central Office before 10 A.M." How can I call Central Office when they don't get in until 9 A.M. and I'm teaching from 8:30 until my lunch break at 11:40?

— Winston-Salem, NC

Dear Winston-Salem:

Ms. Class agrees that the overnight paper pileup is a mystery, but short of nailing your mailbox shut, there is no solution to the accumulation of this paper. This does not mean that Ms. Class does not have a suggestion for making your mornings more pleasant. Ms. Class herself achieves morning calm by never approaching her mailbox until after lunch. Since you cannot act on early-morning imperatives anyway, why subject yourself to them?

MAINSTREAMING CHILL INDEX

Dear Ms. Class:

There are six mainstreamed children in my fifth-grade class: a Down's syndrome girl, an emotionally disturbed boy, three physically challenged children, and a child labeled as dyslexic. That leaves nineteen other children whose skills range from first-grade to tenth-grade level. The physically challenged aren't really that much of a problem—other than getting things transcribed into braille for the blind child and that sort of thing. I wonder, though, what the people who make decisions about mainstreaming expect me to do for the other children? What am I supposed to teach a girl who can't even tie her shoes or remember her address or phone number? Or a boy who rolls up in a fetal position and sucks his thumb—when he isn't quacking like a duck?

— Binghamton, NY

Dear Binghamton:

What few people making education policy will acknowledge is that mainstreaming is not a search for the possible. Mainstreaming means having to choose between the regrettable and the catastrophic. When considering the options for mainstreaming a child, the chill factor should always be considered. Mainstreaming is about sentiment, not about teaching, or even training.

Dear Ms. Class:

And you call yourself an educator? I am disgusted by your attitude toward mainstreaming. Differently abled children can achieve the same skills as children termed "normal." Sometimes they just need more support and more time to catch up. A person in your position of influence ought to be ashamed of preaching such ugly negativism.

— St. Joseph, MI

Dear St. Joseph:

Ms. Class never preaches; she comments and leaves it to the educationists to proselytize. She would comment that she finds the term *catch up* curious when applied to the valiant and often futile struggles of damaged children. Who could be so heartless—and doctrinaire—as to claim that there is enough time for a child with Down's syndrome to "catch up" with his classmates?

Ms. Class has never discounted the power of a good slogan to move mountains. Now she sees that even a mediocre slogan can silence sensible opposition to outrageous agendas.

Ms. Class regards this as the Campbell's Soup approach to education. Salt is what gives their soup taste. But salt is also the dirty word of the health-conscious nineties. Campbell's reduced the salt in a soup serving size by twenty percent—by reducing the serving size listed on the label from ten ounces to eight ounces.

MAJORITY-RULE CREDIT CHECK

Dear Ms. Class:

After much rancorous discussion, our department voted on a language arts text. Two dissenters now refuse to use the book agreed on. This smacks of poor sportsmanship to me.

— Cambridge, MA

Dear Cambridge:

Surely English teachers remember that Henry David Thoreau went to jail because he believed that "any man more right than his neighbors constitutes a majority of one."

In *An Enemy of the People*, Henrik Ibsen was even more adamant. His character says, "The majority never had right on its side."

Ms. Class wishes you had offered more convincing evidence for the worthiness of the language arts text than a faculty vote. She has been privy to too many departmental book selection votes to put much faith in the outcome.

MARTYRDOM-POTENTIAL REALITY CHECK

Dear Ms. Class:

I've been teaching for more than twenty years, and still I get to my classroom an hour and a half before school begins each day. I stay an hour after school to give students extra help. I don't understand this new breed of teacher who dashes in at the last minute and leaves as soon as the last bell rings. What's happened to professionalism?

— Salt Lake City, UT

Dear Salt Lake City:

Ms. Class humbly asks you to consider two important principles about professionalism:

1. Time expended has little relationship to excellence achieved.

2. Everybody hates a martyr; it's not surprising they were burned at the stake.

MASTER PLAN SPIN-OFF

Dear Ms. Class:

My principal wants us to form committees and develop a Master Plan for Education. Can you explain exactly what this means?

— Perth Amboy, NJ

Dear Perth Amboy:

It means that if your plans are big enough, you'll never have to change a thing.

Dear Ms. Class:

Are master plans related to mastery learning? I'm always suspicious of anything that claims teachers or children "master" something, suspicious of claims that anyone knows everything they need to know about something and that they know it forever. I mean, I sometimes forget my own husband's name when I go to introduce him. I worry that in the name of professional standards teachers are being driven to claim some sort of grand expertise that doesn't exist. I know I'm a good teacher, but I also know that I am daily humbled by what I don't know.

— Waterloo, IA

Dear Waterloo:

Ms. Class salutes you. A sure sign of a teacher's true professionalism is her daily recognition and acknowledgment of the alarming increase in the number of things that baffle her.

MASTERY LEARNING JETSTREAM

Dear Ms. Class:

I serve on a school report card committee that includes parents, teachers, and administrators. Parents want the report card to indicate exactly what their children have learned and are pushing for a report card checklist of skills mastered. This makes me nervous, as I know that students learn something and then forget it.

— Poughkeepsie, NY

Dear Poughkeepsie:

Of course you are right. *Mastery* is a nonsense term. Learning is not something that takes place in finite steps at finite times. Ms. Class suggests turning the table on any adults who profess a belief in mastery and asking them to list exactly what skills they have mastered. If you are feeling really devious you could give them a test on apostrophes, dividing fractions, or listing the planets in order of their distance from the sun.

Dear Ms. Class:

Surely you aren't trying to make a case for ignorance. Surely you believe there are things that students need to know and it's a teacher's job to teach these things.

— Virginia Beach, VA

Dear Virginia Beach:

Ms. Class wants her students to know lots. She's just not willing to make a finite list. When E. D. Hirsch came up with his list of five thousand things everybody should know to be culturally literate, the idea was so deliciously awful that Ms. Class phoned *Education Week* and insisted they let her write a review of Hirsch's work.

Ms. Class then amazed and alarmed strangers on airplanes and in hotel lobbies by reading portions of Hirsch's list aloud and asking them, "What do you know about Leyden jars and when did you know it? How about Mach numbers, biochemical pathways, and liver detoxification?

Professor Hirsch says his lists are necessary because schools "have shrunk the body of information." Ms. Class thinks teachers should send him their curriculum mandates. If the school day wasn't so overcrowded already by the pressures of the factologists, maybe students would have time to learn things that really matter.

MATH FACTS UPGRADE

Dear Ms. Class:

I am very interested in integrating the arts across the curriculum and wonder if you can point me in the direction for connecting dance and mathematics.

— Muncie, IN

Dear Muncie:

Ms. Class wonders what you have in mind: the Virginia reel, the hula-hula, or the hokeypokey. In all earnestness, Ms. Class advises you to make sure those kids know their math facts before you start tap dancing.

MEDIA-MONITORS REMOTE ACCESS

Dear Ms. Class:

I guess I'm lucky. I teach in a school where the parents don't seem to have many complaints. We are by no means perfect, but the parents seem to be pleased with what we are doing. But you would never know this by reading the local paper. When they bother to report on schools at all, they pick up some Associated Press story about a disaster somewhere else in the country. The only time they print news about a local school is when something negative happens. The most recent example was kids spray painting graffiti on the outside gym wall on Halloween.

— Portland, OR

Dear Portland:

Except when local scandal erupts, the media reports education news as disinterested bystanders. Ms. Class wonders if the public would permit this same disengagement—and lack of on-site information—from our sports reporters.

Ms. Class was once the public relations committee for her teacher association. Yes, she was a one-person committee. It makes scheduling meetings a whole lot easier. Every week for eight months, she sent the local newspaper a press release on teacher association letterhead highlighting a noteworthy happening in the district. To her knowledge, not one of these events received mention in the paper.

MEMO DESTABILIZATION

Dear Ms. Class:

My principal stuffs our mailboxes with memos detailing every aspect of our professional lives. We get a memo on what time to be at school, a memo on how to dress, a memo on how often to give homework, on how to figure out grades, and so on. I find it demeaning for this petty tyrant to insist he knows how I should conduct my professional life.

— Richmond, VA

Dear Richmond:

No one feels more important than when he has written a memo of more than twenty-five words. Ms. Class suspects most teachers can appreciate the advice of Vladimir Kabaidze, general director of the Ivanovo Machine Building Works near Moscow. In 1988, talking of the proliferation of paperwork, he advised that it's useless to fight the memos and papers: "You've got to kill the people producing them." Ms. Class advises you, Richmond, to consider slightly less drastic measures.

Ms. Class would remind you that a memorandum is written not to inform the reader but to protect the writer. The principal writes memos about proper dress so that if a teacher ever appears topless, he, at least, is covered.

Dear Ms. Class:

I thought you might enjoy the enclosed memo, which is typical of the matter that fills our boxes.

TO: All Staff

RE: SIGN-IN/OUT SHEET

The sign-in/out procedure has been established in order that the administration may have some feasible way of keeping track of the staff as to who is present and who is not present in the school premises at specific times. It is also very beneficial in meeting the needed clerical work for payroll purposes. Therefore, it is expected that all staff members initial and indicate their time of arrival and departure from the school premises on the sign-in/out sheet daily.

Please omit the city name. The principal doesn't read, but I don't want someone telling him that his memo went public. He'd get a court order to make you reveal who sent it.

— Paranoid, USA

Dear Paranoid:

Thank you. The writer could have just said, "I want everyone to sign in and sign out." But that is too personal and too direct. You could hold a faculty contest to figure out to what (or whom) the "it" in the last sentence refers.

As a rule, the length of a memo is in inverse proportion to the information it contains. The more trivial the information, the longer the memo.

Environmental Impact Warning: Memos multiply when left in the mailbox.

MERIT PAY SKILL MAINTENANCE

Dear Ms. Class:

My district has a system of merit pay, based on a teacher's taking extra courses and achieving a certain score on a rubric devised by the district. I need the money, but part of me resents this imposition of one more hurdle to achieve a living wage.

— Knoxville, TN

Dear Knoxville:

Merit pay is an idea passed on to schools from the business community. Ms. Class wonders why, if it is such a terrific idea, the business community does not impose it on their own leaders? The notion that private industry rewards workers according to their productivity is a myth on a par with the tooth fairy and the Easter bunny. Ms. Class knows of what she speaks. She worked in business for a number of years. The notion that such a payment system can improve education is worse than a joke; it's a mistake.

METACOGNITION TOXIC HAZARDS

Dear Ms. Class:

I want to make my students aware of the bipolar, metacognitive power of their minds. Can you offer advice?

— Laramie, WY

Dear Laramie:

Robert Parker's fictional Boston detective Spencer warns his school psychologist lady friend that talking this way will cause her teeth to rot.

Dear Ms. Class:

I've been hearing a lot about metacognition lately, but I confess I'm not sure what it is. Can first graders do it?

— Helena, MT

Dear Helena:

Metacognition is one of those five-dollar words that make one feel ten feet tall just by saying them. Anyone who can keep this kind of language up for half an hour is eligible for a government grant, if not a university appointment. You are unique in admitting you haven't yet grasped its subtleties. Many people feel it's easier to admire something than to admit they don't understand it.

As for those first graders: Ms. Class appreciates your desire to remain up-to-date and not get left behind when the pedagogical Rollerbladers whiz by. Relax. Not only can first graders metacognate; they do it even when you aren't looking. When your first graders talk about the fun of sharing a good book, you can impress the administrators by writing "metacognition" in your plan book.

METRIC SYSTEM DIVINE RIGHT

Dear Ms. Class:

I don't understand what's holding up this country's move to the metric system.

— Wausau, WI

Dear Wausau:

There is a sizable block of citizenry who insist that if God had intended us to use a metric system, then His Son would have had ten disciples, not twelve.

MINIMUM COMPETENCY LIFE EXPECTANCY

Dear Ms. Class:

I'm confused by our district's minimum competency tests. They reflect such a low level of achievement and yet we are expected to spend a lot of time drilling kids to pass them. I am depressed at the thought of directing my energies—and those of my students—toward such a low-level accomplishment.

— Lewisburg, WV

Dear Lewisburg:

In *Twenty Teachers*, Ken Macrorie writes about teachers who have been identified by their peers as exemplary. These teachers include a first-grade teacher, a high school teacher of woodworking, and a professor of space engineering. After discovering that all these teachers believe in pretty much the same ideas and at a deep level use pretty much the same methods, Macrorie concludes that "it is good works, not minimum competency, that these enablers bring about in their classrooms."

Ms. Class invites you to consider how schools would be transformed if we helped students concentrate on good works rather than minimum competency.

MISSION STATEMENT MIASMA

Dear Ms. Class:

I am on a committee working on a mission statement for our new school. I wonder if you could point us in the direction of some good, inspiring statements.

— San Bernadino, CA

Dear San Bernadino:

Ms. Class admits that she finds mission statements useless—unless they can be recycled as cardboard boxes. Too many of these statements take a missionary tone, portraying school personnel as saviors to a community of savages. If you insist that you must have a statement under which you can march, you can't go wrong by recycling the first part of the Hippocratic oath: *first, do no harm.*

MORAL EDUCATION REVENUE SHARING

Dear Ms. Class:

I am distressed at the lack of moral curriculum in the elementary schools. How can we expect children to learn how to behave if we don't teach them?

— Fargo, ND

Dear Fargo:

When William Bennett was Secretary of Education he made quite a pitch for moral literature in the schools. (Mr. Bennett has since become the author of the best-selling but unreadable *Book of Virtues*.) Ms. Class traveled to Allentown, PA, where Mr. Bennett was speaking, to ask him this question: "Does your recommendation that elementary students be exposed to the great works of literature, works of worthy moral message, include any works published in this century? Do you have any books published after, say, *Heidi* to recommend to elementary students and their teachers?"

Mr. Bennett was startled by the question. He paused for along moment and finally confessed, "No, I don't." Then he launched into a quite witty account of reading to his three-year-old son, sharing such books as Sendak's *Where the Wild Things Are*. Bennett closed his amusing anecdote with, "I don't suppose *Wild Things* has a moral message—except, of course, 'Always obey your parents.'"

Then it was Ms. Class's turn to be stunned. The next day she set into motion a little research study in Allentown. Here are some of the lessons Allentown first and second graders found in Sendak's book:

- If you watch TV and it's scary, don't believe it.

- Never be afraid of monsters because there ain't none.

- Don't chase the dog down the steps with a fork.

When a fourth-grade teacher asked her class if they remembered what the book was about, here's what they said:

- Your imagination can go anywhere—if you command it to.

- You don't always need to be the top person to be happy.

- Being king wasn't enough and Max wanted to go home.

This is powerful stuff, and no teacher who reads a lot of good books with her students will be surprised by the children's insights. Of some eighty children who were asked about the meaning of the book, only one first grader agreed with Mr. Bennett, saying that the lesson was "Listen to your mom." Most of the children got far more out of the book.

Dear Ms. Class:

Nice story, Ms. Class, but I'd like to know what Fargo wanted to know: what moral curriculum can we offer our students?

— Roseville, CA

Dear Roseville:

You are the moral curriculum for your students. In *The Moral Life of Children*, Pulitzer prize-winning child psychiatrist Robert Coles recalled something his teacher Paul Tillich said. "Morality is not a subject; it is a life put to the test in dozens of moments." The scary part of teaching is that every minute of every day you are a moral guide for your students—and not just in what you say. In "Self-Reliance" Emerson reminds us that virtue and vice are communicated not just by overt actions but they "emit a breath every moment." What this means, of course, is that when Ms. Class taught seventh grade, or third, or tenth, she was also teaching Morality 101. The wonder and terror of teaching is that the most important thing we have to offer students is ourselves.

MULTICULTURALISM BROWNIE POINTS

Dear Ms. Class:

Our middle school is about ninety-five percent white, and I guess one might say this makes us nervous. We want our students to have a realistic picture of the diverse nature of American society as well as a sensitivity toward people who are different than they are. The English and social studies teachers are having a relatively easy time bringing in multicultural contributions to the curriculum. Music, food, and folktales are popular with the students. Admittedly, science and math are a bit more difficult, but what bothers me is, two teachers refuse to be bothered.

— Burlington, VT

Dear Burlington:

What bothers Ms. Class is that, realistically speaking, math and science are universal, and English is the language professionals in those fields use for communication. Ms. Class sees value in having students use Chinese tangrams, engage in Japanese paper folding, play Wari (the Ashanti strategy game), but whose culture is being celebrated? Wari is as foreign to a black boy in Harlem as it is to a white boy in Burlington. Most Chinese in America have never seen a tangram puzzle, nor do Japanese Americans sit around doing origami. As a matter of fact, neither to Japanese in Japan. Recently there has been a resurgence of adult education courses in Japan, because people worried that the ancient arts of paper folding and flower arranging were dying out.

Ms. Class worries that most schools engage in multicultural endeavors learned from placemats at the International House of Pancakes and tours of Epcot Center. If teachers want students to understand the peoples of other nations, it does not do a whole lot of good to study Egyptian hieroglyphics as a second language. They'd do better to study what makes Japan such a successful industrial giant rather than the art of paper folding. If we want to appreciate and understand Mexico, NAFTA is more significant than sitting around eating tacos and singing "La Cucaracha."

NEATNESS NANOSECOND

Dear Ms. Class:

I wonder if other teachers have as much trouble keeping supplies in order as I do. I'm in such a long-term muddle I don't even know for sure what I have, and can't find what I think I might have.

— Halifax, NS

Dear Halifax:

You are not alone. Ms. Class, while entirely punctilious about matters of courtesy and sobriety, has her own problems with the notion of every object having its own place.

Noted field anthropologist Erma Bombeck says that the difference between youth and old age can be summed up in a predilection for box saving. When you're young you believe that somewhere around the next bend there will be a box when you need it. Old age means keeping plenty of boxes in reserve; it means saving boxes inside other boxes.

Probably as a result of centuries of working in situations where supply rarely meets demand, teachers suffer from premature saving syndrome. Primary-grade teachers, in particular, start stockpiling supplies at age twenty-seven, and they don't limit themselves to boxes. They save baby food jars, L'Eggs containers, cottage cheese cartons, and Clorox jugs. Three days from retirement, teachers panic when they realize the container fairy isn't going to appear and remove these treasures, leaving $1.25 in their place.

Here are the classroom supplies axioms that Ms. Class has uncovered in her twenty years before the chalk tray:

- If you're looking for something in your center desk drawer, it's in the back. Once you find and remove it, the drawer won't close.

- The only way to prevent the further pileup of junk is to seal your desk drawers with duct tape.

- There are never enough shelves.

- The lunch boxes in the closet don't belong to anyone in your class; they don't belong to anyone who has ever been in your class.

- The student who pays the least attention to academic matters is the student most likely to know where to find what you're looking for.

NEEDS ASSESSMENT MODE CONVERGENCE

Dear Ms. Class:
   Just what is a needs assessment?

                                             — Racine, WI

Dear Racine:
   A needs assessment is a skills checklist with a graduate degree.

NEW IDEAS CLIMATE CONTROL

Dear Ms. Class:
   After fifteen years of teaching, I have become knowledgeable about reader-response theory, and it has changed my life. I've taken several classes and read a lot. What I really need is a cohort to share ideas with. I wonder why it's so hard to get people to even consider doing things differently. Even good teachers just shrug and say, "Not another new idea."

                                             — Amarillo, TX

Dear Amarillo:
   Jonathan Swift once pointed out that "'tis not good manners to offer brains." The teacher with a new idea is first seen as a crank and then, if she's not careful, a bore. Sometimes recent converts have a way of swamping the uninitiated with their enthusiasm. Ms. Class suggests offering a small piece of the theory to one colleague. Be careful not to scare her off with too much information at once.

NURSE'S OFFICE MAGNETIC FIELD

Dear Ms. Class:
   I wonder how to tell if a child is genuinely ill and needs to see the nurse or if he's faking and just wants to get out of class.

                                             — Oakland, MD

Dear Oakland:
   For twenty-plus years, Ms. Class made it her policy never to try to make the distinction between botulism and boredom. The fact is that children occasionally need the diversion that a trip outside the classroom provides. The nurse has the added lure of offering Band-Aid accessorization.
   Teachers occasionally need diversion too, which is why we are rarely ill when we call in to take a sick day.

Ms. Class developed this policy during her first semester as a teacher, when she was assigned a nonteaching duty period taking charge of the health office for a school of thirty-five hundred students. Feeling outraged by the responsibility of being in charge of the health and first aid needs of a community larger than her hometown, Ms. Class let any student who wanted to sit or lie in the health office do so.

Ms. Class was not an absolute softie. If a student did not wish to return to class at the end of the period, Ms. Class phoned the parents, giving them the option of retrieving their child, persuading him to return to class, or meeting him at the emergency room, where Ms. Class would dispatch him by ambulance. An impressive number of students thus received encouragement to return to class after one period.

Ms. Class regards this early experience as formative: she learned that students occasionally need a break from classroom pressures; she also learned that teachers don't need to take on responsibilities, such as the health needs of students, that properly belong to parents.

Dear Ms. Class:

The school nurse yelled at me for "overreacting" when I asked her for news about my student who was sent home with scabies. Today, another student was sent home. The nurse claims it's "the fifth disease," a skin irritation caused by a dry winter and nothing to be alarmed about. Have you ever heard of this fifth disease? I'm worried about the fact that scabies is so contagious and definitely something to worry about. I also worry that the principal is a "good news" fanatic. He will do anything to prevent bad news from leaking out into the community.

— Buffalo, NY

Dear Buffalo:

The fifth disease sounds rather like an invention of the fifth column. Ms. Class does not believe in this fifth disease, not for a moment. Ms. Class has long experience with the double-talk surrounding a school infested with scabies, head lice, and impetigo. Your principal is not unique in being afraid the president of the PTO will find out there's a nasty, contagious affliction in the school. Your story is so similar to a recurring problem at Ms. Class's school that she wonders if all principals don't take Damage Control 104: How to Convince Nurses to Aid and Abet Public Relations Damage Control.

Nevertheless, you must remember that discretion is the better part of valor. Ms. Class suggests confronting the principal, not the nurse. The only persons who don't feel the need to approach school nurses with considerable caution are school secretaries.

OFFICIAL OBSERVATIONS DATA BASE

Dear Ms. Class:

I know this is going to sound foolish, but, anyway, here's the story. I've been teaching seventh grade for twelve years, and I get along with my principal and with the social studies supervisor. Nevertheless, I am petrified about official observations. I've never had a bad report, so I don't know why I'm so worried. Can you give me any advice?

— Erie, PA

Dear Erie:

Ms. Class once traveled to another state to give an inservice course to middle-grade teachers. Somehow, apropos of nothing, she mentioned the farce of teacher observations, how we put on these phony lessons for the administrators. We put on an act, the kids put on an act, and the supervisor goes away satisfied with a Ptomkin classroom in which the warts of reality have remained hidden.

Teachers in the audience gasped. One said, "I thought I was the only one who did that." Others agreed. For years, every teacher there had thought that every other teacher was officially observed teaching a regular, everyday sort of lesson. Every teacher there thought she was the only one with this sneaky little secret of staging an event for occasions of official observation.

This makes Ms. Class wonder if perhaps you are worrying that you are the only one in your school putting on an act, teaching a canned lesson for the benefit of your supervisor. Talk to your colleagues about official observations. When you discover they do the same thing, you'll feel better. Deceit seeks collaboration.

One year Ms. Class decided to abandon the canned lesson and just let the language arts supervisor see a regular day in the life of seventh graders. Sharon, who had just fallen in love, dashed into the room and asked for a pass to the library to get a copy of *Romeo and Juliet,* three students read joke books to each other, four students read notes Ms. Class had written to them and wrote replies, two students quizzed each other for a social studies test in some other teacher's class, Charlie (left behind from the previous class) remained asleep, Raymond picked up his novel where he had left off the day before, and Pete launched into his daily litany about "not doin' no friggin' work in this friggin' school." Interestingly, on other occasions when Ms. Class performed "show" lessons for her administrator, Pete played his role of model student. But since Ms. Class wasn't faking it this time, neither did he.

The language arts supervisor happened to be sitting across the table from Ron, who was working on a poem. Three times he called Ms. Class over to help him, and she persuaded him to stop going for the easy rhyme, nudged him to reexamine his metaphor, and reminded him about the thesaurus when he decided he needed a special word, "something different."

Ms. Class thought Ron's work nothing short of miraculous and was also pleased with the independent work showed by most students in the room. But you won't find any record of these magic moments in an official observation in her personnel file. After ten minutes, the language arts supervisor couldn't stand it any more. She gathered up her notebooks and her checklists and announced, "I'll come back when you are teaching."

One final suggestion: if you continue to be nervous while you're being observed, just think about what your supervisor looks like while taking a shower.

OPEN CLASSROOM POSTTRAUMATIC SHOCK SYNDROME

Dear Ms. Class:

I've recently changed schools and am trying to get used to this new school's "open" arrangement. This is a school without interior walls. I'm finding it very difficult to adjust to the lack of privacy and to the noise. I wonder if I'm just too old and set in my ways to feel comfortable about teaching in a fishbowl. Any advice?

— Green Bay, WI

Dear Green Bay:

Ms. Class commiserates. Good fences may not make good neighbors, but every teacher needs a door she can shut. Denying a teacher a room of her own is LaLa Land gone berserk. Ms. Class knows of a number of open pod schools—in California, no less—where people in charge have come to realize the importance of a teacher's having a room with walls and a door and are bringing in carpenters to build these interior walls. In addition to praying for this administrative awakening to take place in your building, Ms. Class suggests using bookcases, portable chalkboards, filing cabinets, and whatever else you can beg, borrow, or pilfer to create a private nook for you and your students.

Don't feel guilty about your desire for your own space. The people who borrowed the open space concept from England thirty years or so ago did not take into account the fact that Americans are raised with bedrooms of their own; they grow up being able to shut the door.

OPEN HOUSE EMISSION STANDARDS

Dear Ms. Class:

I wonder what I can do about the fact that the parents who come to open house are the parents I don't need to see. The parents of children having difficulties never come.

— Worcester, MA

Dear Worcester:

Open house is an outmoded ritual where the parents of A students visit schools to receive praise about their successful parenting skills. The other parents already know that society has judged them and their children as deficient. They don't need to dress up and leave home to hear their failure proclaimed in public.

Ms. Class must admit that her own rather unique first parent conference made all others in the subsequent twenty years pale by comparison. As she may have mentioned before, Ms. Class began her teaching career in late October, quite literally in the middle of someone else's lesson plan. Ms. Class was told to report to Grover Cleveland High School in Queens, New York, in the middle of the week—on a nonteaching day, a day that just happened to be parent conference day. And so it happened that Ms. Class was supposed to explain the educational program of ninth and tenth graders to parents before she had laid eyes on the students.

Not surprising, Ms. Class does not remember a thing about that conference, other than trying to reassure parents that their children's education would continue uninterrupted. What Ms. Class does remember is the horror of clearing out her desk in June and coming across notes she made of that parent conference. Mrs. Jackson had extracted Ms. Class's promise to contact her at the "very first sign of trouble" from her son Billy.

Billy was the catastrophe of Ms. Class's first year of teaching. Nasty, sneaky, and disruptive, he never turned in a piece of homework or, for that matter, did any assignments. Three months into the term, Ms. Class finally figured out he couldn't read. Twenty years later, Ms. Class still feels guilty that she didn't realize she'd met Billy's mother on her first day on the job and still feels guilty that she broke the promise she'd made. She wonders, though, if Billy's mom might not have been grateful. After all, no news is good news. Maybe Mrs. Jackson thought it was the first good year her son had had.

Dear Ms. Class:

I can't tell you how much I dread parent conferences. I dread being put on the defensive. I teach in an area where most parents are professionals and many of them are condescending. Their favorite complaint is that I don't teach their precious children enough subject matter. Parents complain that they ask their child, "What did you learn today?" and the child replies, "Nothing." How can I answer this?

— Bellevue, WA

Dear Bellevue:

Ms. Class wants to share with you part of a teacher's letter to parents (the letter appeared in the *Wall Street Journal* in January 1985; Ms. Class doesn't feel she should be expected to remember the exact date): "If you promise not to believe everything your child says happens at this school, I'll promise not to believe everything he says happens at home."

Dear Ms. Class:

The pressure of all the parental "involvement" in my every classroom breath is really getting to me. Any suggestions?

— Charlotte, VT

Dear Charlotte:

Teacher observations about parents seem to fall into two categories:

1. Those that complain parents don't get involved enough in what goes on in school.

2. Those that complain parents get too involved in what goes on in school.

OPTIMISM ON CALL

Dear Ms. Class:

I need some advice for creatively channeling Jarrod's boisterous spirits. Jarrod is six years old and an active child: he has difficulty sitting still for storytime, other children complain that he fools around too much and resist being his partner, and he never seems to complete projects. He is a bright child, and his mother says that my class bores him. I worry that she may be right. What can I do?

— Santa Fe, NM

Dear Santa Fe:

You and Jarrod's mother are optimists, people who mistake obnoxious behavior for creativity. Although Ms. Class believes that boredom in certain social situations indicates one's good taste, she is reluctant to give six-year-olds the upper hand. First of all, Sante Fe, you and Jarrod's mother should give yourselves a large dose of reality. Big Bird and Cookie Monster to the contrary, learning is not always fun, snappy, or dramatic. For

Jarrod's sake, you cannot accept either brilliance or boredom as an excuse for not working.

That said, take a look at your class routines. Maybe Jarrod needs big jobs broken down into a series of smaller tasks. Talk to a teacher specializing in learning disabilities for some short-term techniques for getting Jarrod on track.

Dear Ms. Class:

I'm really tired of reading all your negativism about teaching. A teacher's day is as good as she makes it!

— Toronto, ONT

Dear Toronto:

Ms. Class is a realistic optimist. This means she takes each day as it comes. Sunshine today doesn't mean that it she isn't prepared for snow tomorrow. As far as a teacher's making her own day, Ms. Class appreciates your willingness to accept responsibility but advises caution.

In *Passages,* Gail Sheehy points out that we need an award for people who come to understand the concept of enough. Good enough. Successful enough. Thin enough. Rich enough. Socially responsible enough. "When you have self-respect," observes Sheehy, "You have enough, and when you have enough, you have self-respect."

OUTCOME-BASED EDUCATION CRAP DETECTION

Dear Ms. Class:

Our local conservative Christian coalition is up in arms about outcome-based education. Why? I thought this was a plan embraced both by the Bush and Clinton administrations.

— Rochester, NY

Dear Rochester:

Translating professional jargon into English is no fun. You're right about the Bush-Clinton education alliance. Outcome-based education is based on conservative educational bean counting, namely, products are more important than processes. Of late, though, the term has become a catchall phrase meaning anything and nothing. Conservatives use it to inspire fear of demonic takeover of the schools. Liberals use it as a euphemism for humanistic education (which conservatives attack). Consultants, who have no philosophy, use the term as a bauble to dangle before school districts with money for inservice training. The rest of us try not to use it at all.

OUT-OF-THE-CLOSET DISCOURSE INTERVENTION

Dear Ms. Class:
I am convinced that one of my colleagues is homosexual. I worry about her being adviser to the girls tennis team. What should I do?

— Pueblo, CO

Dear Pueblo:
There are two possibilities:

You could be right about your colleague's sexual preferences.
You could be wrong.

In either case, why do you think you need to do something? Ms. Class wonders why people think a homosexual female is a greater risk to a girls tennis team than a heterosexual male.

PAPIER-MÂCHÉ CRITERION REFERENCE SCALE

Dear Ms. Class:
Our district has eliminated art teachers. Now classroom teachers are expected to "do" art. Part of the art curriculum for our grade level includes papier-mâché sculpture. I cannot imagine tackling this with thirty-two active sixth graders. Do you have any suggestions?

— Modesto, CA

Dear Modesto:
Yes. The first thing Ms. Class would do is forget the art curriculum. This is a case where the end could not possibly justify the means. If God had intended for people to dip newspapers into water and flour, he would not have made them so convenient as litter box liners and kindling starters in the fireplace.
Ms. Class realizes she will get impassioned letters from teachers who love papier-mâché, teachers whose students have made models of the seven wonders of the ancient world, the Golden Gate Bridge, Mount Rushmore, the White House, Elvis, and Mickey Mouse, as well as death masks

of members of the board of education from papier-mâché. Ms. Class says God bless them and entreats them to keep their nasty, sticky messes to themselves.

PARANOIA PARADIGMS

Dear Ms. Class:

It seems like every five years, schools are accused of not teaching something else. Whether it's bomb shelter sufficiency, the classics, or abstinence, I feel I'm always looking over my shoulder—watching out for whoever is getting ready to pounce with something else for me to teach. Am I being paranoid?

— Salem, MO

Dear Salem:

It is good to hear from a teacher with a sense of history. Remember this: just because a person has an irrational fear of cockroaches in her desk drawers, doesn't mean there aren't any there.

PARTIES: TRUTH IN ENTERTAINING

Dear Ms. Class:

I've noticed you have maxims for just about every school happening. How about classroom parties?

— Cedar Rapids, IA

Dear Cedar Rapids:

Yes, indeed. If Emily Post and Miss Manners found themselves in the extremely unlikely position of hosting a classroom party, here's what they would decree:

- Never serve refreshments earlier than fifteen minutes before the dismissal bell rings.
- Never pour more punch than you can wipe up.
- Include a plate of fruitcake, so children will be grateful for the oatmeal cookies.

PEDAGOGICAL PUNITIVE DAMAGES

Dear Ms. Class:

I am concerned about the fact that your pedagogical position reflects a gender-ist, racist, classist, ablist social structure that oppresses students. Until you deconstruct the historical configurations of oppression and recognize the need to speak out from your particularized semiotic space, your pedagogy will continue to support oppressive ways of knowing.

— Silver City, NM

Dear Silver City:
    You may be right.

PENCIL AFFLICTION SUPPORT GROUP

Dear Ms. Class:
    What can I do about a student who never has a pencil?

— Frankfort, KY

Dear Frankfort:
    You have a choice: You can give him a pencil, or you can drive yourself nuts. You should know, first of all, that your student is not unique. At any given moment, 3.7 students in every classroom across the country are without pencils. Here is a list of dos and don'ts to help you deal with this epidemic:

- DON'T phone the child's home, asking a parent to check for his pencil each morning. This is parental abuse, and forcing a household search for a pencil will only make the child late to school and the parents late to work.

- DON'T make the child write with the biggest crayon you can find.

- DON'T insist the child sit and do nothing.

- DO ask all your students to bring in old pencils from home. Keep a box of spares for emergencies.

- DO ask a miscreant's parents to supply you with ten pencils if the problem persists. Then you can assume responsibility for losing them.

- DO relax. These pencil miscreants grow up to be decent human beings— who lose their keys.

Dear Ms. Class:
    I do have a sense of humor. Occasionally, I even enjoy your weird idea of what's funny. But you don't seem to realize what a seriously annoying problem pencils present to teachers. Recently I begged the school secretary for a box of #2 pencils so my students could take the annual standardized reading test. She counted out each pencil and made me sign an affidavit as to the number I had received. I should

add that after much pleading, she gave me only eighteen pencils. There are twenty-nine students in my class.

I scrounged around and came up with the eleven extra pencils, but when the test was over I was able to return only sixteen new-looking pencils to the secretary, who used this pencil shortfall as an excuse to humiliate me further. I can handle mainstreaming, the gifted and talented, principals, parents, and members of the school board. I cannot handle pencils.

— Gulfport, MS

Dear Gulfport:

Ms. Class is in awe that after the test you had a pencil shortfall of only twelve percent. Just as leftovers in the refrigerators multiply, pencils at school self-destruct. Mere humans have no control over either phenomenon.

If you think you have problems, just reflect on the fact that Henry David Thoreau was killed by overexposure to pencils. If you want to know whether or not they were #2, you should consult a lead historian.

History aside, you need to face facts. Your real problem is not pencils but a nasty secretary, a problem even more prevalent and more intractable than pencil shortfalls.

PENCIL SHARPENER TWO-TIER FUNCTION

Dear Ms. Class:

I have taught in six different schools. Believe it or not, I have never been in a classroom where the pencil sharpener worked.

— Coxsackie, NY

Dear Coxsackie:

Of course Ms. Class believes you. What you exhibit is the classic misunderstanding of the two-tiered function of this classroom convenience item. For students, the pencil sharpener is an excuse for mobility, a chance to walk around the room and observe what one's classmates are doing. For teachers, practitioners of a sedentary occupation, the pencil sharpener is one of the few exercise devices available to develop muscles and improve the pectorals.

PENMANSHIP GRIDLOCK

Dear Ms. Class:

I'm distressed by the abominable penmanship of everybody. Please don't tell me it's the computer age. The real problem is nobody bothers to teach the beauty of a fine hand any more. Call me old-fashioned: I insist that my students practice penmanship for fifteen minutes every day.

— Chattanooga, TN

Dear Chattanooga:

Ms. Class has no problem with that. Just don't give penmanship practice as homework, where it becomes the model of what parents should be doing with their children. One of Ms. Class's own third graders, who was convinced he hated books, had terrible penmanship. Ms. Class begged Chris's parents to stop making him practice handwriting after school every day. She said they'd do better to read joke books with him. They thought she was nuts—until Jack Prelutsky answered a fan letter Chris had written him. Chris's parents put away the penmanship drills and framed Jack Prelutsky's letter. They are convinced Chris will be a poet: Prelutsky's penmanship is worse than his.

In Ms. Class's school, the middle and high reading groups learned cursive on schedule, and they enjoyed showing off their new skill. Her students, the rotten readers of third grade, cried when she introduced cursive in the fall. She nearly cried too. She put away the Palmer charts and told them they could print forever. In mid-March students began to send Ms. Class signals indicating they weren't satisfied with the status quo. When students asked Ms. Class to spell a word on the board, they'd add, "Write it in cursive." Then one day Leslie demanded, "How come we aren't learning cursive? We're supposed to learn cursive."

On the spot Ms. Class taught them to write their names in cursive, then their spelling words. They began to ask for cursive renditions of the poems Ms. Class printed on the board each morning. She felt like a translator at the United Nations.

Just three weeks after this reintroduction of cursive, with great fanfare, Leslie presented Ms. Class with a note that was entirely in cursive: "I love lemon ice cream, vanilla ice cream, butterscotch-swirl ice cream. . . ." Leslie had transcribed—in cursive—all thirty-one flavors from an ice-cream menu.

"Where did you learn that cursive?" Ms. Class asked her in a note. "You taught me," she wrote back. "Don't you remember?" Leslie and Ms. Class obviously viewed this differently. Ms. Class's impression was that once Leslie was ready, she must have taught herself cursive in about two days—when Ms. Class wasn't looking.

One of Ms. Class's few fifth-grade memories is getting her knuckles rapped for (deliberately) slanting her letters in the wrong direction in the official handwriting workbook. Please understand: Ms. Class does not believe any of this penmanship punctiliousness did her any harm; she just knows it didn't do her any good. On most days in education, a draw is the best a teacher can hope for.

Dear Ms. Class:

I am disturbed by your use of the retrograde genderist term pen*man*ship. *Handwriting* is the nonoffensive, nongendered preferred term. A person in your position needs to be sensitive to the language that oppresses women and keeps us in subservient positions.

— Storrs, CT

Dear Storrs:

You have increased Ms. Class's sensitivity. She wonders about your use of the word *person*.

PERMANENT RECORD SUSTAINABILITY

Dear Ms. Class:

Every September and May we are required to record standardized test scores on students' permanent record cards. Between October and April, these cards are locked up in the guidance counselors' offices, unavailable to teachers without a papal dispensation, an act of Congress, or a phone call from a school board member. Everybody acts like we want to use these cards to embarrass the kids on the Sally Jessy Raphael show. If a teacher can't look at these cards, then what are they for, anyway?

— New Castle, DE

Dear New Castle:

Keeping track of statistics is the first requirement of any bureaucracy. Standardized tests are the school's version of catch-22. Standardized tests are taken and their scores recorded in indelible ink on pieces of cardboard called permanent record cards just so that, in case a parent ever tries to sue the school district for not giving (and recording) these tests, authorities will have proof that all tests were in order. Since teachers do not have access to the information, obviously there is no instructional purpose for this number collection.

If it's any consolation, the statistic you need is not on the permanent record card, anyway. And even if it were there, there's nothing useful you could do with it. Even in a bureaucracy, statistics are no substitute for judgment.

Please note: if you are ever given the opportunity to look at the permanent record cards, don't do it until you have known the students for at least six months. One of the immutable laws of physics and pedagogy is that what you see is changed by looking.

Dear Ms. Class:

I disagree with your attitude about permanent record cards. A teacher needs to know as much about her students as possible. I carefully study my students' cards during the summer so that when school starts I know what to expect. If a student has a reading problem, for example, I don't embarrass her by asking her to read aloud. Why should a teacher waste valuable time in the fall, not to mention risk embarrassing students, by pretending her students are blank slates? I respect my colleagues' judgments and do my best to learn from them.

— Middlebury, VT

Dear Middlebury:

A boy named Gary showed Ms. Class a different approach. When she transferred to a new school, Ms. Class scrapped her remedial reading title and filled her room with science equipment. Officially, Ms. Class was still a Chapter I reading teacher and she had a list of students for whose reading progress she would be responsible. But she didn't tell the kids. Instead, she opened the room to any child who wanted to come and who could persuade his teacher to let him out of class. No schedules, no pretests for entry into the room. Ms. Class just opened the door and waited to see what would happen. As it happened, them rotten readers were eager to get out of class and their teachers were not reluctant to release them. Because it was the kids' idea, they came without prejudice, which was the point of the operation.

Ms. Class had two rules: Clean up your mess! and Write up what you do! She was better at enforcing the latter than the former. Starting the second week of school, Gary, a tall, gangly boy with a permanent grin on his face, appeared every day at 2:35 sharp to do color chemistry experiments. Gary put himself in charge of writing up the experiments for his group of four fifth and sixth graders, most of whom were prone to horsing around. His spelling was poor and his descriptions brief, but Ms. Class was impressed with his reliability in keeping track of all the experiments. When his teammates wanted to rush on to a new experiment, Gary would hold them back with the reminder, "First we have to write this one up," even though he was the only one doing the writing.

After Gary had been doing experiments for eight days, Ms. Class said, "Tell me the name of your teacher so I can write her a note about the good work you are doing." Gary looked nervous and then confessed that he was in special class. His school day ended at 2:30. Instead of getting on the bus, he circled the building, reentering through a rear door. He had heard about the room where kids did science experiments and decided to put himself into that room.

Had Ms. Class seen Gary's permanent record card ahead of time, he would never have been able to set a foot through her doorway. After all, everybody knows special ed kids don't belong in a class doing chemistry experiments.

Ms. Class was so shaken by this experience that she sought out the director of special education. "If I didn't recognize Gary as nonnormal, maybe the people who define these things should take another look." Three days later, Gary was assigned to a regular fifth-grade classroom. Three years later, Gary's mother wrote Ms. Class a note of gratitude for giving her son another chance at being regular.

This easy malleability of permanent record card definitions shook Ms. Class to the core. She still gets chills when she thinks about it. The saving grace of the story is the curiosity and audacity of one determined boy who dared to enroll himself in a class—without the accompanying paper trail of six years of test scores and teacher comments.

The eminent newspaper man Walter Lippmann once pointed out, "We do not first see, then define; we define first and then see." Ms. Class tries to defy this tendency by looking first. She pretends that each new student is a blank slate, no matter who his brother was or how many times he got sent to the office last year.

PETTY-CASH LEVERAGED BUYOUT

Dear Ms. Class:

I wonder why my principal, who is in charge of a $15,000,000 building, supervises one hundred two staff members, and oversees the welfare of twelve hundred junior high students, is not trusted to administer a petty-cash fund.

— Cadillac, MI

Dear Cadillac:

A bureaucracy always scrutinizes most closely the things that are easiest to control. That is why a district employs a treasurer, a purchasing agent, a payroll officer, an auditor, a head account clerk, and a cashier to take six weeks to process a teacher's $6.42 petty cash-voucher.

PHONICS PHACTS FANDANGO

Dear Ms. Class:

Phonics has become the battleground for the teachers at my school. I listen to both sides and wonder what's happened to common sense. How can anyone say that we don't need phonics? I just don't see how anyone can learn to read without some understanding of the sounds letters make.

— Broken Bow, NE

Dear Broken Bow:

You may be right. Part of the problem is that phonics gets undeserved credit for efficiency. The fact is that phonics works best when you already know the word. Ms. Class's own disillusion with phonics came early on. One day her first-grade teacher sent her to read with third graders, and Ms. Class suffered acute embarrassment when the teacher corrected her oral reading of "iz-lənd," telling her that it was "ī-lənd." Even though the teacher reassured her that this was an understandable error, Ms. Class suffered the lasting shock of realizing the letter combinations on which she'd structured her brilliant school career were undependable.

In *Reading Without Nonsense*, Frank Smith points out that the initial sound *ho*, for example, has a different pronunciation in each of the following common words: *hot, hope, hook, hoot, house, hoist, horse, horizon, honey, hour, honest.* Smith asks if anyone really believes that a child could learn to identify any of these words by sounding out the letters.

Here is another example from a teacher's guide (the publisher of which shall remain anonymous, to protect the guilty) telling teachers how to teach children to decode the word *check:* "Tell children to decode check by substituting /e/ for /i/ in the known word "chick."

Ms. Class does not regard this as a big help.

Dear Ms. Class:

I read what you wrote about phonics. Surely you overstate the case. Surely you believe that some decoding rules are helpful.

— Cripple Creek, CO

Dear Cripple Creek:

You may be right.

Ms. Class confesses that she used to teach the "final *e*" rule, regarding it as useful information. Then in 1980, she read the results of Ivo P. Grief's research. Professor Grief found that of 7,687 words studied, only fifty-three percent followed this rule. Professor Grief concluded that so unpredictable a rule should not be taught to children. Ms. Class finds herself agreeing. The point is this unpredictable rule is more predictable than most.

Dear Ms. Class:

I don't mean to belabor the phonics issue, but I hope we can regard your off-the-wall remarks as a (misguided) attempt at humor and not your final word on the subject.

— Charleston, SC

Dear Charleston:

How perceptive of you—realizing Ms. Class had more to say. Here is her final word with regard to phonics. She believes that every child should be taught Verner's law with regard to phonics. Verner has since passed to his just desserts, but he has left us with the observation that, in medial or final position in voiced environments and when the immediately preceding vowel does not bear the principal accent, the proto-Germanic voiceless fricatives derived from the proto-Indo-European voiceless stops and the proto-Germanic voiceless fricative derived from the proto-Indo-European *s* become the voiced fricatives represented in various recorded Germanic languages by *b, d, g,* and *r.*

Ms. Class hopes you are satisfied.

PICTURE DEVELOPMENT

Dear Ms. Class:

I have received a grant to buy cameras for my students. Based on the precept that "a picture is worth a thousand words," I am excited about the possibilities of providing a level playing field for students handicapped by less than sophisticated verbal skills.

— Milton, MA

Dear Milton:

Not everyone would accept your premise. The iconoclast and gadfly Edward Abbey, for one, pointed out that "one word is worth a thousand pictures. If it's the right word. The good word."

Models and photographers are the only ones who carry photo albums to job interviews. Ms. Class finds it difficult to believe that the playing field will be level for people who cannot express themselves in words.

PICTURE BOOK PATOIS

Dear Ms. Class:

You can settle a faculty room dispute. Just what is the proper way to read a picture book to an entire class?

— Muskegon, MI

Dear Muskegon:

Wearing an ankle-length dress. Preferable red velvet. Three-quarter sleeves trimmed in Belgian lace.

For pity's sake, what is the world coming to? Anyone who can't read a book for the sheer joy of it shouldn't be let loose around children.

PIZZA BRIBERY REALITY CHECK

Dear Ms. Class:

I heard someplace that you are against the Pizza Hut Book-It reading incentive. I can't imagine why. Why wouldn't you applaud and support anything that encourages children to read?

— Oshkosh, WI

Dear Oshkosh:

The Pizza Hut reading-incentive program and all other such forms of bribery are morally bankrupt. If we want to educate children and instill in them good character traits, then we must help them learn to read and savor books for their own sake, for the information and pleasure they bring, not because someone is keeping a scorecard and handing out stickers or trophies or pizzas. When you offer bribes, you debase both books and children.

Experienced and savvy teachers know that when you keep a scorecard on reading, whether it's gold stars or pizzas, children start paying more attention to the prize than to the books. Even worse, they start lying about the number of books they've read, or they read easy books so they can read more in less time. The result is that instead of encouraging a love of books, participation in such schemes ends up encouraging the development of moral monsters. People who promote such schemes have faith neither in children nor in books. They also lack faith in the abilities of teachers to bring good books and children together without gimmicks.

Educational psychologist John Nicholls warned that pizza incentives are likely to produce fat kids who don't like to read. He facetiously suggested that maybe we should try offering kids a free book for every pizza they eat.

Dear Ms. Class:
I understand your point about pizza bribery. I wonder how you feel about the principal of the school promising to shave his (very curly) head of hair if students read a certain number of books.

— Teaneck, NJ

Dear Teaneck:
It happens all over the country: principals getting dunked in a barrel of water, principals eating fried chicken on the roof of the school, and so on. Ms. Class agrees with the poet John Ciardi, who pointed out that the U. S. Constitution gives every American the inalienable right to make a damn fool of himself. She just wishes the jesters would not tie their antics to the number of books children read. Only people who themselves have never experienced the lure of the books think you have to trick, cajole, or bribe children into books.

POETRY BUFFER ZONE TRIGGERPOINTS

Dear Ms. Class:
When is the best time of day to read poetry to children?

— Ogden, UT

Dear Ogden:
Good times for reading poetry are at the beginning of the day, at the end of the day, right before lunch, right after lunch. And in between. Rainy days, sunny days, fair-to-middling days. Every day offers its own pretext for a poem.

When Ms. Class taught rhetoric at a technological university, none of the engineering students were enthusiastic about a course that emphasized language. These students were aliterate: they *could* read and write;

they simply chose not to. Ms. Class was determined to find some words that would interest and entice these resistant students. She started each day with "good words" on the board. The most resistant young man remained scowling in the back row throughout the semester—until the thirty-fourth day, when Ms. Class wrote the words of an eleventh-century Chinese lyric poem on the board. That scowling student straightened up in his chair and said, "Hey, not bad." High praise indeed.

POSITIVE REINFORCEMENT REACTIVATION

Dear Ms. Class:

I don't understand why you are so negative about assertive discipline and other methods of positive reinforcement that help children learn how to behave appropriately. I'm grateful for every bit of help I can get. And these methods work!

— Pendleton, OR

Dear Pendleton:

Ms. Class would remind you that the scariest part of being a teacher is that we teach who we are every minute of every day. That is why feelings are so important. It simply is not good enough merely to do the right thing at the right time. You also have to do it because you mean it. Children need to know teachers can bleed, as well as be thoughtful, generous, and zany. They most definitely do not need to see us as automatons measuring their lives with knee-jerk check marks and gold stars.

PRAISE JUNKIES

Dear Ms. Class:

I don't understand your stand against gold stars and other forms of acknowledging that a student has done a good job. We all need to be appreciated, to know that other people think we are worthy. If you could see the way my students' faces light up when I hand them a sticker, you'd know that this is not a bad thing. They love these stickers.

— Eugene, OR

Dear Eugene:

Manipulating people with incentives works in the short run, but there's plenty of evidence that, over time, it does lasting harm. Lots of respected educators have told us this:

- Teacher John Holt: "We destroy the . . . love of learning in children, which is so strong when they are small, by encouraging and compelling them to work for petty and contemptible rewards—gold stars, or papers marked 100 and tacked to the wall, or A's on report cards, or honor rolls, or dean's lists, or Phi Beta Kappa keys."

- Constructivist math educator Constance Kamii: "If we want children to become able to act with personal conviction about what is right . . . we must reduce our adult power and avoid the use of rewards and punishments as much as possible."

- Professor of psychology Edward Deci: "Rewards, deadlines, surveillance, and threats of punishment actually decrease intrinsic motivation."

These are not abstract statements from philosophers with their heads in the clouds. They are the conclusions of people working with students. Deci, for example, has conducted a number of experiments to assess how students react to working with and without rewards. Doubters can get full documentation of the evils of rewards in Alfie Kohn's *Punished by Rewards: The Trouble with Gold Stars, Incentive Plans, A's, Praise, and Other Bribes.*

Dear Ms. Class:
  With the exception of John Holt, the people you quote are college professors, and Holt, as valuable as his insights may be, did very little classroom teaching. Mostly he tutored children in small groups or individually. I'd like to know how I can say "Good job!" to a class of obstreperous fourth graders without turning them into praise junkies.
                                                                  — Duluth, MN

Dear Duluth:
  It depends on the activity. Ms. Class believes that the "reward" of reading a good book is to be directed toward another good book. It has always puzzled her that people would reward reading with pizza instead of with books, in effect, saying, "Your reward for reading is not to have to read any more."
  In day-to-day school business, Ms. Class chooses to think of ways to tell students, Take a break, rather than, Here's a reward. Here are some surefire student breaks that are integral to learning:

- Write/draw on the chalkboard. It's amazing, in this era of CD-ROMania, how much students love to do this. Since Ms. Class is allergic to chalk-dust, students appreciate it as an especially rare and privileged treat.

- Take turns being the teacher. Students may not learn much from this, but teachers certainly do. You think you don't have tics and weird habits? Just let a student sit at your desk for ten minutes and you'll never see yourself in quite the same way again.

- Choose a poem, riddle, amazing fact to write on the board and/or read aloud to the class.

- Clean up the top of your desk. Not integral to learning, you say? When the teacher can't find anything, learning is definitely sidetracked. And kids love messing around with the teacher's belongings.

- Rearrange the furniture in the classroom. Give those divergent, spatial thinkers a chance to shine.

Dear Ms. Class:

Don't you think some people are taking this praise prohobition to extreme lengths? I won't say that I work for praise, but when my principal or a parent or a colleague expresses approval of my work, I sure feel good.

— Gatesville, TX

Dear Gatesville:

Good point. Mark Twain confided, "I can live two months on a good compliment." Ms. Class's point is that we should not cheapen praise, should not proffer it indiscriminately like free peanuts on an airline. When a student does a good job, by all means tell her so. Be specfic. Don't say, Great work! What's she supposed to learn from that? Point to some sentence you particularly like in her writing, some way of explaining a math problem, and so on. Praise should not be promiscuous.

PRAYER-IN-SCHOOLS BENEFITS PACKAGE

Dear Ms. Class:

I wonder why I'm suddenly branded as a conservative because I think a moment of silent prayer wouldn't be terrible. I'm not advocating it; I just don't think it would be the end of Constitutional rights. Am I wrong?

— Cleveland, OH

Dear Cleveland:

Ms. Class appreciates your calm approach. Ms. Class agrees that irreparable psychic damage will not occur if children are led in one minute of silent prayer at school. However, Ms. Class believes that "does no harm" is not sufficient cause to institute such a policy. Children and their parents have plenty of opportunity to pray at home. Ms. Class does not want to add prayer instruction to her long list of curriculum duties (should it go before or after swish-and-spit?). And she wonders why a religious person would want someone like herself leading children in prayer of any kind.

Having stated her opinion, Ms. Class cannot resist pointing out that the schoolhouse is ever filled with irony: the people who want to continue the ban on prayer in the public schools on the grounds that religion should be a personal and private matter are usually the same people who favor compulsory sex education in those same schools.

Ms. Class no doubt dates herself when she confesses a nostalgic longing for the days when sex was as personal and private a matter as religion.

Dear Ms. Class:
Just what is wrong with a moment of silent prayer?

— Topeka, KS

Dear Topeka:
What is wrong with a moment of silent prayer is that it is hypocritical and developmentally unsound. Has forcing six-year-olds to parrot the Pledge of Allegiance led to greater patriotism than would be obtained by the daily singing of "Itsy Bitsy Spider," which would at least have the virtue of making some sense to young children? Ms. Class believes children can pray in church and pray at home. They can pray at McDonald's, should they be so inclined. In school they should sing songs, read good books, discover patterns in numbers, and marvel at the wonders of nature.

PRESENTS-MINIMIZATION NEGOTIATIONS

Dear Ms. Class:
I wonder what to do about the really awful presents my students give me.

— Knoxville, TN

Dear Knoxville:
Putrid perfume and crocheted catsup covers won't kill you; they can't even be regarded as health hazards. Nonetheless, there's no point in continuing this ritual in hopes that one day the gift will turn out to be tickets on a Carnival Cruise or even to a mud-wrestling match or the symphony. Tell students that you do not accept gifts and stick to it. Encourage children to concentrate their holiday spirits of good will on a food collection drive for a local food pantry.

PRINCIPAL PRINCIPLES ACCESS

Dear Ms. Class:
Although you are notoriously harsh on administrators, I'm still going to risk asking you for some words of wisdom for me. I have just been appointed principal. I'm excited and also scared.

— Bismarck, ND

Dear Bismarck:

You have just satisfied Ms. Class's first rule of successful principalship. My best wishes for achieving rules two through nine. A successful principal is a principal who:

1. Is humble about what she knows and not afraid to ask for help.

2. Takes risks.

3. Keeps her mouth shut and her ears open.

4. Does not allow enthusiastic, environmentally conscious fifth graders to store their compost projects in the faculty room.

5. Confronts the one teacher who is always late rather then sending out sixteen memos reminding all staff of the importance of punctuality.

6. Does not try out his Letterman or her Miss Piggy imitations over the intercom.

7. Does not scratch whenever and wherever it itches.

8. Does not talk to children sent to the office in rap.

9. Avoids the Nixon principle: if two wrongs don't make a right, try three.

PROFESSIONALISM PRECEPTS REINFORCEMENT

Dear Ms. Class:

We have worked without a contract for six months, and the union is organizing all sorts of protests. I think it's unprofessional for teachers to walk in picket lines. I'd rather light a candle than curse the darkness. What do you think?

— Detroit, MI

Dear Detroit:

It depends on where you plan on putting the lit candle.

Dear Ms. Class:

Our faculty room is more like an off-track betting parlor than a meeting place for professionals. And I'm not referring to the pit-stop decor. My colleagues bet on everything from Monday night football to the next snow day to the delivery date of a teacher's pregnant wife. I feel like an old fuddy-duddy for refusing to participate in the betting pools, but I feel even more strongly that these pools are a bad image to hold up to students. It's no good suggesting I talk to the principal about it as he's the ringleader. He often goes from room to room collecting the bets.

— Fargo, ND

Dear Fargo:

Ms. Class does not have a clever quip to describe people who would bet on the duration of a woman's pregnancy, but she does suggest that you bring up the matter of illegal behavior to your union teacher-administrator liaison representative. Illegal behavior is illegal behavior and should not be tolerated, even in the name of good old boy fun. A school should be a school and not an off-track betting parlor.

Dear Ms. Class:

My district is subtly pressuring teachers to earn national certification. For starters, they are paying the exorbitant application fee and providing a salary bonus to anyone who puts himself through the procedure, never mind the gold stars for those who pass. I'm annoyed. I am torn. Part of me resents the added pressure; part of me wants that official stamp of approval. What do you think? Please withhold my city. Public relations are vital, and I don't want anyone to know a teacher from our fair city might have doubts about getting certified.

— Anonymous

Dear Anonymous:

Ms. Class understands your ambivalence. It seems ironic that a teacher's professionalism is determined by people who have never set foot in her classroom. Ms. Class's own version of professionalism is contained in a wonderful little story that appeared in the Metropolitan Life column of the *New York Times* in 1989. A woman, in a hurry, made an illegal turn in midtown Manhattan. A policeman pulled her over and took all the necessary information preliminary to giving her a ticket. Then he said, "Okay, you can go now, but please drive more carefully."

"That's it?" she blurted. "Why aren't you giving me a ticket?"

"Because you were my first-grade teacher," he replied.

This story gives Ms. Class chills every time she reads it, and she rereads it every few months. She tried reading it in a keynote speech and started crying. But mostly she reads it, and she makes lists of her students—those who would give her a ticket and those who wouldn't. Somehow, Ms. Class finds this a better model for teachers and teaching than a national exam.

Dear Ms. Class:

Just when I'm beginning to like you, you say something really stupid! Professionals are recognized by being board certified, not by telling cute anecdotes. If teachers are to be ranked with doctors and lawyers then they are going to have to join the ranks of those willing to be scrutinized by a rigorous, impartial procedure.

— Morristown, NJ

Dear Morristown:

In her book *Confiding: A Psychotherapist and Her Patients Search for Stories to Live By*, psychotherapist Susan Baur contends that professionals are missing the boat when they fail to see the importance of stories that relate to patients' experiences. Baur describes an experiment where she compiled a monologue of a patient's feelings, complaints, and delusions. She then asked professional therapists, people in the community, and mental patients to respond to this monologue.

Lay people in the community were confused and uncomfortable, admitting they didn't know how to respond.

Mental patients responded first with sympathy and then with stories. They told their own stories and finally offered advice, "Stop crying! Fight back!"

The professional clinicians responded with "doctor talk." They wanted to know the facts and to see charts of the diagnosis. They offered no personal response to the patient; they offered dosages but no stories.

Ms. Class, of course, reads this sort of thing to confirm her prejudice that the professionalism of charts and graphs and board certification isn't all that it's cracked up to be. Ms. Class does not believe that education can be neutral. The teacher who sits in the middle of the road is going to be run over by the school bus.

As far as board certification goes, Ms. Class wonders why educationists always point to the tests taken by doctors and lawyers. Why not be inspired instead by the great Renaissance buildings designed by such nonarchitects as Brunelleschi, Michelangelo, Leonardo, and Alberti? These men were called architects not because they were board certified or even schooled in architecture but because they created architecture. Closer to our own times, Frank Lloyd Wright, Ludwig Mies van der Rohe, and Le Corbusier were not schooled as architects. Louis Sullivan studied at Beaux-Arts but did not complete the degree requirements. Again, they were architects because that's what they did. The proof in our teacherhood lies not in standards and certificates but in what we do in the classroom.

PROGRESS DECONSTRUCTIONISM

Dear Ms. Class:

I work in a district that seems to be moving toward the nineteenth century instead of the twenty-first century.

I'm trying to find another job and wonder if there is a way of determining if a district is truly progressive.

— Athens, GA

Dear Athens:

There is actually much less progress than you might think. Ms. Class would advise you not to be distracted by things that school officials often mistakenly label as progress. For example, here are a few education innovations of the past that were not progress:

1. Film strips were not progress.
2. Computerized workbooks were not progress.
3. Eliminating classroom walls and doors was not progress.
4. Students' calling staff by their first names was not progress.

Here are a few present education innovations that are not progress:

1. Wholesale mainstreaming is not progress.
2. Fat-filled jargon—*facilitator, implementation, management systems*—is not progress.
3. Career ladders are not progress.
4. Shared decision making is not progress.
5. Sitting in a circle is less progress than people think.

PUBLISHER TRUTH IN ADVERTISING

Dear Ms. Class:

I wonder if you have any advice regarding publishers' catalogs. Can we trust them? I teach in a small, poor district. We don't get to conferences. These catalogs are our only source of information about new products.

— Beaufort, SC

Dear Beaufort:

Henry Ward Beecher offered advice to nineteenth-century gardeners that teachers would do well to follow. Beecher warned gardeners not to "be made wild by pompous catalog." Ms. Class acknowledges that this is hard advice to follow, no less in classrooms than in gardens.

Publishers are no better or no worse than any other for-profit conglomerate, which means that that good old adage applies: *let the buyer beware.* ITT Continental's Fresh Horizons bread is a good case in point. The bread was advertised as containing five times as much fiber as whole wheat bread. That was true, but what ITT did not point out was that the extra fiber came from wood. The Federal Trade Commission obtained a consent order against ITT, ruling that wood is "an ingredient not commonly used, nor anticipated by consumers to be commonly used, in bread."

So when a catalog bills twenty-eight activity cards as "a comprehensive teaching kit" or "everything a teacher needs," Ms. Class hopes that you will remember the wood in the bread.

Dear teacher, you may not be able to go to conventions, but you can subscribe to professional journals. Think about this: of approximately one and a half million K–8 teachers in this country, just thirty-six thousand subscribe to the official NCTM publication *Teaching Children Mathematics.* Subscription statistics for journals in the other curriculum areas are similarly dismal.

PUNCTUALITY IMMUNITY PROVISIONS

Dear Ms. Class:

I teach in what used to be called a deprived neighborhood. I think it's now an opportunity zone. I feel that if I don't manage to teach my students anything else, I will teach them punctuality. I insist that they appear in class on time and turn in their assignments on time. I have developed an incentive program for low achievers that instills this virtue. I wonder how I would go about getting it published.

— Denver, CO

Dear Denver:

Although Ms. Class is herself never late, "On time" is not what she would choose for her tombstone. Punctuality is an agreeable habit; it is neither a virtue nor a curriculum. The British writer Evelyn Waugh said punctuality is the virtue of the bored.

There are three important things to remember about punctuality:

- You aren't late until you get there.

- People who are always on time spend a lot of their lives waiting for people who aren't.

- There's no evidence that the bird with the worm is any better off than the one who stayed home in bed.

PUNCTUATION ABSOLUTION DUE PROCESS

Dear Ms. Class:

I'm embarrassed to admit that the most recent argument between the other third-grade teachers in my school and me is over the comma in apposition. Instead of having my students do mindless exercises in the language arts texts, I have them write every day. My colleagues insist that it is my duty to make sure students learn the comma in apposition simply because it's there in the text and on the drill sheets accompanying the text. I became so frustrated over this impasse that I cried. Now I feel like a fool.

— Troy, NY

Dear Troy:

Keep two things in mind. First, no comma is worth a single tear. Second, and this is more difficult, you have to let this matter lie. A camel can sooner pass through the eye of a needle than can you convert a commaphile. The only person more intransigent than commaphiles are the apostrophists.

All you can do is smile and apply the Mencken retort. Just say, "You may be right." Save your energies for battles you can win—and for continuing to encourage your students to write, with or without commas.

Please don't construe Ms. Class's advice of silence as advice that you should teach the comma in apposition. No, no, a thousand times no.

Dear Ms. Class:

It's easy for you to say we should ease up on grammar vigilance. What about the standardized tests? What about the parents? Even if I didn't have these pressures, I would still believe in standards. We can't just sit back and say anything goes.

— Pierre, SD

Dear Pierre:

Ms. Class is very aware of parents and teachers who could find a grammatical flaw in a stop sign. She once lived in Pennsylvania, where pedants bemoaned the grammar of the license plate. However, the fact of the matter is that when we try to teach what is developmentally inappropriate, we end up teaching it over and over. Year after year we teach the very things that people don't learn until they are thirty-five, if ever.

Eudora Welty, who experts acknowledge as writing a pretty fair paragraph, said her own teachers never managed to scare her into grammar.

And here's some classroom proof. One year Ms. Class had a group of rotten readers who had so many problems that she never got around to teaching any grammar. None. Ms. Class pretty much scrapped science and social studies too and concentrated on reading aloud to the children and having them read silently as well as write. They wrote a lot—at least three times a day. And Ms. Class is not talking about the phony writing of filling in worksheets; she's talking about the kind of writing that starts with a blank piece of paper.

In the spring these rotten readers took the dreaded standardized test and the results were rather stunning. The children scored on or near grade level in reading comprehension. They scored way above grade level in grammar and spelling. Even Ms. Class was rather startled. After all, she didn't teach them. All she could figure was that "grammar" on a standardized test is really proofreading—choose the right answer. Ms. Class postulates that her students had read so much, written so much, that they could guess what looked right (even if they couldn't produce it in their own writing). The one part of the test on which they did poorly was phonics. Not surprising, considering they wouldn't have been judged as rotten readers if they'd been any good at phonics.

QUARREL CONFIGURATIONS

Dear Ms. Class:

Most of the time I avoid the faculty room, but I feel I should make the effort to be sociable. The only trouble is every time I go there I get in an argument with someone. Anything from single-parent families being the cause of the national debt to the futility of dragging kindergartners through calendar math—we get into arguments. Any suggestions?

— Greenville, MS

Dear Greenville:

Ms. Class would caution that it is futile to argue with people who are too ignorant to recognize when you have won. Now that dueling is illegal, silence is the only way to settle such arguments—unless you want to get blood on your plan book. If you must visit the faculty room, then Ms. Class recommends adjusting your discourse to the audience. Read aloud knock-knock jokes, risqué limericks, or *Soap Opera Digest* in the faculty room.

QUESTIONING STRATEGIES BIODIVERSITY

Dear Ms. Class:

I try to employ higher-level thinking strategies with my students, but I seem to be the only one in my classroom asking questions.

— Baton Rouge, LA

Dear Baton Rouge:

Forget the ed-whiz-biz jargon and encourage your students to ask the simplest question of all: why? It's a question that will hold them in good stead wherever they go, whatever they become.

Dear Ms. Class:

I know this will sound naive, but I wonder how a teacher knows when she's taught something? I get the feeling that giving a test isn't good enough. Kids can memorize for a test and then forget. How does a teacher know that something is ingrained for good?

— Grand Rapids, MI

Dear Grand Rapids:

Don't ever feel you need to apologize for asking a question. But also remember that in teaching, as in life, one of the hardest lessons to learn is that some questions have no answer. Yours doesn't. Ms. Class can only tell you that fifteen years after David, a boy with serious learning problems, was in her class, she learned that he is living a productive life. It's a long story, much too involved to summarize here, but Ms. Class has reason to believe David learned an important lesson from her and that she can take satisfaction in claiming one small part of his success. Ms. Class can only tantalize you further by saying that although she was David's language arts teacher, it was her approach to asparagus and avocados that impressed him.

Ms. Class learned about David's success only through a chance conversation with someone who knows someone who is a neighbor of David's mother. In other words, it was one of those once-in-a-decade miracles that sustain teachers and keep them going. Hundreds of other students passed by Ms. Class's desk and she is still waiting to hear that they learned something that lasted.

A teacher must learn to live with uncertainty. She rarely knows for sure that her students have learned anything important. Nonetheless, she acts each day on the belief that they do.

Dear Ms. Class:

I have moved from teaching first grade to sixth grade. I know this sounds ridiculous, but I worry that I won't be able to answer the children's questions.

— Fargo, ND

Dear Fargo:

Not to worry. As humorist James Thurber reminded us, "It's better to know some of the questions than all of the answers." Adults in general and teachers in particular answer far too many questions. It is not a teacher's task to answer questions but to get students to ask them—and then look for answers.

What the teaching profession really needs is more people to question all the answers given so glibly by consultants, publishers, politicians, and media pundits.

QUID PRO QUO TAXONOMY

Dear Ms. Class:

Although we have never articulated this agreement, my principal and I have reached an accommodation of sorts. He ignores the fact that I don't turn in lesson plans; I help him out by writing his monthly school progress reports to the board of education. My husband says I'm crazy to flout such basic school rituals as lesson plans. I say we have a mutual assistance pact, and if you don't look for trouble you won't find it.

— Salem, OR

Dear Salem:

Your husband is right. Although Ms. Class hates to discourage you and your principal from working from your individual strengths, quid pro quos are dangerous, and yours is destined to come to a bad end. What happens when your principal needs to enforce the lesson plan rule on an inadequate teacher and that teacher points out you haven't turned in a lesson plan for sixteen years, or whatever? And don't think for a minute that your colleagues don't know about your sweet little deal. Schools have no secrets.

By all means, keep writing the principal's reports if you want. That's the principal's problem. Just make sure you fulfill your own professional obligations, including the dreaded lesson plans.

QUIET ATTITUDE BY-PRODUCTS

Dear Ms. Class:

I'm a new teacher, and things seem to be going pretty well—except for the noise. Nothing has prepared me for the constant chatter of fifth graders. I don't seem to be able to keep them quiet for more than twenty minutes. Help!

— Durham, NC

Dear Durham:

Don't mistake children's quietude for thinking or learning. Sometimes still waters don't run deep; they're just stagnant. Ms. Class always tells people, "If you can't stand noise, don't be a teacher." Of course there are times when you want and need quiet. If you can get fifth graders to remain silent for twenty minutes, you are already doing better than the average. Research shows that the average fifth grader can keep his mouth shut for just fourteen minutes, twenty-six seconds. That's longer than teachers can go without making noise. The average teacher, when pressed, can keep quiet for eight minutes, seventeen seconds.

Encourage trade-offs with your students: ask them to respect your need for some silence. Uninterrupted Sustained Silent Reading (USSR) and Drop Everything And Read (DEAR) are productive ways for all of you to keep quiet. Once you've all read silently for half an hour or so, give students opportunities to chatter. Invite them to talk to each other about what they've read.

RAMONA THE BRAVE HERMENEUTICS

Dear Ms. Class:
What texts do you consider most vital for teacher development?

— Grand Island, NE

Dear Grand Island:
What's good enough for Katherine Paterson is good enough for Ms. Class. Katherine Paterson once observed that *"Ramona the Brave* should be required reading for all teachers, just as *Ramona and Her Father* should be read by all parents."

READING RESEARCH MEDIATION

Dear Ms. Class:
What is the proper way to teach reading?

— Spokane, WA

Dear Spokane:
In our culture, from left to right.

Dear Ms. Class:
I am a primary-grade teacher, and I teach in a whole language school. Although I subscribe to whole language tenets, I do want to teach my students some phonics skills that are helpful. How can I do this without incurring the wrath of my colleagues?

— Kenosha, WI

Dear Kenosha:
Ms. Class deplores the sight of vigilante squads roaming school hallways with the purpose of enforcing phonics-free zones. Ms. Class advises: don't call your lessons phonics lessons. Do call them literature enhancement strategies.

Dear Ms. Class:

I resent the fact that students are pulled out of my classroom to go to corrective reading classes. All they do there is fill out worksheets on consonant blends. I'd rather keep these kids in my class and try to help them find a reason to read. What can I do?

— Clarksville, TN

Dear Clarksville:

Regrettably, some teachers and many administrators are rather like the character in a Nabokov novel who, had he been condemned to spend a whole day shut up in a library, would have been found dead about noon. A good question to ask on interviewing candidates for corrective reading positions in your district is, Read any good books lately?

Ms. Class advises inviting the reading teacher into your classroom to work with students there. Perhaps the high quality of the reading material you make available to students will inspire her to mend her wicked ways.

Dear Ms. Class:

My third graders finished the year being able to read silently for an hour. Not fake reading but sitting with a book and concentrating on it for one hour. When they reached fourth grade, the teacher complained (loudly) that my reading program had failed because it had failed to prepare students to choose the best title for the disembodied paragraphs in the workbook exercises she assigns.

— Schenectady, NY

Dear Schenectady:

Ms. Class confesses she has never been able to choose the best title either. Tell your colleague that in the real world the only people who get to choose titles are editors.

Ms. Class wonders why we have thirty-five varieties of mustard in our supermarkets but insist there should be one true way to teach reading.

Dear Ms. Class:

I encourage my second graders to read whatever they want to read, but when I choose a book to read aloud to them, I want it to be special. How do I handle kids bringing in quite dreadful supermarket books for me to read aloud?

— Columbia, SC

Dear Columbia:

Tell the truth. Don't be hesitant to tell your students that some books are more worthy than others. Tell your students that Eudora Welty's mother ran back into a burning house—on crutches—to rescue her set of twenty-four volumes of Dickens. She threw the books out the window and then jumped out after them. If students bring in books featuring TV cartoon characters or other such objectionable matter, explain that you are delighted that they enjoy a wide range of reading material, but when choosing a book to read aloud, you only read books that you'd run back into a burning building for. Ms. Class's students knew that she would not run back into a burning building for *Curious George*, for example, so they tried to tease her by sneaking his books in her book bag.

Dear Ms. Class:

I teach fourth grade in a district where the parents put a lot of pressure on us to maintain high standards. Reading seems to be their criterion for excellence. I assign vocabulary development homework every night. I have developed extensive study guides for the books I assign for extra credit. I am worried sick about what eight parents will do when they find out that their children are reading below grade level.

— Doylestown, PA

Dear Doylestown:

In *Reading Without Nonsense*, Frank Smith observed, "Children cannot be taught to read. A teacher's responsibility is not to teach children to read but to make it possible for them to learn to read."

Ms. Class worries about all those extensive study guides. She advises the anxious teacher to ask herself which would be more disastrous to her reading program: for the copy machine to break for a week or the library to close for a week.

Dear Ms. Class:

I'm surprised that a woman of your obvious intelligence hasn't pointed out that reading is an overrated skill. A few centuries ago the King of England could not read at all. In more recent times, Nelson Rockefeller was dyslexic and had great difficulty with the printed page. It is time the schools took reading off its pedestal and developed other important skills.

— Princeton, NJ

Dear Princeton:

Pardon me? Ms. Class finds it hypocritical—and worse—that people who are themselves able to read disparage the importance of other people's being able to read. Ms. Class wonders how you'd feel if your son couldn't read or if your daughter wanted to marry someone who couldn't read. Ms.

Class wonders why you failed to mention Leonardo da Vinci, Albert Einstein, and Thomas Edison, geniuses who had difficulties in school.

Kings, millionaires, and geniuses can probably get by in any century without reading, but the rest of us need to be able to do it. It is insane to claim otherwise.

RELUCTANT READER FLASHPOINT

Dear Ms. Class:

About one third of my sixth graders are reluctant readers. I wonder what I can do to turn them on to reading.

— Minneapolis, MN

Dear Minneapolis:

Ms. Class wonders, reluctant to read what? Ms. Class has never found a second grader reluctant to read Beatrix Potter's little books or *The Stupids*, or a sixth grader reluctant to read *The Great Gilly Hopkins* or novels by Gary Paulsen or a ninth grader reluctant to read *The Outsiders* or novels by Walter Dean Meyers. If children don't like their texts, the texts are wrong, not the children. We may deplore the fact that kids read the *Goosebumps* books, but kids have devoured thirty million copies of this popular series, demonstrating that not only will kids read, they will even buy books. So if all else fails, start with Stine and move on from there.

REPORT CARD RECONCILIATION

Dear Ms. Class:

I am bothered by the fact that a star player on our high school football team has been passed along through academic classes year after year even though he can't read. How can this happen in a district that prides itself on excellence?

— Pawtucket, RI

Dear Pawtucket:

Experience has taught Ms. Class that star quarterbacks are always assigned to classes with teachers who give passing grades.

Ms. Class does not mean to engage in one-upmanship, but she would like to tell you Jackson's story. A very athletic seventh grader with severe learning problems, Jackson had been retained twice by the time he reached seventh grade. This is significant information: it made Jackson eligible for junior varsity sports at the high school. During football season the principal drove Jackson to the high school each afternoon to play junior varsity football; football season slid into basketball season, which slid into baseball season. Neither Jackson nor the principal were ever at school during seventh period.

By the end of seventh grade, Ms. Class thought she and Jackson were making some progress in reading. When he did not appear for eighth grade, she asked where he was. "Jackson's in high school," the students told her. Ms. Class did not believe them; she knew this couldn't be possible. But she discovered that nothing is impossible to people who think the ends justify the means. Because of his age, Jackson's junior varsity eligibility was due to run out while he was still in eighth grade, so school officials bumped him right past eighth grade and into high school.

Dear Ms. Class:

Even though I have been teaching for fifteen years, I'm still not reconciled to report cards. Four times a year, grading students is the trauma of my life. I find it impossible to grade students on some objective scale of material mastery, whatever that means. I always worry over differing abilities, family circumstances, and other extenuating conditions. Can you offer any advice for getting through report cards quickly?

— Casper, WY

Dear Casper:

This is one of those areas in which Ms. Class can claim no expertise. In her many years in teaching she has uncovered just one report card maxim: the last four take as long to fill out as the first twenty-two. We're not worried about the A students here, are we? They and their parents love report cards.

For the rest, Ms. Class also knows that the bitter pill of quantified marks is easier swallowed when accompanied by a friendly letter from the teacher making note of the students' strong points. Such letters won't increase the time you spend by all that much, and they'll make you, the student, and the parents feel a whole lot better.

Ms. Class received a report card at the end of her first year of teaching. A neophyte who got into the school through the back door of emergency credentials and no student teaching, she felt lucky to scrape by with a C. She felt lucky, too, that her department chairman wrote a personal message on her report cart, noting that she "has a good heart and goes out of her way to help handicapped students. With a bit more experience, this teacher will excel."

That appraisal has stuck with Ms. Class through her career. The sting of the C didn't last; the commentary on the good heart is sustaining.

RESEARCH RETROFIT

Dear Ms. Class:

I get frustrated because our school can't seem to commit to any particular agenda. We try a bit of this and a bit of that. I wonder why we don't gather the appropriate research and do things right.

— Baltimore, MD

Dear Baltimore:

Why does Ms. Class suspect that you are a retired Marine Corps sergeant or other recent recruit to teaching as a second career? The reason most schools do exactly what your school does—an inservice course on whole language, followed by an inservice course on mastery spelling, followed by an inservice course on how to increase memory power—is because for every research study there exists another research study giving opposite and contradictory conclusions. Few educators have the nerve to put all their eggs in one basket—or to ignore contrary research. Ms. Class's short-term answer is to tell you to relax and learn to live with contradiction. Her long-term answer is to tell you to gnaw your own bone.

RESPONSIBILITY REINFORCEMENT SIMULATION

Dear Ms. Class:

I worry that my fifth graders are so irresponsible. They don't remember their homework, they don't hand book reports in on time, they don't even remember things they care about—like permission slips for field trips. Do you have any advice on teaching children to be more responsible?

— St. Joseph, MO

Dear St. Joseph:

Your fifth graders sound rather like Ms. Class's husband, who forgets to tell her about phone messages, locks the keys in the car, and forgets to pay phone bills. Twenty-two years has shown Ms. Class that there is no cure for husbands, but Booker T. Washington advised not giving up so easily on children. He said that few things help a person more than to give him responsibility and then to trust him to be responsible. Too often in schools we give students responsibility for trivial things and then plan an "out" for them if they don't come through.

RETENTION YELLOW BRICK ROAD

Dear Ms. Class:

I teach in a school where it is definitely not politically correct to retain students. Our parents have their eyes on the Ivy League colleges that will lead to successful Wall Street careers; they definitely will not tolerate any detours on the career paths they have chosen for their children. On the other hand, we are under a lot of pressure from the school board to establish standards, to make sure that students are not gliding along on social promotion with no evidence of skill mastery. So our principal has come up with the following attempt at obfuscation. She sends this letter to parents of children who teachers want to retain:

Your child is being considered for a special educational opportunity. We would like to include your child in a group being given "the gift of time." These children will remain in our primary cluster for four years instead of three.

This special consideration is not viewed as a retention. Your child will be able to proceed to the next grade level in those areas deemed appropriate. In addition, each child in this program will have an individualized instructional plan that will establish clear and attainable goals. This presents the possibility of accelerating those children who begin to grow at a faster rate.

This office hopes you will consider that childhood should be a journey, not a race.

If you have any questions, please feel free to call us.

Ms. Class, who's kidding whom? I wonder what you think of this?

— New York, NY

Dear New York:

Ms. Class always gets a kick out of official obfuscation, but she is more concerned with the policy of retention than with the language used to disguise it. Statistics show that children who are held back do not catch up.

RETIREMENT PLANNING CLIMATE CONTROL

Dear Ms. Class:

I have been teaching for thirty-eight years. I will admit that I find today's children much harder to manage than children were even ten years ago. Many children I see these days are seriously damaged. It isn't just that they aren't nurtured. They are victimized: there's sexual abuse, drug abuse, and general neglect. These days, few children come from homes that can offer the support that schools could once draw upon. Nonetheless, I know I still have a lot to offer children, and I bitterly resent all the hints from colleagues and administrators that maybe it's time that I retire. Teaching is my life. Without it, I'd be lost.

— Savannah, GA

Dear Savannah:

Ms. Class has always known that giving advice is not for weaklings. O teacher of so many years, Ms. Class must ask you to stop being a clinchpoop. Retirement is not euthanasia, not unless you insist on making it so. Just because your school is the place where, when you go there, they have to let you teach, doesn't mean there's no limit. We let people in their seventies lead the country but are smart enough to know that teachers are worn out by sixty, if not before. When a teacher finds herself starting her sentences with "These days. . ." as she considers yesterday's students through rose-colored glasses, it's definitely time for her to take a look at her retirement plan.

Start thinking about your going-away gift. Which would you prefer: an electric peanut butter maker or a buttermatic popcorn popper with caramel corn capability?

RIDDLE RIGOR BY-PRODUCTS

Dear Ms. Class:

I'm in hot water because I have substituted riddle writing for haiku writing in our language arts curriculum. I've done this—with great success—for years. But the new coordinator, a stickler for following the curriculum guide, is pressuring me to stick to that guide. What argument can I offer?

— Overland Park, KS

Dear Overland Park:

A first-rate riddle is more creative than a second-rate poem any day, any time, any place. Tell your coordinator that for children raised in a western culture, writing haiku involves just counting syllables. Writing riddles involves understanding word roots, suffixes, and prefixes, not to mention homonyms and such. Let Ms. Class know if you want to be on her mailing list for her doctoral thesis containing the skill continuum of riddle writing.

ROOM MOTHER DELIVERY SYSTEM

Dear Ms. Class:

Every year the PTO assigns me a room mother, and every year she "forgets" the Halloween party, brings ice cream two hours before the Christmas party is scheduled to begin, brings food the children won't eat, or causes some other bit of chaos. I'd rather just handle the parties myself. How can I do this gracefully?

— Long Beach, CA

Dear Long Beach:

No way. You need to put this blasphemous thought from your mind. Nothing in this life is inevitable but death, taxes, and room mothers. You can remind her of the date and the time and tell her not to bring ice cream. Then when she brings oat bran health squares, just smile, say "Thank you," and supplement them with your emergency supply of Oreos and Reese's Pieces.

RULER RULE

Dear Ms. Class:
I need tips on helping my fourth graders draw straight lines with rulers.

— Rapid City, SD

Dear Rapid City:
Her own experience with rulers has shown Ms. Class that there is no such thing as a straight line.

SALARY DESTABILIZATION

Dear Ms. Class:
Our teachers union is negotiating a new contract. The only thing they seem to care about is money. I wonder what all the complaint is about. I've been teaching sixth grade for twenty-two years and make $56,000. Where else could I make that?

— Yonkers, NY

Dear Yonkers:
It's all a matter of perspective. You might not be as well off as you think you are. Studies have shown that people gauge all future wages by their first paycheck, regardless of the changes in the cost of living. So if, like Ms. Class, your first annual salary as a teacher was around $6,000, $56,000 does indeed look good. But consider this: in the 1960s, a CEO made 38 times as much as a public school teacher. By 1994, CEO pay was 160 times greater than that of teachers. Dollar amounts? Michael Eisner, the head of Walt Disney Company, earned two hundred million dollars in 1994. There's a good math problem for your students: this is half a million dollars a day, $78,000 an hour. Of course all this seems like peanuts when you consider that Wall Street trickster and later convicted felon Michael Milken earned $550,000,000 one year in his heyday.

On the other hand, if you consider that as a free-lance education writer, working weekends and with no summer break and no health insurance, Ms. Class considers it a really good year when she makes $30,000, your salary is very good. Ms. Class is not complaining. That's $28,971.50 more than she'd make as a poet.

SCHOOL BOARD SITCOM

Dear Ms. Class:

Our school board is impossible. I am insulted that I have gone to university for seven years, earning two master's degrees, so that my professional life can be ruled by nine oafs who barely got out of high school.

— Anonymous

Dear Anonymous:

Just for you, Ms. Class will publish the school board dozen, formulated from years of watching school boards in action.

1. *School board teacher relations principle*
   We don't care. We don't have to.

2. *School board contingency plan*
   If we wait, it will go away. If it doesn't go away, we'll hire a consultant.

3. *School board cover-your-behind rule*
   If we wait and it doesn't go away, blame the lack of professionalism of today's teachers, single-parent families, and Dr. Spock.

4. *School board Borgia principle*
   It is better to be hated than ignored.

5. *Abraham Lincoln principle*
   You can fool enough of the people enough of the time.

6. *Check-all-your-options rule*
   We will consider behaving wisely only when we have used up all other options.

7. *John Henry legacy*
   When all you have is a hammer, everything looks like a nail.

8. *The magnification maxim*
   Nothing is too small to be blown out of proportion.

9. *The yellow journalism principle*
   The degree to which a school board overreacts to information is inversely proportional to its accuracy.

10. *School board addition facts*
    When you have seven board members, you'll have eight opinions.

11. *School board deficiency principle*
    There are only eleven in a school board dozen.

SCHOOL CRITICS FLASHBACK

Dear Ms. Class:

Every time I pick up the paper I see someone else attacking schools—a corporate leader, a governor, a senator, a Hollywood actor, a news reader on the nightly news—all saying we aren't teaching enough stuff, the right stuff, or whatever. Why do the media hang on every word the president of IBM spouts about elementary education but ignore the opinions of fourth-grade teachers?

— Erie, PA

Dear Erie:

Ms. Class's short answer is that the media confuse wealth with virtue and wisdom and that the president of IBM makes a lot more money than a fourth-grade teacher.

Here is her long answer. Complaints about schools have long been a popular national hobby. In 1932, popular pundit Will Rogers wrote a column attacking schools. It could have come from yesterday's op-ed page. "All the kids I know, either mine or anybody's, none of 'em can write so you can read it, none of 'em can spell. They can't figure and don't know geography, but they are always taking some of the darndest things like Political Science, International Relations, Drama . . . ." Rogers sums up the curriculum of the day as "punk and hooey" and complains that schools have gyms and swimming pools and tennis courts "but not a spelling book in a carload of schools."

Such complaints entertained the public then and continue to do so today. Response to criticism is difficult because much criticism has a degree of merit. Certainly the critics go overboard in their enthusiasm for denunciation, but any rebuttal that begins "Yes, but . . ." is dead in the water before it gets away from the dock.

Ms. Class suspects that what you want is not a homily along the lines of Benjamin Franklin's *Poor Richard* offering "Blame-all and praise-all are two blockheads," but a comeback with more vinegar. Okay, here goes: longtime Speaker of the House of Representatives Sam Rayburn once observed that "any jackass can kick down a barn, but it takes a good carpenter to build one."

SCIENCE FAIR HEADACHE RELIEF

Dear Ms. Class:

Every year I swear I won't participate in another science fair. It's too much of a hassle, and, more and more, it becomes a contest to see whose parent does the project with the most light bulbs. What can I do?

— Albany, NY

Dear Albany:
There are two alternatives for science fairs:

1. Decree that all projects must be done in school. Dust projects for alien fingerprints (ambitious parents with no shame have been known to sneak into the building after hours to insert those light bulbs).

2. Put the PTO in charge and insist that no part of the project can be done in school. This makes it a parental free-for-all, leaving teachers free to do something worthwhile after school: bake cookies, read *War and Peace*, take the cat to the vet, practice that acute-right-angle turn on Rollerblades. A word to the wise: it is your duty as a concerned citizen to make sure the number of the rescue squad is handy during the judging of these projects.

SCIENTIFIC METHOD BALDERDASH

Dear Ms. Class:
In different textbooks I have seen different versions of the scientific method. Can you tell me whether the correct scientific method has has four steps or five?

— Austin, TX

Dear Austin:
Neither. The mystique and mistakes surrounding scientific method are even more muddled than those surrounding writing process. Nobel prize–winning scientist P. B. Medawar pointed out that there is no such thing as "the" scientific method. Medawar noted that a scientist uses a very great variety of exploratory stratagems and that these explorations can't be written down as steps in a process. Underlying every advance in information about the natural world is not a particular process but an act of imagination and a speculative adventure that, more often than not, is not neat and tidy.

Dear Ms. Class:
Now wait just a minute! Scientific method is one of the foundations of progress in the Western Hemisphere! It does not behoove you to belittle the benefits it has provided for humankind.

— Alexandria, VA

Dear Alexandria:
As noted Harvard professor of biology and geology and McArthur genius award recipient Stephen Jay Gould has observed, different people solve

problems in different ways. Gould describes himself as "hopeless at deductive sequencing," someone who can never work out the simplest Agatha Christie or Sherlock Holmes plot. What we need to recognize, says Gould, is that while some people prefer Arthur Conan Doyle's Sherlock Holmes, others are partial to Dorothy Sayers's Lord Peter Wimsey.

SCOPE-AND-SEQUENCE FREE AGENCY CLAUSE

Dear Ms. Class:

I worry that more and more teachers seem to assume that it's enough to put children in a room with beautiful books and they will learn to read. Most teachers don't have a clue of when, where, or how to introduce important skills. I'd really like to see a scope-and-sequence chart of the important reading skills posted in every primary-grade classroom.

— Rochester, MN

Dear Rochester:

"Important" is the key word in your argument. The last time Ms. Class looked, the New York State Education Department had 1,800 reading skills in their data bank. Most basals have a few hundred. Ms. Class is bothered by the image of scope and sequence, which connotes an excessive orderliness. Think of that kitchen scene in Anne Tyler's *The Accidental Tourist*. Rose has a kitchen that is so completely alphabetized that you find the *allspice* next to the *ant poison*. Rose and her siblings argue whether noodles should go with *n* for noodles or *p* for pasta. Then Rose announces the solution: she puts them with *e* for elbow macaroni.

Rose would definitely want a scope-and-sequence chart of skills in her classroom. Rose can't send out the manuscript pages of her brother's book until she buys nine-by-eleven envelopes. All they have in the house are ten-by-thirteens, and Rose can't bear it when things don't fit precisely. The only problem with this scenario is that children don't come in neat and tidy packages, nor do real books.

SCOTCH TAPE TEMPLE OF DOOM

Dear Ms. Class:

I wonder if every school district is as penny-wise and pound-foolish as mine. Every year I order Scotch tape. Every year I receive brand X cellophane tape, the kind that one can't get off the roll except in two-millimeter, jagged strips. Last year I ordered a pair of shears and received two dozen left-hand children's scissors. All children's scissors are impossible to cut with. Left-hand scissors are torture that should be outlawed by the Geneva Convention.

What can a teacher do about this ridiculous state of affairs?

— Pittsburgh, PA

Dear Pittsburgh:

Save those scissors. Some day you may be able to trade them for a box of humped-crown staples.

Just know this: you are not alone. A teacher in California reported that for two years she requested that the lock on her supply cupboard be repaired. The third year, when she complained again, and more loudly, the broken lock was removed, leaving a hole in the cupboard door. A teacher in New Jersey sent Ms. Class twenty-three pages of memos regarding pull-down maps in her classroom that did not pull down. Paper is rationed in upstate New York schools, and PE teachers, who are given the same amount as English teachers, barter their allotment for hall-duty relief.

Like you, Pittsburgh, teachers send these horror stories to Ms. Class because they know that these peculiar events, which would cause any sane person some doubt, will find a believer in Ms. Class.

SECRETARIAL STRESS DISORDER

Dear Ms. Class:

Our school has two secretaries. One is pleasant, kind, and helpful. The other is not. She is a vicious, vindictive, petty tyrant. I do my best to avoid her, but she is in charge of school supplies. She is stingy. You'd think she gets a rebate on unused supplies the way she guards them. You almost need a court order to get a pencil out of her. The other day I asked for a box of staples. She snarled, "Hold out your hand!" I did, and she dumped seventeen staples into my extended palm. Of course they separated into individual bits before I could get back to my classroom. Take it from me: it is very difficult to insert staples one by one into a stapler. It is also dispiriting and demeaning to try. How can teaching ever be a profession when we are subjected to such abuse?

— Trenton, NJ

Dear Trenton:

One of the most important things a teacher can learn is how to distinguish between the things that she can change and the things she cannot. Obviously, secretary B believes that no one is useless in the world if she can increase the burdens of others. Although Ms. Class realizes there is a principle involved (as well as a principal who is afraid to tell the secretary to behave), in the short term she advises you to buy your own box of staples (at $1.98, are a thousand staples worth such agony? ulcers? spilled blood?). In the long term, choose your battle carefully. The day you need a class set of #2 pencils may be the day you need to stand up to the secretary—or force the principal to confront her. Most bullies back down when someone dares to challenge them.

SELF-ESTEEM EUPHORIA TOOL KIT

Dear Ms. Class:
How can I best nurture my students' self-esteem?

— Jackson, MS

Dear Jackson:
Late in the last century, philosopher-psychologist William James noted that self-esteem is what you get when you divide pretensions by success, but in the last decade or so there has been a strident effort in some educational circles to view self-esteem not as something earned but as a biological right. School psychologists and other happy-time specialists hold group sessions on enhancing self-esteem. Too often, these turn out to be nothing more than cheap nostrums administered in the form of parroted slogans to a group of kids who find it easier to be losers than to learn something. As noted black educator Kenneth Clark pointed out more than two decades ago, you don't get pride by singing a song about it. The truth is that nothing enhances self-esteem so much as the ability to do something well. Teaching chants or songs or self-congratulatory phrases is a particularly noxious fraud because it betrays the weak with kind words.

People of all ages gain pride and self-respect through the hard work of developing skills and capabilities. Skill is an outgrowth of curiosity. When a child is interested in something, he wants to learn more about it, and as he learns he becomes proud of the fact that he knows something. So, dear reader, by encouraging your students to be curious, you increase their chances of developing self-esteem.

Ms. Class's own sixth-grade teacher was proud of having been a Marine during World War II, and Ms. Class and her classmates became proud of that fact too. Ms. Class does not recall if there was any connection, but this sixth-grade teacher taught everybody in the class to play the harmonica. This, too, was a source of great pride. On the teacher's birthday, the class, with the collusion of the music teacher, surprised him with a spirited rendition of "The Marine Hymn." The fact that Ms. Class grew up to be a pacifist in no way diminishes from the pride in that moment and the pleasure she still feels when she hears that song.

SEX EDUCATION MANAGEMENT CRISIS

Dear Ms. Class:
I'm a sixth-grade teacher, and although I see the need for sex education, I confess I'm very nervous about being the one to deliver the information. I just can't

picture myself standing up in front of my class and explaining how to use a condom. Do you have any advice?

— Dade County, FL

Dear Dade County:

Ms. Class wouldn't volunteer to put herself in your shoes for all the proverbial tea in China. Not even for all the humped-crown staples in the school district's storehouse.

Traditionally, schools have intellectualized sex education: students watch film strips made by the same people who produce educational explanations of the metric system and the migratory paths of salmon. Then students take multiple-choice tests. One of Ms. Class's students, reputedly the stud of seventh grade, failed the multiple-choice sex quiz in his health class four times. He even missed the definition of *penis*. No one in the faculty room believed Heywood didn't know what a penis was or how to use it. Certainly, failing a penis quiz is more of an indication of the school's failure than Heywood's.

But even if schools have failed abysmally in their presentation of sex education, what is the alternative? Ms. Class would not be first in line to advocate a more practical course. The real dilemma is that schoolteachers do not have it in their power to convince adolescents and preadolescents not to experiment.

Schools shouldn't be trying to take on the parents' responsibility. Ms. Class suggests sex education is a good topic for which to solicit parent volunteers.

SEXUAL ACTIVISM DECONSTRUCTION

Dear Ms. Class:

I teach language arts to eighth graders. Several girls have let me know that they are sexually active. They cut classes a lot and spend time in the dorms at a nearby college. I wonder how I can help them understand the possibly serious consequences of the choices they are making.

— New Haven, CT

Dear New Haven:

Ms. Class wonders how it came to be that we decided to rename promiscuous activity and call it just another life-style choice available to thirteen-year-olds. In calling fornication sexual activism, we seem to pretend it is in the same category as environmental activism, political activism, or whatever. We never seem to hear about abstinence activism.

Semantics aside, Ms. Class cautions you to remember, first of all, that the sexual habits of these girls are not your responsibility. You are not their parent. You should contact the parents or ask the school nurse, social service worker, or principal to do so. Someone can also contact the dean of students at the university, who might want to point out the ramifications of statutory rape to the young men in the dorms.

Your job is to teach language and literature. That, by itself, is difficult enough. It is not your job to teach birth control, parenting skills, religion, or values clarification. Although it is not your job to monitor your students' sexual behavior, you would be doing them a service (and relieving your own worry) by asking school personnel to put them and their parents in touch with Planned Parenthood, people who are professionals in these matters.

SHARED DECISION MAKING AUTONOMY TASK FORCE

Dear Ms. Class:

Our school instituted shared decision making three years ago. Since then, five faculty have been hired without any teacher input. Central office says that because of special circumstances these hirings were done in the summer, when the shared-decision-making team was not available. When the bus schedule for our school was changed, we were not consulted, nor were our protests and recommendations acted on. More and more, I've noticed that important decisions are made at central office and our shared-decision-making team is left to decide the protocol for putting memos in teachers' boxes.

— Springfield, MA

Dear Springfield:

Giving a committee a high-sounding name doesn't change the fact that it's still a committee. The British scientist Sir Barnett Cocks said that a committee is "a cul-de-sac down which ideas are lured and then quietly strangled." In the case of shared-decision-making committees, blame is dispersed. The principal no longer has to take responsibility for the fact that the school lavatories are filthy when there's a committee set up to share decisions.

When all is said and done, shared decision making ends up being an agreement whereby all parties get what none of them want.

Dear Ms. Class:

My principal doesn't want to admit that there's a firebug in the school. When smoked poured in the window of my third-floor classroom—from the room below me—I picked up the intercom phone to report a fire. The secretary said she had orders not to ring the alarm without the principal's permission—and he was out of the building. All of us teachers on the third floor evacuated the building with our students. We were later told we "overreacted."

I have seen the principal using a garden hose to put out a fire in a dumbwaiter shaft. He doesn't want to ring the fire alarm because it's directly connected to the fire department, and once the fire company comes to the school our firebug problem will be public knowledge. The principal says he doesn't want the public to be "overly alarmed" about the situation.

Can you give me advice on what an overly alarmed teacher should do?

— Troy, NY

Dear Troy:

Ms. Class advises that this is an example of the golden rule of teaching: never leave the principal's office angry. Stay and fight.

You must advise—and convince—the principal that fires in the building are not good times to practice shared-decision-making skills. If he seems reluctant to agree, point out that schools are required to have alarm boxes so that when a teacher smells smoke, she does not have to consult a committee; she can pull the alarm herself.

Dear Ms. Class:

Just because the writer from Springfield, Massachusetts, taught in a substandard school district doesn't mean you have the right to universalize what happened there. A school district's commitment to learn from such corporate strategies as shared decision making is proof of a district's ability to meet the requirements of the twenty-first century. Maybe you should get your fuddy-duddy head out of the sand and get ready for the twenty-first century.

— Orlando, FL

Dear Orlando:

Linking shared decision making to the corporate world only confirms Ms. Class's worst suspicions. The lasting lesson Ms. Class learned from the corporate world was when corporate guru Michael Milken (before he went to prison as a felon) addressed the graduating class at the University of California, advising graduates that greed is good.

SILAS MARNER STICKER PRICE

Dear Ms. Class:

I don't understand all the fuss about whether high schoolers should have to read *Silas Marner* and *Great Expectations*. I read them and they did me no harm. Who knows? Maybe they even did some good. Why shouldn't today's youth read them?

— Kansas City, MO

Dear Kansas City:

Ms. Class notes that the best you can say is that the books did no harm. Ms. Class does not believe teachers should select curriculum on the basis of "if I suffered, why shouldn't my students?" Ms. Class is of the opinion that teachers at every grade should help students find books that will knock their socks off, books that will make them laugh and cry and, most important, reach for another book.

SINCERITY INFRASTRUCTURE

Dear Ms. Class:

The teacher across the hall is an enigma. She is more sincere in her devotion to children than anyone I've ever seen. She's always baking cookies for her class, taking them to her house for cookouts, spending a big chunk of her paycheck for beautiful books, and so on. And yet her curriculum is workbook skill drill. She spends more money on blackline master drill books than anyone I know. I just can't figure her out.

— Hoboken, NJ

Dear Hoboken:

What's the question? Surely you are aware that it is possible to be sincere *and* stupid.

SINGLE-PARENT FAMILIES SEISMOGRAPH

Dear Ms. Class:

Of twenty-eight students in my class, only twelve come from intact families. I wonder how a society that sanctions the deterioration of family values expects teachers to make a difference.

— Richmond, VA

Dear Richmond:

Although Ms. Class regards one good parent as being more valuable to a child than one hundred good teachers, she is not eager to proclaim what an "intact" family is or what kinds of family configurations lead to high SAT scores and a growing GNP. And a seat in the Oval Office. From George Washington on, we are a nation led by the products of single-parent families. George Washington was eleven when his father died (and Washington raised his own fatherless grandchildren); Thomas Jefferson was fourteen. Andrew Jackson was posthumous and was fourteen when his mother died. Abraham Lincoln was eleven when his mother died. That's just the beginning.

We give children history lessons about some presidents who could not tell a lie and others raised in log cabins. Maybe it's time we offered the children in our diverse society some narratives about presidents whose lives were shaped by family values in alternative configurations.

Dear Ms. Class:

It's outrageous for you to claim that children in single-parent homes are as well off emotionally and educationally as children who have a father who goes to work and a mother who stays at home and provides for the family.

— Boise, ID

Dear Boise:

Ms. Class would not presume to claim whether the children of, say, Ronald and (homemaker) Nancy Reagan were better or worse off than the children of, say, (widower) Thomas Jefferson. But consider this: according to a study at the University of Michigan Institute for Social Research, the child of a working mother watches television for an average of 111 minutes on a weekday. The child of a nonworking mother watches television for 139 minutes on a weekday.

SKILLS OVERFLOW MOBILIZATION

Dear Ms. Class:

I am upset to see skill checklists for books children love. I saw a one-hundred-page study guide for *The Very Hungry Caterpillar,* and I wanted to vomit.

— Vergennes, VT

Dear Vergennes:

This is the American way. Any kind of skill, no matter how trivial or how significant, begets entrepreneurial opportunities among the publishing tribes.

But as you point out, recognizing reality doesn't mean accepting it. The teacher who survives and even triumphs is the teacher who learns to just say no and to resist much.

Dear Ms. Class:

I have carefully taken my students through a scope-and-sequence chart of reading mastery appropriate to their age level. I am worried about assuring skill maintenance. I am very aware that students often forget things they have learned. How can I help my students maintain their skill mastery?

— Staten Island, NY

Dear Staten Island:

Skill maintenance? Ms. Class is suspicious of anything that sounds automotive—too subject to breakdown. She advises that you get your desk out from behind the counter of the Qwik-Stop Skill Shoppe. A school is not a garage or a service center where one takes children in for a tune-up.

One problem with following skill scopes and sequences is that half the time we spend teaching specific skills is wasted. The trouble is, we don't know which half.

SOB TAKEOVER BID

Dear Ms. Class:

Something unbelievable is happening at my school. The joke about our district is that the only way a teacher would not get tenure is to be caught *flagrante delicto* with a student. And yet a young teacher of impeccable probity has just received a letter telling him he won't be getting tenure. He has two years of good observation reports from two principals and from the elementary supervisor. The only negative thing I can think about this fellow is that he isn't the best speller in the world. It's a joke with the faculty and with his fifth graders. He's earnest, enthusiastic—and, my god, he's a black male in a school with thirty-six percent black students and no black tenured faculty and only one tenured male teacher. The only possible explanation we can come up with is that a school board member's daughter is looking for a job, and the market in this area is very tight. She does a lot of substitute work in our building. Is this theory too bizarre to be believed? Is there anything we can do to help this young teacher?

— Name Withheld on Request

Dear Name Withheld:

No, of course your theory is not bizarre. It has come to Ms. Class's attention that in some school districts SOB means scion of board member. In Ms. Class's district, it was of longstanding tradition to hire teachers to teach summer school and, at the same pay, hire college student SOBs to paint, count books, answer phones, and talk to custodians.

With regard to your colleague: you must not feel helpless. You can fight back. Ms. Class has personal knowledge of a school district with exactly the scenario you describe. Teachers there organized a letter-writing campaign. They wrote letters testifying to their colleague's competence. They attended board meetings when tenure decisions were scheduled. The teacher in question was given a year's extension on the tenure decision, and the SOB is still unemployed.

SOLID WASTE MANAGEMENT CYCLE

Dear Ms. Class:

My cupboards and file drawers are a disgrace. I have been teaching for fifteen years and just don't seem to be able to throw anything away. I know I'll never again use the St. Patrick's Day dittos or the camel bulletin board. But I feel that I'd be throwing half my life in the trash if I just dumped them. Help me!

— Lincoln, NE

Dear Lincoln:

Ms. Class thought of suggesting you hold a closet giveaway. Invite colleagues to come take what they want. But you sound like a sensitive person, and you might not bear up well under the knowledge that nobody wants that junk—even when it's free. Why not hold a classroom lottery and let your students take what they want? Ms. Class is always amazed at the number of students who don't get enough of school at school and love to play it at home. Students love old dittos and that camel bulletin board will be a prized item.

SPECIAL EDUCATION MARKET INCENTIVES

Dear Ms. Class:

I teach in an economically deprived school in a black neighborhood. I am outraged that twenty-one percent of our students are labeled as needing one sort of special education or another. Is this a racist policy to keep nonwhite people in their place?

— Newark, NJ

Dear Newark:

Special education labels in poor districts are not so much a policy as an opportunity. The number of students assigned to special education classes expands to fit the economic needs of the school. Schools in affluent districts have a stronger tax base, as well as parents who wouldn't stand for having their children so labeled. Special education labels are one of the few economic incentives left to schools without a strong tax base.

SPELLING CASUALTY LOSS

Dear Ms. Class:

I know spelling bees are controversial, but so many of my students love them. What do you think?

— Troy, MI

Dear Troy:

Ms. Class will let Josh McBroom have the first word on this one. In *McBroom's Almanac*, he says, "First student to teach a bee to spell, wins."

Ms. Class has a modest proposal: line up all teacher candidates. Last one standing in a spelling bee gets the job. Any candidate who can spell *onomatopoeia*, *algorithm*, and *occurred* should be given an administrative position. Think about the results if school boards were chosen by spelling bee performance.

Dear Ms. Class:

I'd like to share a spelling procedure that's proved very effective in my classroom. After years of having children memorize words for the test and then promptly forget them, I came up with a plan to jazz up spelling, to make it memorable. I ask each student to stand and spell a word, but they don't just spell it. One student must spell it backwards, another must spell it while standing on one leg. I ask students to spell while hopping, holding their breath, patting their heads, rubbing their bellies, and so on. I try to come up with a wide variety of different body movements to accompany the spelling. Students love it—and it aids their concentration. They remember their spelling words, too!

— Reno, NV

Dear Reno:

Thank you for sharing.

STANDARD ENGLISH DEBT CEILING

Dear Ms. Class:

Our English department is torn in two over the issue of standard English. Some of us feel that this is not so much a linguistic issue as a political one. We feel that students have a right to their own language and there is no such thing as "incorrect" language. Others feel that disagreement between subject and verb is only slightly less reprehensible than incest. I wonder if there is any chance of such polar-opposite viewpoints coexisting.

— Chicago, IL

Dear Chicago:

Ms. Class does not see a peaceful settlement on your horizon. She is fascinated, however, that people who proclaim the merits of nonstandard dialects do not themselves use these dialects in public discourse. How do you feel about your daughters and sons marrying somebody whose subjects and verbs are at odds with each other?

Only a person who has command of standard English can choose to reject it. Ms. Class believes every student should be taught standard English and then allowed to use whatever language he wishes.

Dear Ms. Class:

I object to your deliberate misinterpretation of linguistic necessity. Black English is a perfectly legitimate means of communication, one of the many dialects of English, and, as such, just as valid as the dialect known as standard English. The First Amendment to the Constitution gives every American the right to choose the language through which she or he will communicate.

— Urbana, IL

Dear Urbana:

The Constitution, like the devil, can be quoted for many purposes. When Ms. Class taught eighth grade, she had a set of books written in black dialect. It seemed like a good idea, a way to lure her black students into books and to help them see that their spoken language was legitimate. The only trouble was the students hated the books, denouncing the characters as "dumb."

"They don't talk right," protested one student.

"Don't they talk the way you talk?" Ms. Class queried.

"Yeah, but that don't be the way you suppose' to talk in school."

Would it not have been just a bit perverse for Ms. Class to have insisted that her students read stories written in black dialect rather than accede to their vehement demands to read stories written in standard English?

Ms. Class is very aware that the acquisition of standard English does not guarantee financial or social or moral advancement. However, this doesn't mean we teachers can abdicate our responsibility or to lead our students in singing "We Shall Overcome" in place of presenting a writing lesson.

STANDARDS AND PRACTICES OZONE LAYER

Dear Ms. Class:

My school district bought copies of the NCTM *Standards* for every mathematics teacher. Now we are being given the arts standards, the social studies standards, and god only knows what else. I suppose it is good to have goals, but these standards documents become more and more impossible. What good is it to have the NCTM *Standards,* for example, when we have no money for manipulatives or technology? What good is it to have the social studies standards when our school library is open only two days a week and then is staffed by a paraprofessional with a high school education? Never mind that there is no money to buy library books or to update our textbooks: our school board can boast that we teachers have copies of the standards in all these disciplines.

— Roanoke, VA

Dear Roanoke:

Ms. Class agrees that we seem to be entering a purgatory of standards documents. Ms. Class questions the fact that practicing teachers are so infrequently involved in writing these documents. Ms. Class thinks it fair to ask: would you rather have your dinner cooked by a food consultant or a chef?

Dear Ms. Class:

I agree that the proliferation of standards documents in every curriculum area is daunting, but surely you believe that this move to upgrade education is a good thing?

— Oxnard, CA

Dear Oxnard:

Perhaps. But twenty years of hanging around schools has shown Ms. Class that any definition in education is ten percent axiom and ninety percent exception.

STATISTICS GROWTH FUND

Dear Ms. Class:

As if it wasn't bad enough that our district publishes the reading scores of every school in the newspaper, now they have come up with the notion of comparing our scores with the scores of children in other countries. I wonder what purpose all these statistics serve—and where they will end.

— Council Bluffs, IA

Dear Council Bluffs:

Statistics are just numbers with hollandaise sauce. Statistics are a school's way of demonstrating to the public they are getting their money's worth. Ms. Class believes the only way to stop this abuse of children is to start a grass-roots movement to publish the results of reading and math tests administered to every public official—from the mayor and city council members in every village and hamlet to the members of Congress.

SUFFICIENCY RULE

Dear Ms. Class:

Ordinarily, I don't consider myself a pessimist, but lately I'm beginning to wonder. I seem to be paddling upstream—without a boat. I teach in a dilapidated school where parents don't come to open house, the principal doesn't care enough about anything to bother with holding faculty meetings, and most of the faculty gave up teaching a decade ago. I've only been here two years, but I worry that my own conviction that I can make a difference to children is being worn away.

— Atlanta, GA

Dear Atlanta:

Ms. Class suggests the Theodore Roosevelt tenet: do what you can, with what you have, where you are, rather than than whining about what you can't do. But she would add one further suggestion: find one more person in that building who does not accept the crumbling status quo. It may be a teacher, a librarian, a nurse, a secretary. Find that person and cultivate her. You need a shoulder to cry on and a person with whom you can share the triumphs that will come to any teacher who has not lost faith in children.

SUPPLIES ADVISORY BULLETIN

Dear Ms. Class:

I wonder why school supplies are never available when school begins. We place our orders in June and supplies don't begin arriving until November. Can you explain this?

— Holyoke, MA

Dear Holyoke:

If you are receiving your school supplies by November, you're better off than 63.7 percent of U. S. teachers. A school's fiscal year begins in July. That means that administrative personnel might look at your orders in September—if they weren't so busy straightening out the beginning-of-year bus snafus.

Ms. Class's School Supplies Advisory Bulletin

1. Don't count on having any. Although a teacher's year begins on the first Tuesday after Labor Day, no purchase orders go out before the second Wednesday after Halloween.

2. Black chalk theory: you get most of those things you need the least. That's why your school has six basals per student and only two dictionaries in the entire building. Corollary: teachers with staplers

requiring flat-top staples have access to an unlimited amount of humped-crown staples.

3. The number of rolls of cellophane tape ordered is inversely proportional to the number of left-hand scissors received. Corollary: three cellophane tape dispensers are ordered each year for a district, whether they are needed or not.

4. Anything described as "new," "innovative," and "individualized," isn't.

5. If it doesn't say "new," "innovative," and "individualized" in the catalog, your supervisor won't be interested in getting it for you, which is why you never receive pencils, lined paper, glue, or staples. Corollary: it is easier to get a "new," "innovative," and "individualized" reading program for $650 than a decent dictionary for $29.

6. Never order any learning aid requiring batteries.

7. If it doesn't work, learn to do without it; no one can fix it. Corollary: nothing gets fixed in schools. Broken things are moved around. If things can't be moved, then the teachers are.

8. If it still works after three months, order half a dozen more immediately. Anything that good will soon be unavailable.

9. The farther a company is located from your school, the more likely your request will be approved. If you say you could pick up the item on the way home, you haven't a chance of approval. Corollary: it is easier to get five hundred textbooks from Des Moines than five copies of the local newspaper.

10. No matter how many workbooks, texts, or protractors you order, you will have three more students in your class.

11. On your requisition, always include at least one item on which your supervisor can exercise administrative option: mink-covered beanbag chair, combination pencil sharpener-ice crusher, term-paper shredder.

12. If you order twenty-eight items, you will either receive twenty-two or sixty-nine, depending on how eager you were to use this item. This is why teachers lie on the requisition about their class size.

Dear Ms. Class:
    Who were your district's suppliers? I find it hard to believe anyone would send you three times as many items as you ordered.

— Columbia, MO

Dear Show-Me Stater:
    Ms. Class wonders who your supplier was, if this sounds unusual to you. Haven't you ever received twenty-two books when you ordered two?

Eight chairs when you ordered twenty-eight? Actually, this phenomenon is not unique to school suppliers. At home, Ms. Class has had Sears leave an (unordered) set of kitchen furniture in her driveway (and had a damn hard time convincing them to pick it up), two sets of china from Macy's, a set of encyclopedias. One item caused a moment of panic. When Ms. Class took a job a continent away, her husband ordered her a small flashlight. One. She received a box of 144 from the mail order company. When she opened the box and saw all those little black tubes, she had this fleeting panic that he had sent her a do-it-yourself television set. Ms. Class reflects how much cheaper things would be if suppliers employed more expert typists.

SYLLABIFICATION AMORTIZATION UPDATE

Dear Ms. Class:

I suppose I'm naive, but I'm confused by all these workbook activities on dividing words into syllables. If a student can't read the word, how can he divide it into syllables? If he can read it, why does he need to divide it into syllables?

— Shelton, WA

Dear Shelton:

In regards a topic of this kind, it becomes more than a moral imperative to speak one's mind. It is a delight. Do you realize that 99.7 percent of the population has never heard of the word *syllabification?* This is a first. In twenty years of research, Ms. Class has never found occasion to use it in casual (or serious) conversation. Nor has she found anyone who can tell her why we teach children to divide words into syllables. Copyreaders formerly needed this skill. Now computers syllabificate for them.

TALENT AMPLIFICATION FLAGSHIP

Dear Ms. Class:

Some colleagues and I have been arguing about whether teachers are born or made. Do you have an opinion?

— Rutland, VT

Dear Rutland:

Ms. Class wonders: aren't there any boards to erase, any smokers to catch in lavatories, any #2 pencils to sharpen? Ms. Class is aware that tall oaks from little acorns grow, but like Queen Victoria, she is calmed by great events and irritated by trifles.

Nonetheless, you asked; Ms. Class answers: the disposition for teaching is two percent inborn and ninety-eight percent reinvented every day of one's career. Please note: this is a fact. Ms. Class does not indulge in idle speculation.

TEACHABLE MOMENTS METAPHYSICS

Dear Ms. Class:

I'm fed up with teachers who talk of "teachable moments" as though no child can learn without some metaphysical beacon from the zodiac. It sounds more like loosey-goosey Shirley MacLaine astromuddle than professionalism. I just walk into my classroom every day ready to teach and expecting my students to be ready to learn.

— Sacramento, CA

Dear Sacramento:

Ms. Class notes that you're from *northern* California. Even so, Ms. Class would point out that your utilitarian, workaday expectations do not contradict the notion of the teachable moment.

Ms. Class is as hard-nosed as anyone about the pragmatism involved in teaching, but, be that as it may, she knows the mystic teachable moment most certainly does exist. The poet William Stafford observed that "poetry is the kind of thing you have to see from the corner of your eye." Stafford adds that to concentrate too much on the form of poetry is "like boiling a watch to find out what makes it tick." Ms. Class feels the same way about teaching. A teacher must prepare herself for the task by being the smartest, toughest, most caring person she can be. But she must also be ever wary of boiling the watch. Students are far more mysterious than watches. The best of us can't control their ticking.

Dear Ms. Class:

There you go with metaphors again. I'm a practical person. I don't believe teaching is a science, but I do believe we can learn certain principles to help us do our jobs. Maybe that's a good definition of education itself: finding the guiding principles to help us do our jobs and lead our lives.

— Omaha, NE

Dear Omaha:

Maybe so. Nineteenth-century English biologist T. H. Huxley put it this way: "Perhaps the most valuable result of all education is the ability to make yourself to do the thing you have to do when it ought to be done, whether you like it or not."

Ms. Class rather likes onetime schoolteacher Robert Frost's twentieth-century addendum. This Pulitzer prize-winning poet said that "education is the ability to listen to almost anything without losing your temper or your self-confidence."

TEACHERS AND TEACHING CRITERIA REFERENCES

Dear Ms. Class:

I am so tired of hearing that old line: "Those who can, do; those who can't, teach." Can you suggest a snappy comeback?

— Ambler, PA

Dear Ambler:

Relax. To worry about the kind of person who sneers at teachers is to worry about being called ugly by a toad. School is the place where the expert is told how to do her job by people who have themselves never done it. Ms. Class suggests reminding those who would sneer at the intellectual attainment of teachers that fifty percent of doctors and lawyers graduated in the bottom half of their class.

Here's another provocative bit of information that may come in handy at a cocktail party, Little League game, or ballet recital intermission: a *New England Journal of Medicine* study found that thirty-six percent of patients admitted to hospitals developed new illnesses as a result of the treatment they received. Ms. Class has not seen any studies documenting that students leave school worse off than when they arrived.

There's more to the medical analogy. In *Doing Better and Feeling Worse,* Aaron Wildavsky makes the point that the medical system (doctors, drugs, hospitals) affects about ten percent of the usual indices for measuring health. The remaining ninety percent are determined by factors over which doctors have little or no control: smoking, exercise, worry, income, eating habits, inheritance, air and water quality, and so on.

Dear Ms. Class:

My best friend is a great teacher, but I can't get her to see that if you believe in the importance of authentic reading, of children's choosing their own books, then you can't give isolated vocabulary quizzes.

— Providence, RI

Dear Providence:

Ms. Class would advise that you be not so fond of censure. Ms. Class is not aware of either any religious commandment or a Constitutional amendment on the topic of vocabulary quizzes. Therefore, Ms. Class questions whether your best friend's vocabulary quizzes are really any of your business. Ms. Class believes all teachers need to have the courage of their contradictions.

Instead of worrying about your colleague's correctness, you might consider concentrating on cleaning up your own language. Authentic reading, indeed.

Dear Ms. Class:

I've been teaching for ten years, and I wonder when I'm going to get it right. Mostly, I enjoy what I do, and I think I make a difference. Nonetheless, things rarely go just right. I'm always conscious of things I could have changed for the better. Other teachers don't seem to have my problem. I see some good teachers going home without lugging two book bags that weigh ten pounds each. What's their secret?

— Memphis, TN

Dear Memphis:

The secret of teaching is, of course, that there is no secret. Teaching does prove one thing: practice doesn't make perfect. But take heart. A fourth-grade teacher of Ms. Class's acquaintance, a teacher of some twenty-four years' experience who is admired by children, colleagues, and community alike, says the year she gets things right, the year she's satisfied, will be the year she knows it's time to retire.

The eminent Edwardian gardener Gertrude Jeckyll noted that it takes "half a lifetime to decide what's worth doing in a garden and another half to try to do it."

Pablo Casals put it this way: "I never play the same piece twice in the same way. Each time it is new." Likewise, the wonderful thing about teaching is that it's new every day. Wendell Berry, a farmer-poet-teacher much admired by Ms. Class, says, in his poem "Traveling at Home":

Even in a country you know by heart
it's hard to go the same way twice.
The life of going changes.
The chances change and make a new way.

Now to some particulars. About those ten-pound book bags. First, why don't you ask those colleagues the secret of their light-handedness? Second, if you look into the bags you drag home from school, you'll find at least nine things you could have thrown away three months ago. The national average of useless, out-of-date, and/or Toxicogenic book bag items is 13.6.

Dear Ms. Class:

You write about teaching having no secrets. How about principles? Aren't there some general rules one can count on?

— Rugby, ND

Dear Rugby:

Yes, indeed. Here they are:

1. You never teach an easy class.

2. Teaching consists of equal parts perspiration, inspiration, and resignation. Gail Godwin puts it another way. She says, "Good teaching is one-fourth preparation and three-fourths theater."

3. For unsuccessful teachers, teaching is not a career of one year building on the preceding years but one dreadful year repeated over and over.

4. The real rule of teaching is that it's no easier when you're forty-four than when you're twenty-four. The only difference is that at forty-four you know this.

5. Some people do fine in teaching with a second-class intellect, but every teacher needs a first-class temperament. To be able to teach, you have to be able to love and be loved; you need patience, compassion, humor, faith, and the ability to tolerate ambiguity. If you have all that, pray for a little magic, too.

6. Don't badmouth your students' former teachers. Even when there's sore provocation, such as the sixteenth time Emily proclaims, "Ms. Fizzle didn't do it this way," when the truth of the matter is you'd rather die than do anything the way Ms. Fizzle does it, you must smile and say, "I know but we like trying new things, don't we?"

TEACHER SAVVY THREE-STEP PROGRAM

Dear Ms. Class:

I've read what you've written about the temperament for teaching, and it all sounds too mystical for me. Can you offer some practical advice for a new teacher?

— Elko, NV

Dear Elko:

Certainly. Here goes.

1. If it moves, tell it to sit down.

2. If it doesn't move, ask the custodian to clean it up.

3. If disinfectant doesn't eradicate it, tape crepe paper around the edges.

Dear Ms. Class:

Take off your Groucho moustache for a minute and get serious. I'm not looking for a twelve-step recovery program or for closure; I'm not looking for a chuckle, either. What I need is something to make me feel more secure as a teacher. It just seems like kids' needs these days are so vast, and I really have doubts that I'm doing an adequate job. I may be doing them some good; I question whether it's enough.

— Cheyenne, WY

Dear Cheyenne:

Dr. Benjamin Spock's famous book *Dr. Spock's Baby and Child Care* was published in 1945, and it begins, "You know more than you think you do." What revolutionary and yet reassuring words for parents. Ms. Class would like to offer those same reassuring words to teachers. Too many of the courses we take are disempowering, convincing us that we can never know enough. Of course it's true that we always need to learn more, but it is also true, Cheyenne, that you do know more than you think you do.

Begin each school day by reminding yourself: *you know more than you think you do.* Then tell your students to remind themselves of the same thing: *you know more than you think you do.*

Finally, a cautionary note: every time you are tempted to say something about kids "these days," reflect on what Virgil said some decades B.C.: *perhaps one day this too will be pleasant to remember.*

TEAM TEACHING PEER PRESSURE

Dear Ms. Class:

My principal returned from an administrative conference gung ho for teamwork. I have been placed on a seventh grade team with three other teachers. The idea is that we will have our planning period together and thereby be able to integrate language arts, social studies, science, and mathematics instruction and present a holistic learning package to our students. Fine. The only problem is it was a unilateral decision: teachers were not consulted. The principal chose the teams. The science teacher on my team is an idiot, and the language arts teacher isn't much better. As I look at the other teams, I can see a similar pattern. The principal has deliberately paired weak teachers with strong teachers. I work hard at my job. Isn't it enough that I teach difficult students? It is just too much to have to drag along lazy, incompetent colleagues.

— Wilmington, DE

Dear Wilmington:

First, stop crying in your soup. There is hope. You didn't say, but Ms. Class can deduce that you teach either social studies or math. Since you didn't complain about that fourth member of your team, Ms. Class suggests you try planning with that person. Start small. Find one thing that interests both of you and do it together. You can hope the two laggards will be inspired by your stellar example. If they aren't, not to worry. At least you've found a partner. Although you can probably rely on your restless principal to find a new bandwagon before long, Ms. Class recommends trying to make the new partnership work.

Dear Ms. Class:

Your advice on team teaching just proves you don't know what you're talking about. If team-teaching partners are not carefully self-selected for philosophy, style, and outcome goals, the experience not only won't work, it will be a nightmare and a real disservice to children. For the sake of the children you pretend to care so much about, Ms. Class, why don't you just admit when you don't know anything about a topic?

— Hot Springs, SD

Dear Hot Springs:

Have we met? Ms. Class does not recall such an occasion, nor does she recall your visiting her classroom. Ms. Class does not take offense when people disagree with her. She would warn you, however, that it is both misguided and atrocious to make assumptions about someone's teaching qualifications based solely on the fact you disagree with her opinions.

Although Ms. Class feels somewhat disinclined to explain herself to someone of your disposition, she will yield to the benefits of a good story. One late August morning, Ms. Class walked into her classroom a few days before school started and discovered a second teacher desk—and another teacher—in the room. Over the summer, in a fit of imaginative abandon or, perhaps, indigestion, the language arts coordinator had created a teaching team—without informing either party. Being teachers, Ms. Class and her cotenant consulted neither lawyers nor psychiatrists but set about dividing the room in half; they produced some pretense of privacy by stringing up old bedspreads on a clothesline down the center of the room. Quite literally, students were expected to toe the mark: seventh graders on one side of the bedspread, eighth graders on the other. The two teachers never crossed this line either.

This jerry-rigged divider didn't help the noise. Ms. Class is a noisy teacher and the other half of this odd couple was restrained. Every time Ms. Class's students read knock-knock riddles, she had to wonder how much the students and teacher on the other side of the bedspread were suffering as they worked their way through the sixteen rules of syllabification. When Ms. Class and her classroommate replaced the bedspread dividers with a row of portable chalkboards that they begged, borrowed, and stole from throughout the school, Ms. Class's seventh graders had a penchant for turning these chalkboards into rudimentary skateboards, riding them around (her half of) the classroom.

Ms. Class and her cotenant eventually decided that any demarcation line was silly, as was dividing up the students. They worked together for six years, not caring who was officially a seventh grader and who an eighth.

Although Ms. Class never learned how to divide words into syllables, she and her colleague did learn a lot from each other. The fact that they worked together in harmony for six years was a result not of some natural affinity or similarity in temperament, style, or outcome goals; it was a result of their own hard work and the fact that they gave themselves the time and space to accept and learn from each other's strengths and weaknesses. This experience taught Ms. Class that Carl Jung wasn't whistling "Dixie" when he pointed out (in *Memories, Dreams, Reflections*) that "everything that irritates us about others can lead us to an understanding of ourselves". The teacher who realizes this finds herself getting along better with difficult students as well as with difficult teachers, including herself.

TECHNOLOGY HYPERBOLE STRESS TEST

Dear Ms. Class:

Our superintendent has announced that books are an antiquated information-delivery system and that libraries should put money into software, not books. I teach reading and we've been ordered to key all our materials to a computerized skill-maintenance system. What do you think of this? Am I old fashioned in holding on to my belief in books?

— Atlanta, GA

Dear Atlanta:

No. You must not go down without a fight. Resist much. As seductive as the computer chorus line may be, the mechanical miracle is not about to sweep aside low reading scores with a flutter of the video display screen. A workbook skill is a workbook skill even when it lights up, dances a jig, and whistles "Flight of the Bumblebee." The student who is plugged in for an electronic fast fix is just participating in refuse management: garbage in/garbage out.

The fault, of course, is not in the computer but in a wrongheaded notion of reading. Decoding a screen filled with type is neither amusing nor inspiring. It is acutely painful, and people who are forced to do it should receive adequate monetary compensation. Certainly it is not something we should inflict on children who have not yet experienced the power and the joy of the printed word that appears on paper they can run their hands over. Maurice Sendak and Gore Vidal, among others, speak passionately of the wonderful tactileness of the books of their childhood.

Dear Ms. Class:

You seem to be prejudiced against all sorts of technology. Why don't you get your head out of the nineteenth century?

— Trenton, NJ

Dear Trenton:

Ms. Class is not prejudiced. She just believes in keeping technology in its place, and she recognizes that forces are at work to increase this place exponentially. Ivars Peterson relates a popular joke in the aircraft industry: automated airplanes of the future will have only a pilot and a dog in the cockpit. The pilot is there to reassure old-fashioned, fuddy-duddy passengers. The dog is there to bite the pilot if he tries to touch any of the computerized equipment that is flying the plane. Professor of computer science Nancy Leveson adds, "The pilot will also be there so that there's someone around to blame in case of an accident."

Since eighty percent of all new products never make it past the test market stage and since Ms. Class lived for sixteen years in a test-market area, it is her custom to wait for the ballyhoo and bombast to settle before letting any new products into her life. Case in point: whatever happened to Top Coverage, a hair-colored spray paint for bald spots? Northwood's Egg Coffee? Parsnip chips?

Ms. Class is not going to retire quietly while her students plug into computers. She learned early in her career that technology should aid teaching, not drive it. Ms. Class went from teaching in a huge high school where the only technology available was an antique ditto machine to teaching in a new college where officials insisted the staff should be on the technological cutting edge. For starters, the English faculty was called in for a preopening-day pep talk on how the overhead projector should transform each lesson. Each faculty member was given hundreds of transparencies and scores of felt-tipped markers. In a variation on the publish-or-perish theme, faculty were told to turn in transparencies with which they had augmented lectures. In other words, ultimately faculty would be judged by the height of the pile of the transparencies in their file.

Pleased to be on the forefront of the technological revolution, Ms. Class threw herself into making wonderful transparencies in every color of the rainbow. She had produced a six-week supply before school even opened. On the first day of class, she put one of these masterpieces on the overhead projector and continued talking. Students began to titter. She talked faster. The tittering increased. Finally, Ms. Class looked at the screen . . . and watched the last of her beautiful words disappear. She grabbed another transparency and put it on the machine. Line by line, the words vanished. The same thing happened with a third transparency and a fourth.

The person in charge of technology at the college had purchased the wrong type of felt-tipped marker: heat caused the ink to evaporate. By that time new markers arrived two months later, Ms. Class was well into teaching without the marvel of the new technology that should have/could have transformed her professional life.

Ms. Class would add that that same English department was gung ho on showing films to students. When some staff members complained that the announced films, carefully scheduled to match their lessons, did not always arrive on time and the machinery did not always work, the person in charge of technology replied, "Be innovative. Improvise!"

Sometimes it was a blessing when the technology broke down. Ms. Class did not have a clue why her students were supposed to view a surrealist film in which the most powerful image is an eyeball being slit with a knife. Difficult to understand, impossible to improvise—so she just skipped it altogether.

Dear Ms. Class:

The stories you tell may be funny, but they are beside the point. One instance of a machine not working does not undercut the technological revolution.

— Darien, CT

Dear Darien:

Ms. Class does not tell stories as an attempt to undercut anybody's revolution or even to rain on his parade. Ms. Class offers her stories as emblems of teaching, scars from the field. If they do not resonate with the reader's own experiences, then so be it. However, over the years Ms. Class has learned that her stories do resonate with teachers and with administrators too. An assistant superintendent in Michigan once wrote her a fan letter; she wrote a few more articles and he wrote again, offering her a job.

Certainly Ms. Class is not alone in feeling that in the end most innovations are only so much foofaraw. In the end, a teacher can rely only on herself. Over a century ago education was symbolized by the image of educator Mark Hopkins on one end of a log and a student on the other. Ms. Class does not think electronic marvels have changed teaching essentials all that much. A teacher and a student, without claptrap, is still what education is all about.

Stubbornly, Ms. Class offers one more emblem of technology. Early in her career she received a federal grant to study innovative ways to encourage the "culturally deprived" to read. Officially labeled culturally deprived eighth and ninth graders were bused into the pristine refinement of Princeton University, which is an interesting anomaly that Ms. Class won't dissect just now. The innovative course was structured around showing movies made from provocative books. Every day students were given a paperback book, barely given time to look at the cover, and then the rest of class time was taken up in watching a full-length movie version of that book.

The thing that most impressed Ms. Class was those students' devotion to the books. Every day they carried all the books to class, so that by the end of two weeks they were juggling fifteen paperbacks. But even more impressive was the students' determination to read the books. The image of technical innovation that lingers after all these years is of the power of the book: the sight of black teenagers struggling to read *Grapes of Wrath* by the light of the movie projector while *On the Waterfront* played on the screen.

Dear Ms. Class:
Can't you think of any technology that has improved your life as a teacher?

— Minneapolis, MN

Dear Minneapolis:
No, though an electric pencil sharpener comes pretty close. Ms. Class does have a modest proposal for technological innovation that would play well at the principals' convention—the administrative answering machine:

- If you have a question about yard duty, press one.
- If you wish to make a discipline referral, press two.
- If you wish to speak to a hall monitor, press three.
- If you need Valium, Halcion, Atarax, or Prozac, press four.
- If you wish to order pizza, press five.
- This machine neither records nor acknowledges excuses for missing the faculty meeting.

Dear Ms. Class:
I can tell you of a technology innovation that is sure to blow your mind: we took a field trip on the information highway. My students visited the Berlin Wall for the fiftith anniversary of Victory in Europe Day and asked questions of Germans via the America Online network. This possibility comes from the Turner Education Service's Adventure in Learning Program, which collaborates with Indiana University's Center for Excellence in Education, a research-and-development center that specializes in classroom technology.

— Alexandria, VA

Dear Alexandria:
The idea of a virtual field trip over the real kind has obvious appeal for Ms. Class. But Ms. Class must admit she finds the cost of the necessary computer equipment mind-boggling. And the telephones. For years, teachers have begged for phone access to make a dentist appointment or call a parent. There are plenty of school districts where teachers do not have

access to an outside phone line. Now you say students are calling Germany?

Not to throw a wet blanket on all this electronic wizardry, but let us remember that Ted Turner is the fellow who colorized *Casablanca*. Ms. Class is almost as nervous about Ted Turner's psyche taking over a part of our school day as she is of Chris Whittle's. These men are excellent packagers: they know glitz; they know marketing; they know grand ambition. We have no evidence that they know anything about what children need.

Isn't it enough that Ted Turner's short attention span dominates television and that his megalomaniacal vision has changed classic movies forever? Are we going to let him into our schools without even a whimper?

TEENAGER JUST DESSERTS

Dear Ms. Class:

I pride myself on being tolerant, but I've had it with teenagers. They have no respect for authority, short attention spans, overwhelming devotion to the faddish and the sensational. What can we do?

— Omaha, NE

Dear Omaha:

Despite international pressure, teenagers have not been outlawed by the Geneva Convention. Nineteenth-century English clergyman J. B. Priestley had it right when he pointed out that like its politicians and its wars, society has the teenagers it deserves. If you are serious about changing teenagers, then the first thing you have to do is change the adults who bring them into the world and continue to be in their close proximity. Take a look at the adults who appear on TV. They exhibit no respect for authority, have short attention spans, are overwhelmingly devoted to the faddish and the sensational. For that matter, take a look around your faculty room or at the U. S. Congress.

TELEVISION EASEMENT

Dear Ms. Class:

Our school has received a big grant to rewire every classroom for television. Last year we got rid of librarians. Next year we'll have television in every classroom. What's wrong with this scenario? It doesn't make any sense to me.

— Buffalo, NY

Dear Buffalo:

Ms. Class knows of no study proving that watching TV causes irreversible brain damage. It only seems that way.

Many people agree that *Sesame Street* is one of the best shows available in children's programming, and yet a growing number of people who know a lot about young children express concern about the sensory assault the Muppets and friends proffer to preschoolers. Typical segments on the show run thirty or forty-five seconds. Three-minute segments are the exception.

In *Endangered Minds*, psychologist Jane Healy observes that our "uncritical acceptance of *Sesame Street* as a model for 'learning' has been part of a larger infatuation with expedient, product-oriented approaches that denigrate the essence of the educational enterprise. Its substitution of surface glitz for substance has started a generation of children in the seductive school of organized silliness, where their first lesson is that learning is something adults can be expected to make happen for them as quickly and pleasantly as possible." Healy goes on to observe that "*Sesame Street* has overemphasized letters and numerals and underemphasized the language and thinking skills necessary to make them meaningful."

And the thing you have to remember is that *Sesame Street* is one of the best shows.

TEMPERAMENT-OF-THE-TRADE MODULE

Dear Ms. Class:

I've been teaching for three years, and I wonder if I've chosen the wrong career. I like the kids and think I do a good job most days, but I have to wonder if I have the right temperament for teaching. I rarely relax, I'm always tired, and I seem to be anxious all the time. I wonder if I'll ever reach the point where I'll feel at ease with this job.

— Cincinnati, OH

Dear Cincinnati:

Nothing is more exhausting than trying, and teaching is the profession of trying. Anxiety is the companion of trying. Freud called it the essence of conscience. The opposite of anxiety is not happiness. The opposite of anxiety is death. The grave is a quiet, stress-free place.

Your job will get easier. Just don't expect to reach a state of peace, relaxation, and contemplative quiet. After all, whatever else it may be, this thing called teaching is a noise forever.

THEMATIC UNIT OMINIPRESENCE

Dear Ms. Class:

Theme units have changed my life. I have organized all my materials into themes and have made an index card file of books in the library that match these units. I have extensive units on fire safety, old people, disabilities, and the seasons. I also have units centered on specific books. For *The Very Hungry Caterpillar,* for example, I have compiled a six-week across-the-curriculum theme unit on time, agriculture, the cycles of nature, ecology, and nutrition. I wonder if you can offer me advice on getting some of these units published.

— Provo, UT

Dear Provo:

Ms. Class worries that thematic units have become the oat bran of curriculum, promising to deliver everything from high reading scores to pimple eradication. Ms. Class has some doubts. She does not see how organizing the entire school day around a caterpillar or, say, a banana, will enrich children's lives.

Ms. Class does not jest. She has in her possession a comprehensive banana theme unit. It does not look like the professor who wrote it was jesting either.

Ms. Class worries about your students' spending so much time on *The Very Hungry Caterpillar,* one of her favorite books. Surely it was written for children's joy, not for their agricultural or nutritional enhancement.

THINKING TAUTOLOGIES BANKRUPTCY
PROTECTION (ALSO SEE *CRITICAL THINKING PRETEST*)

Dear Ms. Class:

Could you explain the different between critical thinking, creative thinking, logical thinking, and problem solving?

— Wilmington, DE

Dear Wilmington:

No. And anyone who says she can has something to sell.

Dear Ms. Class:

Surely you don't reject the notion of children as thinkers?

— Baltimore, MD

Dear Baltimore:

Of course students think. On occasion Ms. Class is pretty sure she has caught one of her cats thinking. But children's thinking is one of those metaphysical concerns about which experts know less than they pretend. Ms. Class wonders if what John Holt called "strategy" isn't what most people mean by thinking.

In *How Children Fail*, Holt says, "Strategy is an outgrowth of character. Children use the strategies they do because of the way they feel, the expectations they have of the universe, the way they evaluate themselves, the classroom, and the demands made of them."

TIME ON TASK TAXONOMY

Dear Ms. Class:

My first graders are good kids. They can get rambunctious, but, by and large, they offer few serious discipline problems. What worries me is that they waste so much time in class. I know they are capable of doing so much more if I could only figure out how to keep them on task and not fooling around. Help!

— Anchorage, AK

Dear Anchorage:

Time on task is one of the greatest frauds in the history of education. Ironic, isn't it, that the teacher effectiveness movement has made it so difficult for teachers to do their jobs?

A great mistake of teaching is to insist on creating an artificial distinction between work and play. This distinction need not be made, particularly for primary graders. Ms. Class must confess that she herself has not been a primary grader for a number of decades, but still, housework aside, there is little distinction between work and play in her life. She gets most of her best ideas while she is wasting time, and she expends ceaseless effort to bring play into her work.

TRADITION TESTIMONIES PRICE RANGE

Dear Ms. Class:

I teach in a district that demands excellence. We are under a lot of pressure to teach the great books. My principal has agreed on a compromise: individual teachers can continue to use the books they love, but at each grade level teachers must agree on one great book that all students will read. Do you have any suggestions for sixth grade?

— Bakersfield, CA

Dear Bakersfield:

Ms. Class sincerely hopes not too much blood is shed over this. One person's great book is another person's fate worse than death. She also hopes your faculty doesn't insist that authors must be dead before their books can be considered great.

Beware of advisers who tell you what great ideas children need. In *What Your First Grader Needs to Know*, Professor E. D. Hirsch says that six-year-olds should learn the legend of Oedipus and the Sphinx, as well as a minibiography of Nicolaus Copernicus. Professor Hirsch commends *Frankenstein* and *Alice in Wonderland* for third graders; *Gulliver's Travels*, *Robinson Crusoe*, Alexander Fleming, and Marie Curie for fourth graders; *Julius Caesar*, *Don Quixote*, Rene Descartes, and Isaac Newton for fifth graders; *Romeo and Juliet*, *Oliver Twist*, *Animal Farm*, and Albert Einstein for sixth graders. Hirsch hopes the short adaptations he offers will inspire youngsters to read the unabridged works. To know how absurd Professor Hirsch's assertions are, all you have to do is try reading these works yourself, never mind trying to pull young children through them. Ms. Class brings up Hirsch's tomes only to forewarn you about what parents and your principal will see at K-Mart.

Ms. Class thought these books were singular in their awfulness—and then she came across a number of little books in the Altemus One Syllable Series, published in 1899. She could not resist buying *Robinson Crusoe in Words of One Syllable*, and she must admit the book is rather a marvel of its ilk. It suggests great possibilities to supplement charades as a parlor game: hand out pages from classic books and challenge contestants to offer line-by-line translations in words of one syllable.

The culturally literate may wonder how the one-syllablist handles the name of Crusoe's trusty assistant. It is printed Fri-day. Some interesting complications: apparently reading experts in 1899 felt children who couldn't cope with words of more than one syllable should be able to multiply. Where Defoe wrote "seventy-two years," the one-syllablist wrote "three score and twelve."

T. S. Eliot once told us, "Tradition cannot be inherited." The wonderful thing about being a teacher is getting the chance to create new traditions in the classroom. It is a teacher's duty, as well as her delight, to find books that students can read and relish on their own. Ms. Class hears from students who, fifteen years after laughing over Jeff Brown's *Flat Stanley* in her classroom, report they are enjoying it again with their children. It may not be Dickens, but it is great fun.

Ms. Class realizes, perhaps somewhat tardily, that you asked for a recommendation, not a proclamation. For sixth graders, this week Ms. Class would recommend *Owl in Love*, by Patrice Kindl. It is a funny, moving, and engrossing account of a fourteen-year-old girl who can transform herself into an owl. When she isn't flying around the neighborhood, she's falling in love with her science teacher.

The humor is delicious. The young heroine can't eat lunch in the school cafeteria, for example. If she eats human food she'll lose the ability to fly, but she can hardly eat the rodents and grasshoppers she needs in front of her peers. This is a dilemma fit for the sensibilities of sixth graders—and their teachers.

Next month Ms. Class might well recommend a different book. But never mind: this month you and your students will do fine with *Owl in Love*.

TRAUMA COUNTDOWN

Dear Ms. Class:

I know it sounds sort of silly, but I wonder if you can rate, on a scale of one to ten, the most difficult tasks facing teachers.

— Rochester, NY

Dear Rochester:

Yes, such lists are silly, but never let it be said that Ms. Class can't occasionally kick up her heels, throw her schedule out the window, and bray at the moon. Here goes.

Teacher Traumas

   1. Bulletin boards

   2. Stapler-staple incompatibility

   3. Shelf space

   4. Bus duty

   5. Lesson plans

   6. Cafeterias

   7. Discipline policies

   8. Field trips

   9. Petty cash paucity

   10. Developing tolerance, accommodation, and compassion for titular superiors whose cognitive endowment would embarrass a sprig of parsley

TROUBLEMAKER TRADEMARK

Dear Ms. Class:

I have taught three older brothers of a fifth grader whom I shall call Joe. The boys were all troublemakers. I wonder if there's anything I can do to prevent trouble with Joe.

— Doylestown, PA

Dear Doylestown:

Your question forces Ms. Class to amend her long-held principle that teachers should change schools every three or four years. Obviously, it would be better if they are periodically run out of town.

A teacher who is convinced a student will be a troublemaker is seldom disappointed. For your sake and Joe's, if you can't relocate, pretend Joe is a recent immigrant, an only child. Students taught Ms. Class to regard each day as a new beginning. No grudges. Certainly every student has the right to start each school year with a clean slate, that is, with no faculty-room gossip about his past.

TRUTH-IN-DISCOURSE CONVERGENCE

Dear Ms. Class:

I seem to find myself in a predicament where telling the truth means letting colleagues know I think their taste in everything from television shows to novels to Avon products is questionable. I don't want to appear snobbish, but I really wonder if I should lie.

— Medford, OR

Dear Medford:

Ms. Class advises that you tell the truth—unless lying is one of your strong points. When you tell the truth, you don't have to worry about remembering anything. Of course, you should realize that telling the truth means you probably won't have any friends left. Ms. Class suspects there are only two ways to tell the one hundred percent truth: anonymously and posthumously.

Dear Ms. Class:

I used to look for the right method, the truth, if you will, in teaching. But the teacher next door and I have totally different styles. We have different beliefs about how children learn and what they should learn. The funny thing is we get along well. I think I'm a good teacher, and I think she is too.

— Deadwood, SD

Dear Deadwood:

Congratulations to you and your colleague for recognizing that the opposite of one great educational truth is not necessarily a lie or even a mistake. The opposite of one great educational truth is often another great educational truth. Ms. Class is distressed by the acrimony surrounding teaching method, as though phonics charts and picture books must wage a holy war for the minds and hearts of every teacher.

Someone wise once said that whenever everybody agrees, nobody is thinking very much. In *The Art of the Obvious*, Bruno Bettelheim observed that "people who know *the* right answer always end up burning other people at the stake."

Dear Ms. Class:

No way. I don't accept that two opposites can both be true. This sounds like moral relativism to me. In my book, right is right. Truth is truth and it always will be.

— Jerome, AZ

Dear Jerome:

Ms. Class wonders what book it is you revere. In all the great books known to Ms. Class, including the Bible, truth is not always so easily discerned. Ms. Class suggests that you dip into the work of the sixteenth-century French essayist Montaigne, who notes that truth is not permanent but fleeting and that lies both outnumber and outlast truths. In our own time, humanities professor and writer William Gass says, "There's a lie on the tip of every tongue like a bubble of spit." Ms. Class tells you this not to depress or disillusion you, but to arm you. Someone who believes that "truth is truth and always will be" needs all the help she can get.

UNCALLED-FOR EXHORTATION

Dear Ms. Class:

I wonder why junior highs exist. Why do we fill one building with the craziest kids? At least in the old K–8 schools, we had the leavening effect of a majority of students not suffering from raging hormones and psychological meltdown. It's easier for everybody when only twenty-five percent of the kids in a building are crazy.

— Ft. Worth, TX

Dear Ft. Worth:

The reader is mistaken. Junior highs were invented by superintendents to gather the craziest teachers in a district together in one place. Before you pick up your pens to denounce Ms. Class, please know she taught in a junior high for ten years.

Ms. Class would remind you that junior highs are not totally negative. They have enriched our vocabularies. For example, "uncalled for" and "under no circumstances" were invented by a seventh-grade English teacher the day after the first junior high opened in Columbus, Ohio, on September 7, 1909.

UNINTERRUPTED SUSTAINED SILENT READING RELIABILITY

Dear Ms. Class:

A parent brought in some research published in an IRA journal showing that kids don't become better readers by reading independently. Does this mean we should replace our schoolwide Drop Everything and Read program with intensive skill drill? Help!

— New Orleans, LA

Dear New Orleans:

Only in reading education would the professionals work at proving the disadvantages of reading. Of course you shouldn't abandon a noteworthy attempt to encourage faculty as well as student reading such as DEAR. Ms. Class finds it disquieting that your belief in reading could be shattered by such a paltry thing as an article in an IRA journal.

UNION RABBLE-ROUSING CONFIGURATIONS

Dear Ms. Class:

My school district participates in some sort of closed-shop agreement with the union. That means whether I join or not the dues will be deducted from my pay. This seems unconstitutional to me, especially since I can't see any benefits the union offers me.

— Syracuse, NY

Dear Syracuse:

If you have toilet paper in your lavatories, thank the union. Seriously. When Ms. Class read the toilet paper provision in the union contract of the first district she taught in, she thought it was a joke. Then, sadly, she taught in a district where the union had not specified toilet paper as one of the teacher benefits.

Ms. Class sees teacher unions as necessary to preventing superintendents and boards of education from running school systems entirely like plantations.

The one grievance Ms. Class will hold forever against the union is its lack of guts. When the superintendent reprimanded Ms. Class for insubordination for wearing a T-shirt with "Support Troy Teachers" emblazoned across the front, Ms. Class was disappointed that the union did not uphold her right of free speech. Instead, union officials told her to take the T-shirt off. Ms. Class, not exactly of a Betsy Ross temperament, had spent hours the night before sewing lace trim on the T-shirt to circumvent any charge of sloppy attire or attire unbecoming to a female or whatever. The lace was quite an attractive touch. Nonetheless, three administrators objected and when Ms. Class stood firm, asking exactly which letters of the alphabet were objectionable (since PE teachers wear T-shirts with various messages every day), they passed their complaints on to the superintendent, who stood firm, whereupon the union caved in. Ms. Class had visions of going home and embroidering "Support . . . Teachers" on a dress, a jacket, a mantilla. But faced with the reality that the teachers union was not interested in free speech, she capitulated. Fifteen years later, she still has the T-shirt and still regrets the missed opportunity to make a point.

Be that as it may, if you make more than minimum wage, thank a union. Ms. Class grew up hearing her father express outrage that teachers made about as much as grocery clerks—and less than just about everybody else—but were afraid to ask for a raise for fear of being fired. Amazingly enough, Ms. Class's father went to the teachers he perceived as leaders and persuaded them to present a salary proposal to the school board. This is amazing because Ms. Class's father was at that time president of the school board. If you know board members like that, maybe you don't need a union. Otherwise, pay up.

VACATION VANISHING POINT

Dear Ms. Class:

When will teachers get it? Teaching will never be regarded as a profession until teachers work a full work year. Their current work year of 180 days is ridiculous.

— Jersey City, NJ

Dear Jersey City:

Listen, Jersey, try picking on a worthy opponent. Try looking at the work schedule of your Congress person. The average teacher works fifty-five hours a week, thirty-six weeks a year. She needs reflection time scattered through the year because teachers cannot teach and think at the same time. And you can't think about something, really think about what matters, until you've taught it. That's why teachers speak a different language from professors and textbook organizers. It's also why they need time off.

VACUUM OPERATIONAL DESIGN

Dear Ms. Class:
  What does the U. S. Secretary of Education do?

— Kent, OH

Dear Kent:
  No one knows—unless it's to prove that vacuums can exist inside the Washington Beltway. During George Bush's administration the name of the First Dog, Millie, appeared in the news thirty-six times more often than the Secretary of Education's name. During Bill Clinton's administration, people weren't sure there even was a Secretary of Education.

VALUES CLARIFICATION SUPERFUND

Dear Ms. Class:
  I wonder why you are so negative about values clarification. It is helpful for people to sort out what they really believe.

— Muskogee, OK

Dear Muskogee:
  That may very well be true for teachers—and Jesuits, from whose sophistry the values-clarification games used in schools were borrowed. It is one thing for adults in a religious community or even a faculty room to talk about whether the one space left on a lifeboat should go to a seventeen-year-old pregnant African American prostitute, a blind rabbi who survived the Holocaust, an HIV-positive Native American medical researcher, or a Hispanic rock star who has made 650 platinum records before the age of twenty-two and tithes seventy-two percent of his income to the homeless, but it is outrageous to inflict such an exercise on children.

VENN DIAGRAM TUNE-UP

Dear Ms. Class:
  Just when are Venn diagrams used in the real world?

— Shreveport, LA

Dear Shreveport:
  What makes you think school isn't the real world? Venn diagrams are lines drawn in the chalkdust to separate those who embrace change in the teaching of elementary math from those who don't.

VISUALIZATION TRACK RECORD

Dear Ms. Class:

My team-teaching partner and I get along pretty well. Television is our major source of disagreement. I believe we should help our students become good consumers of television. My partner wants to ban the TV set from the classroom.

— Mayesville, SC

Dear Mayesville:

Ms. Class wonders how students can become good consumers of something that is so dreadful. When television is bad, nothing is worse. When television is good, it's not much better. Why do you think it's called a medium?

VOCABULARY DOCUMENTATION PARAMETERS

Dear Ms. Class:

I worry that my fourth-grade students, who come from solid working-class families, are hampered by underdeveloped vocabularies. For the most part, their parents are willing to help with any homework I send home. The PTO is even willing to buy vocabulary workbooks. The plan is that every student would be given a workbook and each night he'd do a page at home. This work would then be reinforced in school. Can you think of a better plan?

— Fayetteville, AR

Dear Fayetteville:

Most definitely. Research shows that the best way to increase one's vocabulary is through reading. The least effective way is through isolated vocabulary drills.

The PTO has two excellent options for supporting vocabulary enhancement:

- Take all fourth graders to a bookstore and let each child choose a paperback book.

- Distribute riddle books to fourth graders. Genre riddles (a series of riddles on the same topic) show young readers how language works. These riddles also demonstrate the fun reading can bring.

The grade level doesn't matter. If the program operates yearly, every child will be in the selected grade and benefit.

VOLUNTEER VIRTUAL REALITY

Dear Ms. Class:

In an avalanche of cost cutting, our school district has wiped out teacher aides. The superintendent has told the principals that we should all recruit volunteers to "take up the slack" left by the disappearance of the aides. I think you get what you pay for and have no faith in volunteers.

— Stockton, CA

Dear Stockton:

Ms. Class feels your economic theory is overgeneralized. Schools get much more than they pay for from teacher aides, who, after all, are paid only minimum wage (and are laid off every summer).

The fact is that even the best of volunteers cause extra work for teachers; the worst of volunteers are more trouble than most students (and a teacher can't send them to be disciplined by the principal).

Ms. Class suggests that to be a volunteer in a school, candidates should complete a four-week inservice training course given by the teachers willing to have volunteers in their classrooms. This will give the volunteers and the teachers a better idea of what's ahead and a better opportunity for the volunteers to be productive.

VOMIT CONSTANCY FUNCTION

Dear Ms. Class:

I'm a new primary-grade teacher, and I wonder if you believe in any "universals" of primary teaching.

— Narragansett, RI

Dear Narragansett:

Vomit is the universal constant of primary grades. Funny, isn't it, that they never tell you this in teacher-training courses. Children between the ages of five and eight vomit when they are upset. They also vomit when they are bored, happy, or sad. (See Classroom Management Flapdoodle for the rules of vomit.)

In times of stress, middle graders and even junior high students regress to the vomit stage. Only experience in the field can show teachers how to recognize environmental cues and move out of the zone of proximal upheaval.

No matter what the provocation, it is regarded as unprofessional for teachers to vomit.

VOUCHER SHORT-TERM COVERAGE

Dear Ms. Class:

Our state legislature is under a lot of pressure to pass a voucher bill. I say it's about time. I am a taxpayer as well as a teacher. I send my children to private school. Why should I pay twice?

— Terre Haute, IN

Dear Terre Haute:

By your reasoning, then, why should people with no children pay school taxes? We pay school taxes not to pay for the cost of educating our individual children but because we know that society is better for having an educated citizenry.

Financially supporting every crackpot idea for a school is democracy run amok. Besides that, it is dangerous to the well-being of children. It is curious, in a nation clamoring for standards, that we would say any witches' coven, religious sect, or flat-earth society should be able to operate a tax-supported breeding ground just so long as they call it a school.

VOWEL EXTRASTRENGTH FORMULA

Dear Ms. Class:

I am aware that experts recommend that phonics drill be minimized. I'm also aware that students use consonants before they use vowels. I'm wondering, though, exactly what vowel competence I should look for by the end of first grade.

— Marquette, IA

Dear Marquette:

Thank you for asking. Despite the risk of provoking thousands of letters of tedious explanation, every few years Ms. Class leaps at the opportunity to point out that she taught reading for some dozen years without ever knowing what a schwa is.

Furthermore, during one brief period of economic desperation, Ms. Class found herself teaching the *Distar* reading program. It was at that time she discovered she cannot distinguish between various vowel sounds. She survived by relying on the cues from a student who always raised his hand first. (She was suspicious of the student who waved her hand most violently.)

Please don't send Ms. Class letters explaining the schwa. She's had it explained countless times. Ms. Class used to confess her ignorance in front of large audiences. Helpful teachers rushed to the podium to render aid and comfort. Their explanations of the schwa always made perfect sense. Alas, by the next day Ms. Class had always forgotten again. Don't waste the stamp.

VYGOTSKY VARIEGATION

Dear Ms. Class:

I'm taking a course in children's literature, and people keep quoting Vygotsky. Who is this Vygotsky and should I worry about him?

— Akron, OH

Dear Akron:

Don't worry. Ms. Class will tell you the three things you need to know about Vygotsky:

1. Everybody quotes him.

2. Nobody reads him.

3. The devil quotes Vygotsky for his own purposes.

All you need to do is say "zone of proximal development" once a week, and you'll be okay.

WASTE WATCHDOGGERY

Dear Ms. Class:

I'm worried about conserving our natural resources and wonder if you can direct me to a clearing house that can give me advice.

— Manassa, CO

Dear Manassa:

Ms. Class believes we don't waste enough in schools. Think of the things we hoard: old dittos, stale grudges, apostrophe errors . . . . The list is endless. None of these things would be missed if we could only learn how to stop hoarding them. Start each day by telling yourself: today is a new day. I will throw something away, preferably something from my top desk drawer.

WEBBING WAIVERS

Dear Ms. Class:

I am an experienced trainer in writing process and yet this year I am having great difficulty in getting one girl to participate in our prewriting webbing activities. She insists she knows what she wants to write and just wants to do it. I want students to experience the entire process real writers go through. What do you recommend?

— Tacoma, WA

Dear Tacoma:

Maybe your student is a real writer and should on those grounds be given a waiver from writing process.

Ms. Class confesses she has never liked the term *prewriting*. People who write for a living recognize only two states of being: writing and making excuses.

As for webs: webs have a lot in common with charades. They are a social activity done with a group of people who make quick word associations and want to show how clever they are. Ms. Class would not presume to speak for real writers, but she does know that people who write for a living don't brainstorm ideas radiating from a central thesis. Maybe they'd be better off if they did, but people who write for a living rarely do what's good for them. If they did, they'd do something else for a living.

WHAT IF? WISHFUL THINKING JUNK BONDS

Dear Ms. Class:

I am so sick and tired of all the snide attacks on the schools. Even commentary I usually respect and enjoy—National Public Radio, *The New Republic, Washington Monthly, Atlantic,* and others, spew forth sarcasm and stupidity about the schools.

What would happen if these commentators sat in our chairs for a day? What would happen if the public stopped expecting schools to solve the problems of society?

What would happen if parents accepted some responsibility for their children? What if they turned off the TV and read to their children? What would happen if they didn't let kids come to school dressed like hookers and hoodlums? And so on.

— Lansing, MI

Dear Lansing:

Although Ms. Class sympathizes with your frustration, she feels impelled to point out that you are engaging in malignant wishful thinking. What ifs? don't butter any bread. Nor do they make any contribution to the problems that beset the schools.

Ms. Class, who herself feels these stings of sarcasm, is not unsympathetic to your pain. She would only tell you that the hardest truth teachers must face is that the world is not just. Nonetheless, life goes on. So does school.

WHOLE LANGUAGE WATERSHED

Dear Ms. Class:

Why are whole language advocates so intolerant? The teacher across the hall "caught me" photocopying a class set of a quite wonderful activity. She acted as though by exposing innocent young children to a reproducible master I was violating their innocence, damaging their psyches, and stunting their growth. Why should I have to sneak in on weekends to use the copy machine?

— Washington, DC

Dear DC:

Ms. Class would remind you that just as every cannibal needs a pot, every missionary needs a disbeliever to convert. Remember that passion poisons reasonable discourse. Even Ralph Waldo Emerson admitted that transcendentalism, in its daily practice, often gave him a headache. In his words, "It's faith run mad." The Spanish Inquisition was carried out by people who knew they had a direct line to God.

Please remember also that good causes often attract poor advocates, and the price of a democracy is seeing good ideas go too far.

Dear Ms. Class:

I didn't know anything about whole language and asked a pro in my school. She was very helpful, lending me books and answering all my questions. We spent a lot of time together after school hours and became close. Then, when I decided, despite her advice, to continue giving weekly spelling quizzes, she dropped me flat.

We exchange morning hellos and that's it. She rebuffs all my overtures. I'm devastated, as I can't believe weekly spelling quizzes could come between friends. What can I do?

— Topeka, KS

Dear Topeka:

You have just learned a difficult lesson: hell hath no fury like a whole evangelist scorned. Although Ms. Class tries to avoid dealing in absolutes, she advises avoiding both evangelists and vigilantes.

The trouble with whole language advocates is that they read only studies supporting whole language; the trouble with skills checklists advocates is they don't read anything.

Of course, Ms. Class regrets that a friendship could founder on so slight a thing as a spelling test, but she would point out that if it hadn't been spelling it would have been something else. No corner of your classroom is safe from the vigilant eye of the zealot. You can't reason with zealotry, which is what happens when what began as rebellion ends up as blind faith.

Dear Ms. Class:

My principal just declared whole language a failure. We only dropped the basal in favor of literature sets two years ago. In just two years, how could we know if it's a failure or not?

— Peoria, IL

Dear Peoria:

Rapid obsolescence is not just the province of the manufacturers of cars, washing machines, and toasters. Ms. Class would note that school systems are not willing to give whole language the chance it deserves, any more than they gave open schools or computer-assisted instruction a fair trial. After all, blame is safer than praise; it is also easier to blame something for not producing miracles than to adopt a wait-and-see attitude.

Publishing conglomerates and education consultants flourish on the death of new ideas. Take Bill Honig, former California superintendent of schools, as a small example. He took credit for popularizing literature-based reading in the schools and now that California fourth graders scored lower than fourth graders in any state or territory except Guam on a reading test, he is back as a consultant explaining why his plan for a different scheme is needed. The disappointment Ms. Class sometimes feels toward doctrinaire devotees of whole language does not approach the ferocity of the scorn she feels toward ed-whiz-biz turncoats and charlatans.

WORD PLAY DIRECTORY PATHS

Dear Ms. Class:

I have read your claims that riddles show children how language works, but to my knowledge you've never demonstrated your point. Please do so, particularly as regards fourth-grade curriculum.

— St. Cloud, MN

Dear St. Cloud:

From the tone of your letter, Ms. Class suspects you could do with a good chuckle. She recommends, for starters, *Remember Betsy Floss and Other Colonial American Riddles* and *The Purple Turkey and Other Thanksgiving Riddles*, both by David Adler.

Ms. Class questions that there can be any better way to demonstrate that words have multiple meanings than to ask students:

What do you get when you cross an ocean with a thief?
   (A crime wave)

Ask students to make a list of common idioms. Then challenge them to figure out how some of these idioms take on new meaning when applied to historical characters. For example:

What did Benjamin Franklin's brother say to him when Benjamin pestered him?
   (Go fly a kite!)

What did Sacagawea say to Lewis and Clark?
(I'll paddle my own canoe.)

WORKDAY WHEREABOUTS

Dear Ms. Class:

I am really tired of people sneering that a teacher's life is easy because of her short workday. Just because my students get to school at 8:30 and go home at 2:15, doesn't mean I do. I have been teaching for ten years and cannot think of a time I did not arrive at school by 6:30 A.M. I could count on one hand the times I've been home by 5:00 P.M. in the last decade. My question is, How can I answer the people who insist I have a short workday?

— Pittsburgh, PA

Dear Pittsburgh:

Ms. Class would advise you to remember three things:

1. Trying to answer criticism is as profitable—and as possible—as gathering dandelion fluff.

2. More important, just because a teacher's work is never done doesn't mean she should start earlier or stay later. Why don't you try sleeping an extra hour—or going home when the kids do, putting up your feet, opening a box of bonbons, and reading a mystery just for the fun of it?

3. Nobody loves a martyr.

WORK SKILLS HOCUS-POCUS

Dear Ms. Class:

As a parent as well as an entrepreneur, I am very concerned about today's youth being taught the skills necessary to be successful members of the work force in the twenty-first century. I worry that all this new emphasis on communication in math is producing students who think that the answer to two plus two is up for discussion. I have formed a grass-roots organization to help combat the insidious softness of the school and to help our children grow up to be skilled, productive workers. I hope you will print our 800 number.

— San Jose, CA

Dear San Jose:

In the spirit of capitalism, Ms. Class suggests you buy an ad to disseminate your phone number. Also in the spirit of capitalism, Ms. Class offers the findings of the U. S. Census Bureau. In the summer of 1994, the Census Bureau surveyed three thousand employers across the country, asking, "When you consider hiring a new nonsupervisory or production worker, how important are the following in your decision to hire?" A score of 1 indicates "not important" or "not considered." A score of 5 indicates "extremely important."

Skills Employers Want

Attitude	4.6
Communication skills	4.2
Previous work experience	4.0
Recommendations from current employers	3.4
Recommendations from previous employers	3.4
Industry-based credentials certifying skills	3.2
Years of schooling completed	2.9
Score on tests administered as part of interview	2.5
Academic performance (grades)	2.5
Experience or reputation of applicant's school	2.4
Teacher recommendations	2.1

Ms. Class is bemused and bewildered that employers care more about how many years students spend in school than about what they do there. The low regard in which employers hold teachers' judgment is a message that students understand.

WORKBOOK GRIDLOCK

Dear Ms. Class:

Even though I can predict your answer, I would like to hear any rationale you can offer for keeping—or getting rid of—workbooks.

— Chattanooga, TN

Dear Chattanooga:

A workbook should be carefully structured, analyzed for appropriate reading level, matched to every student's individual learning styles, and then thrown out the window. The finest of workbooks is no substitute for even a mediocre trade book.

Cautionary note: Ms. Class would remind you to keep a low profile while undertaking to rid a class of workbooks. The teacher who has given up workbooks can be just as revoltingly smug as the three-pack-a-day smoker who has given up cigarettes or the dieter who has reached her goal at Weight Watchers.

WRITERS' IMPACT STATEMENT

Dear Ms. Class:

I am a science teacher who would like to make a career change. I wonder if you can give me some advice about how I can become a writer.

— Berkeley, CA

Dear Berkeley:

Ms. Class would advise you to reconsider. Writers are not customarily persons in the best mental health. Physicists, for example, live longer than writers. Keats died at twenty-six, Shelley at thirty, Thoreau at forty-five. Copernicus died at seventy, Galileo at seventy-eight, and Newton at eighty-five.

If you persist, however, you should know that there is no problem: anyone can be a writer. The trick is to find someone who will pay you for it.

WRITING, PROCESS AND OTHERWISE

Dear Ms. Class:

I teach in an affluent school. There is a lot of parental pressure to produce error-free writing. I try, but my seventh graders still make the usual their/there, your/you're mistakes . . . along with apostrophe and comma errors. What's a teacher to do when he believes in process but is judged by product?

— Milford, DE

Dear Milford:

Although Ms. Class would not mistake seventh grade as the threshold for the age of reason, she believes twelve-year-olds can become responsible for checking their papers for a finite number of errors. Ten seems like a reasonable number. Give students a (short) list of commonly committed faux pas that drive parents crazy. Tell them you will not accept any work that contains these errors. Allow students to consult any resources, including each other, they wish to use to vet their papers, but insist that papers cannot contain these particular errors. When you're feeling brave, you can gradually up the ante, adding another five items to the list. If you can get teachers of other subjects to cooperate by adopting this list, too, parents will be ecstatic, and it does seventh graders no harm. After all, computer spellchecks do not distinguish between *their* and *there*.

X CHROMOSOME AFFIRMATIVE ACTION

Dear Ms. Class:

I'm distressed that school staffing practices have changed so little in the past half-century.

A child can go through elementary school never seeing a male—except in the principal's office.

— Moscow, ID

Dear Moscow:

Ms. Class doubts that the ratio of male to female principals will be reduced until coaching a winning football team fails to be a prime asset for principal candidates.

As for male elementary teachers, that's another matter. Ms. Class would suggest some sort of affirmative action plan. Here are some bonuses a school might offer successful male applicants:

1. A three-year moratorium from taking bus duty.

2. Free lunch.

3. No parent conferences scheduled on sports playoffs nights.

4. A lifetime supply of staples and Scotch tape.

5. Six "freedom passes," allowing bearer to skip inservice staff development sessions of his choice.

6. Reserved parking.

XENOPHOBIA DISEQUILIBRIUM MAINTENANCE

Dear Ms. Class:

I am disturbed and frightened by the hostility of the " English Only" activists. Our school board has gone so far as to forbid our library from buying books in any language other than English.

— Monterey, CA

Dear Monterey:

Ms. Class would venture to guess that none of your school board members have traveled to Europe or South America. There is nothing like foreign travel to make one wish one had paid attention in foreign language class—or read a few books in Spanish.

Ms. Class ventures to guess that the United States is the only nation on earth that tries to prohibit its citizenry from learning foreign languages.

XEROX MACHINE AND OTHER COPIERS

Dear Ms. Class:

I am tired of your elitist snobbery—making snide remarks about copy machines and blackline masters. Maybe you don't remember the old days of dittos? The days when we couldn't copy a journal article for a friend? Why don't you just take the next logical step and banish the printing press? Why don't we return to the days of handwritten manuscripts?

— Cody, WY

Dear Cody:

Make no mistake: Ms. Class is grateful for her copy machine. She just finds it necessary to face reality and admit that such a convenience makes it easier to for us to duplicate mediocrity as well as the Declaration of Independence and Calvin Trillin's columns.

YARD-DUTY VARIANCES

Dear Ms. Class:

I teach eighth grade, and our entire faculty agrees that student behavior is worse after lunch than before. I think I have a solution to this, but don't know if I have the nerve to bring it up at a faculty meeting. Our lunch periods last twenty-seven minutes. Students eat in seven and a half minutes but are kept cooped up in the cafeteria for the remaining nineteen and a half minutes. We don't have any recesses, no time when students can let off some of their excess energy. My idea is that we'd let them out of the cafeteria, let them wander around outside for that nineteen and a half minutes.

The problem is that teachers would have to do yard duty. Teachers are already on hall duty, but it's one thing to check for kids smoking in the lavatory and another thing to chase them around outside. As I said, I don't know if I have the nerve to suggest it.

— Albany, NY

Dear Albany:

Ms. Class confesses she is puzzled why a school thinks any good can come of cooping adolescents up for six hours, with no time off for good behavior.

As for teachers being required to chase students around the school yard, Ms. Class would only remind you that those same students manage to get to school and get back home on their own. Perhaps the following story will be of some use. If not useful, it is sure to blow your principal's mind.

Ms. Class once had the occasion to observe two dozen eighth graders tour Japan with their art teachers. They visited Japanese schools and toured notable landmarks. On the first two evenings students, teachers, and Japanese hosts ate dinner together and walked around the neighborhood of their center-city Tokyo hotel. On the third evening, the Japanese hosts handed each student the equivalent of fifteen dollars, reminded them where McDonald's was located, and told them to get back to the hotel by 10 P.M.

Ms. Class admits to having been shocked. Letting eighth graders out alone in Tokyo? after dark? We did it, and they did it. We didn't lose a single student (or teacher). Ms. Class confesses she felt enormously relieved to be present at this incident as a reporter, not as a teacher responsible for the welfare of those eighth graders.

YEARBOOK PRECOCITY FEEDBACK LOOP

Dear Ms. Class:

The PTO in our middle school is very active and, I must admit, very helpful. They work hard to raise money to buy computers for our school, to buy library books, and so on. But such volunteerism has its price. Last year they lobbied successfully for a cheerleading squad. This year they are exerting pressure for a school yearbook. I hope you can offer some advice for keeping a middle school developmentally appropriate and not letting it slide into being a pre-high school.

— Hannibal, MO

Dear Hannibal:

Ms. Class agrees with you on all counts. Once volunteers are let loose, it's difficult to rein them in. When you add money to the mix, their power increases exponentially. Believe it or not, your faculty is the key. Do not engage in argument or even discussion with individual parents. There's strength in numbers, so take a poll. If teachers vote against having a yearbook (and you can certainly point out that yearbooks and cheerleading squads are what makes high school special; you don't want kids going to high school feeling they've already done it all), then the principal and/or a teacher committee can—and must—tell the volunteer vigilantes to back off.

Zz

ZEALOTRY OPTIMIZATION

Dear Ms. Class:

Two teachers in our school are causing a furor that threatens to engulf the rest of us. Both are excellent teachers, but philosophically they are far apart. One teaches *Distar;* one teaches whole language. They engage in nasty confrontations about everything from the presence of chocolate milk in the cafeteria to field trip destinations. Our school has always been a place of "live and let live," a place that accepts diversity among its teachers as well as its students. I'd go so far as to call us a family. Neither of these teachers is a bad person. I just wonder if there is anything the rest of us can do to prevent them from tearing our faculty—and themselves—apart.

— Dearborn, MI

Dear Dearborn:

A lot of blood has been shed over religious conviction. As H. L. Mencken once pointed out, the devil doesn't have to fight the Catholics; he leaves that to the Methodists and the Baptists.

Ms. Class advises that a committee of teachers sit these two warriors down and talk turkey. Tell them that any time they start arguing with each other, the rest of the faculty will refuse to listen. Since most zealots engage in combat in order to win converts, vacating the faculty room whenever they start in on each other should make an impression. Ms. Class predicts fighting will cease when there is no audience.

ZIPPER MILLENIUM-APPROVED MICROCONTROL

Dear Ms. Class:

What do you think of passing a rule that children cannot attend school until they can dress (and undress) themselves? In winter, I spend half the day unsticking zippers, tying shoelaces, and so on. I wish parents would multiply by thirty when considering the educational impact of the clothes they buy for their children.

— Jefferson City, MO

Dear Jefferson City:

Yes, zippers are the curse of primary-grade teachers. But you are asking for the impossible if you expect parents to worry about this. Do any of us really consider the impact of zippers and shoelaces when we are snatching up bargains at the January sales? If we couldn't come to school until we could work our zippers, some of us would never be allowed in the door. Ms. Class admits to owning a full-length down coat that she steps into and out of rather than suffer the consequences of unzippering it all the way. Rather than curse parents, who are looking for bargains, not zipper maintenance, Ms. Class suggests enlisting the aid of upper-grade students to help you get your primary graders in and out of their clothing.

ZONE OF PROXIMAL DEVELOPMENT DIFFUSION NETWORK

Dear Ms. Class:

I just want to know one thing: do you or don't you believe in the zone of proximal development?

— Brunswick, ME

Dear Brunswick:

Ms. Class wonders why her personal life-style choices are any of the teacher's business. Ms. Class decries the incivility of wielding arcane lingo for the purpose of making people out of the loop feel isolated and inferior.

That said, Ms. Class wonders if the letter writer accosts strangers on the street and interrogates them about how often they change their underwear.

Envoi of an Unknown Teacher

Dear Teachers:

It is time for Ms. Class's annual homage to the unknown teacher among us.

The Unknown Teacher
(TO 54-65-8923)
This Acrylic Monument
Is Erected by the
Board of Education

She was found by the board of education to be
One against whom there was no official complaint;
And all the reports on her conduct agree
That her professional behavior and attitude were without taint.
For in everything she did she served the board of education
With the proper degree of subjugation.
In union plans she never was mired,
She'd accrued 999 sick days by the time she retired.
She satisfied administrators at her school,
Dressed in polyester or double knit.
Ne'er a controversial act did she e'er commit.
Her reactions at faculty meetings were normal in every way
Sitting quietly with nothing to say.
She was fully sensible to the advantage of long-term annuity
And had everything necessary to the modern class—
Electronic marvels for each lad and lass.
When State Ed commended trade books, she put in a request;
She could adapt to most any incongruity.
She held the proper opinions for the time of year:
When there was IPAC, she was for IPAC; when there was SAPPA,
    she SAPPED.
She followed every supervisory behest,
She even had a propensity
To accommodate behavioral objectivity.
She knew
One need not PATL one's own canoe
But could find safety remaining supine
While others walked a lonely picket line.
She belonged to four committees—
Which the board said was the right number for a teacher on Step 19—
And the administrators said she never interfered with their
    occupational mien.
Was she free? Was she happy? The question is absurd.
Had anything been wrong we should certainly have heard.

(with apologies to W. H. Auden)

Dept. of Treasury, Infernal Revenue Service
1043 U.S. Individual Classroom Return 1996

USE D.O.E Label or Print. No Cursive.	Your first name and initial (if joint return, also give principal's name and initial)		Last name
	Present school address	School lunch ☐ Yes ☐ No	☐ White milk ☐ Choc. milk

FILING STATUS
(check only one box. If you check more than one, we will send you 16 more forms to fill out.)

☐ 1. Minority
☐ 2. Underachiever
☐ 3. Overachiever
☐ 4. Chapter I (with qualifying percentile) (see p. 68 of instructions)

☐ 5. Gifted
☐ 6. Mainstreamed
☐ 7. Up the creek
☐ 8. Ditto overdosse

Enter number ➤ _____ of boxes checked

INCOME
Please attach Copy B of your lesson plans, bus list, class picture. If you don't have Copy B, why not?

9. Wages . . . . 9 _____

10. Career ladder . . . . 10 _____

11. Gifts ☐ Avon ☐ Mary Kay ☐ Maybelline 11 ➤_____

12. Media credits ☐ Competency ☐ Master ☐ Mentor ☐ Phonics ☐ Values ☐ Just say no 12 ➤_____

13. Media debits ☐ NEA ☐ AFT ☐ Whole language 13 ➤_____

14. Multiply number checked in line 13 by today's date 14 ➤_____

15. Losses ☐ Picture money ☐ Book clubs ☐ Raffle tickets 15 ➤_____

16. Moving expenses (attach form 4216)
☐ Yard duty ☐ After school clubs
☐ Lunch duty ☐ Janitor's closet 16 ➤_____

Do you wish to contribute 69¢ to William Bennett Nostalgia Fund? Yes☐ No ☐

ADJUSTMENTS

17. Anticipatory sets ☐
    Total observed _____

18. Guided practice ☐
    Total coached _____ Won _____ Lost _____ Tied _____

Subtract line 17 or 18, whichever applies, from line 19.

17 _____

18 _____

19. Penalty for early closure ☐
    How early? _____ 19 _____

20. Multiply line 19 x $12.42 20 _____

CREDITS

21. Is your class size larger than line 16? ☐ Yes ☐ No
    If 'yes,' file form 1634
    If 'no,' file form 2278
    If you don't know, take the National Teacher Exam.

Do you think teaching is a profession?
☐ Yes ☐ No ☐ Maybe
(Information requested by the Dept. of Agriculture.)

Please sign here ➤ _____
              (Use cursive)

Custodian's signature ➤ _____

References

Abbey, Edward. 1991. *Abbey's Road.* New York: Dutton.

Adams, Henry. (1918) 1990. *The Education of Henry Adams.* New York: Random.

Adler, David. 1986. *The Purple Turkey and Other Thanksgiving Riddles.* Illus. Marylin Hafner. New York: Holiday House.

———. 1987. *Remember Betsy Floss and Other Colonial American Riddles.* Illus. John Wallner. New York: Holiday House.

Alcock, Vivien. 1985. *The Stonewalkers.* New York: Dell.

Baur, Susan. 1994. *Confiding: A Psychotherapist and Her Patients Search for Stories to Live By.* New York: HarperCollins.

Bennett, William, ed. 1993. *Book of Virtues: A Treasury of the World's Great Moral.* New York: Simon & Schuster.

Berry, Wendell. 1988. "Traveling at Home." In *Traveling at Home.* San Francisco: North Point Press.

Bettelheim, Bruno and Alvin A. Rosenfeld. 1993. *The Art of the Obvious: Developing Insight for Physchotherapy and Everyday Life.* New York: Knopf.

Blume, Judy. 1975. *Forever.* New York: Macmillan.

Brown, Jeff. 1964. *Flat Stanley.* Illus. Tomi Ungerer. New York: HarperCollins.

Burningham, John. 1987. *John Patrick Norman McHennessy: The Boy Who Was Always Late.* New York: Crown.

Byars, Betsy. 1977. *The Pinballs.* New York: HarperCollins.

Carle, Eric. 1981. *The Very Hungry Caterpillar.* Illus. by author. New York: Putnam.

Cather, Willa. (1918) 1994. *My Antonia.* New York: Vintage.

Cleary, Beverly. 1984. *Ramona the Brave.* Illus. Alan Tiegreen. New York: Dell.

Coles, Robert. 1961. "A Young Psychiatrist Looks at His Profession." *Atlantic Magazine.*

———. 1986. *The Moral Life of Children.* New York: Atlantic Monthly Press.

Deci, Edward. 1986. "Motivating Children to Learn: What You Can Do." In *Learning,* 6: 42–44.

Defoe, Daniel. 1961. *Robinson Crusoe.* New York: NAL Dutton.

Dewey, John. 1938. *Experience and Education.* New York: Collier.

Dorris, Michael. 1989. *The Broken Cord: A Family's Struggle with Fetal Alcohol Syndrome.* New York: HarperCollins.

Eckert, Allan. 1971. *Incident at Hawk's Hill.* Boston: Little, Brown.

Eliot, George. 1964. *Silas Marner.* New York: Airmont.

Emerson, R. W. 1983. "Experience." In *Essays and Lectures.* New York: Library of America.

Fleischman, Sid. 1984. *McBroom's Almanac.* Boston: Little, Brown.

Gass, William H. *Habitations of the Words.* New York: Simon & Schuster.

Grief, Ivo P. 1980. *The Reading Teacher* 34 (12): 290–302.

Hawkins, David. 1974. "The Bird in the Window." In *The Informed Vision.* New York: Agathon Press.

Healy, Jane. 1991. *Endangered Minds: Why Our Children Don't Think—and What We Can Do About It.* New York: Simon & Schuster.

Herndon, James. 1969. *The Way It 'Spozed to Be.* New York: Simon & Schuster.

Hirsch, E. D., ed. 1993. *What Your First Grader Needs to Know.* New York: Doubleday.

Holt, John. 1964. *When Children Fail.* New York: Dell.

Ibsen, Henrik. 1977. *An Enemy of the People.* Ed. Arthur Miller. New York: Viking Penguin.

Jung, Carl. 1962. *Memories, Dream, Reflections.* New York: Atlantic Monthly Press.

Kamii, Constance. 1984. "Obedience Is Not Enough." In *Young Children,* 5: 11–14.

Kindl, Patrice. 1993. *Owl in Love.* Boston: Houghton Mifflin.

King, Stephen. 1990. *Carrie.* New York: Doubleday.

Kipling, Rudyard. 1987. *Plain Tales from the Hills.* Ed. H. R. Woudhuysen. New York: Viking Penguin.

Kohn, Alfie. 1995. *Punished by Rewards: The Trouble with Gold Stars, Incentive Plans, A's, Praise, and Other Bribes.* Boston: Houghton Mifflin.

Konigsburg, E. L. 1987. *From the Mixed-Up Files of Mrs. Basil E. Frankweiler.* New York: Macmillan.

Landberg, Michele. 1985. *Michele Landsberg's Guide to Children's Books.* Markham, ONT: Penguin.

Lopate, Phillip. 1989. *Against Joie de Vivre.* New York: Poseidon Press.

Macrorie, Ken. 1987. *Twenty Teachers.* New York: Oxford University Press.

Martin, Ann. Babysitters' Club series. New York: Scholastic.

Medawar, Peter. 1991. *Advice to a Young Scientist.* New York: Basic Books.

Melville, Herman. (1851) 1964. *Moby Dick.* New York: Airmont.

Neill, A. S. 1975. *The Dominie Books of A. S. Neill.* New York: Hart.

———. 1986. *A Dominie's Log.* London, UK: Hogarth Press.

O'Gorman, Ned. 1972. *The Wilderness and the Laurel Tree.* New York: HarperCollins.

Park, Barbara. 1982. *Skinnybones.* New York: Knopf.

Paterson, Katherine. 1978. *The Great Gilly Hopkins.* New York: HarperCollins.

Peterson, Ivars. 1995. *Fatal Defect: Chasing Killer Computer Bugs.* New York: Times Books.

Pickering, Sam. 1994. *Trespassing.* Hanover, NH: University Press of New England.

Rosenhan, David. 1973. "On Being Sane in Insane Places." In *Science* 179: 250–58.

Sacher, Louis. 1987. *There's a Boy in the Girls' Bathroom.* New York: Knopf.

Sendak, Maurice. 1988. *Where the Wild Things Are.* Illus. by author. New York: HarperCollins.

Sheehy, Gail. 1984. *Passages.* New York: Bantam.

Silverstein, Shel. 1974. *Where the Sidewalk Ends.* Illus. by author. New York: HarperCollins.

Slepian, Jan. 1989. *The Broccoli Tapes.* New York: Putnam.

Smith, Frank. 1985. *Reading Without Nonsense.* 2d ed. New York: Teachers College Press.

Spock, Benjamin. (1945) 1992. *Dr. Spock's Baby and Child Care.* New York: Dell.

Stine, R. L. Goosebumps series. New York: Scholastic.

Tyler, Anne. 1985. *The Accidental Tourist.* New York: Knopf.

Viorst, Judith. 1971. *The Tenth Good Thing About Barney.* Illus. Erik Blegrad. New York: Macmillan.

Vygotsky, L. S. 1978. *Mind in Society: The Development of Higher Psychological Process.* Ed. Michael Cole, et al. Cambridge, MA: Harvard University Press.

The Wall Street Journal. 1985. January.

West, Jessamyn. 1980. *Double Discovery: A Journey.* San Diego: Harcourt Brace.

White, E. B. 1952. *Charlotte's Web.* Illus. Garth Williams. New York: HarperCollins.

———. 1970. *The Trumpet of the Swan.* Illus. Edward Frascino. New York: HarperCollins.

Wildavsky, Aaron. 1977. *Doing Better and Feeling Worse.* New York: Norton.

Index